More iPhone Cool Projects

Cool Developers Reveal the Details of Their Cooler Apps and Discuss Their iPad Development Experiences

Danton Chin
Claus Höfele
Ben Kazez
Saul Mora
Leon Palm
Scott Penberthy

Ben Britten Smith
Chuck Smith
David Smith
Arne de Vries
Joost van de Wijgerd

apress®

More iPhone Cool Projects: Cool Developers Reveal the Details of Their Cooler Apps and Discuss Their iPad Development Experiences

ISBN-13 (pbk): 978-1-4302-2922-3

ISBN-13 (electronic): 978-1-4302-2923-0

Printed and bound in the United States of America 9 8 7 6 5 4 3 2 1

The use in this publication of trade names, trademarks, service marks, and similar terms, even if they are not identified as such, is not to be taken as an expression of opinion as to whether or not they are subject to proprietary rights.

Publisher and President: Paul Manning
Lead Editor: Clay Andres
Development Editors: Douglas Pundick, Matthew Moodie, and Brian MacDonald
Technical Reviewer: Ben Britten Smith
Editorial Board: Clay Andres, Steve Anglin, Mark Beckner, Ewan Buckingham, Gary Cornell, Jonathan Gennick, Jonathan Hassell, Michelle Lowman, Matthew Moodie, Duncan Parkes, Jeffrey Pepper, Frank Pohlmann, Douglas Pundick, Ben Renow-Clarke, Dominic Shakeshaft, Matt Wade, Tom Welsh
Coordinating Editors: Candace English and Debra Kelly
Copy Editor: Katie Stence
Compositor: MacPS, LLC
Indexer: BIM Indexing & Proofreading Services
Artist: April Milne
Cover Designer: Anna Ishchenko

Distributed to the book trade worldwide by Springer Science+Business Media, LLC., 233 Spring Street, 6th Floor, New York, NY 10013. Phone 1-800-SPRINGER, fax (201) 348-4505, e-mail orders-ny@springer-sbm.com, or visit www.springeronline.com.

For information on translations, please e-mail rights@apress.com, or visit www.apress.com.

Apress and friends of ED books may be purchased in bulk for academic, corporate, or promotional use. eBook versions and licenses are also available for most titles. For more information, reference our Special Bulk Sales–eBook Licensing web page at www.apress.com/info/bulksales.

The information in this book is distributed on an "as is" basis, without warranty. Although every precaution has been taken in the preparation of this work, neither the author(s) nor Apress shall have any liability to any person or entity with respect to any loss or damage caused or alleged to be caused directly or indirectly by the information contained in this work.

The source code for this book is available to readers at www.apress.com. You will need to answer questions pertaining to this book in order to successfully download the code.

My gratitude and thanks to Mom and Dad (they would have liked this), to my wife Carol for everything over the years, and to our wonderful and artistically, musically talented son Tim. Also, thanks to Robert and Elizabeth Bergenheim, Elise Falkinburg and Errol Frankel, and their wonderfully intelligent sons, John and James Frankel.

—Danton Chin

Thanks to my wife and daughters, who inspire me daily to help make the world a better place. And for letting me buy that awesome new MacBook Pro (you know which one).

—Saul Mora

To my mother, who taught me to pursue excellence, and to my father, who always inspired creativity in me. Also to Andrea Zemenides, for being cute and little.

—Leon Palm

To the beautiful women in my family: Lisa, Julia, and Taylor. Taylor insists I mention our dog, Jack, and Snickers too.

—Scott Penberthy

To my lovely wife Leonie.

—Ben Britten Smith

To my parents, who were always there for me and gave me the joy of reading. Also to my professor, Dr. Gene Chase, who always brought an incredible amount of enthusiasm to everything he taught, and made computer science inspiring.

—Chuck Smith

To my wife and best friend, Lauren.

—David Smith

Contents at a Glance

Contents

Preface

Dear Reader,

This is the fifth in the Apress series of iPhone Projects books and the first to have the word *iPad* mentioned. To say that we're all hyperaware of the iPad and all that it promises is something of an understatement; will eBooks and Apple's new iBooks store be the killer app for iPad, is this really as "magical" as Steve Jobs says it is, and who are all of these people buying every iPad Apple can manufacture? And yet, *More iPhone Cool Projects* is was written about smaller-screen apps for iPhone and iPod touch. Fear not!

When we started putting this book together, it was still 2009 and the iPad had not been announced. As we were finishing the editorial process, each of the ten chapters was reviewed and updated as appropriate to make mention of iPad considerations. At the same time, we discovered an inherent truth about iPhone and iPad development: all of your iPhone knowledge is invaluable for writing iPad apps, as well. We know this, because each of the 11 contributors (one chapter has coauthors) is moving right into iPad app development.

We urge you think of the lessons learned and code shared in this book as applying to any app you might choose to create using Apple's iPhone OS! In fact, the tools remain the same: Objective-C (with a few exceptions), Cocoa Touch, and XTools. Because of this core of Apple technologies, the best practices also carry across all of the various iPhone OS–running mobile platforms. This is a key theme running through all of the Apress Projects books. Somehow, we had an idea that Apple had more things up its corporate sleeve.

As always, I'd like to mention Dave Mark, our tireless series editor and author of several bestselling Apress titles, including *Beginning iPhone 3 Development*, *More iPhone 3 Development*, and, very soon, *Beginning iPad Development*. In many ways, Dave embodies the positive energy and inspirational spirit that makes the iPhone and iPad developer community such an exciting place to be a part of.

It's in this spirit of collegiality that we have done everything we can to ensure that all of the books in this series are truly useful and enjoyable. We've tried to include something for every style of development, or at least to cover a range of tastes. Please let us know what you think, and we'd be happy to hear about new ideas you may have.

Clay Andres
Apress Acquisitions Editor, iPhone and Mac OS X
clayandres@apress.com

Dave Mark
Series Editor, Bestselling Author, and Freelance Apple Pundit

Acknowlegments

What can I say? A book like this cannot exist without the efforts and passion of a great many people. I have read this book. A few times now. It is amazing and I learn new things every time I go through it. It is the product of thousands of combined hours of effort, and I want to give some credit and thanks to the people who made it all possible.

First off, I want to thank all of the authors who took great pains to distill their years of knowledge and experience into words and code for us to learn from, and who patiently took all of our comments, critiques, and requests for yet more code samples but always came back with increasingly better and better material to work with.

I would like to give a shout-out to Clay Andres, the lead editor who originally approached me about this book and basically did all the legwork to gather the authors together and get the project rolling.

I want to give huge thanks to Debra Kelly and Candace English for keeping all of us authors and reviewers herded in the right direction, working on the right things at the right times and keeping the maze of files and revisions and documents in order.

Huge admiration goes out to the development editors Douglas Pundick and Brian MacDonald and our copy editor Katie Stence. They let us authors focus on getting our thoughts onto paper, and they came through and made sure it sounded good and looked professional.

Thanks!

—Ben Britten Smith

Introduction

This is a wonderful book.

I am a working iPhone developer. I spend each and every day of the work week (and most weekends) writing code that is destined to run on someone's iPhone, iPad, or iPod Touch. I have been doing this for a long time now, and yet there is still so much more to learn!

During the course of this book project, I had the task of going through every single chapter, every single line of code, and building every single sample project (often more than once). I don't recall a single chapter that did not provide me with some insight to a problem that I had worked on recently, was currently working on, or am planning to implement in future projects. Some of the stuff I learned I was able to apply immediately to my running projects. I can pretty much guarantee there is something in here for most every developer out there.

Who This Book Is For

This book presupposes that you have some familiarity with iPhone development. Most of the projects presume that you are able to build and deploy apps written in XCode onto your device for testing. If you started with a book like *Beginning iPhone Development* by Dave Mark and Jeff LaMarche (Apress, 2009), then you will be well set to tackle the projects in the following pages.

There are a few chapters that go into some Mac based tools, so it will also be helpful to be familiar with Objective-C and C development with XCode on the desktop. However, if you have used XCode to compile and deploy an iPhone app, then the desktop stuff should be fairly easy to pick up. If you want to learn more, have a look at some books like *Learn C on the Mac* by Dave Mark (Apress, 2009) and *Learn Objective-C for the Mac* by Mark Dalrymple and Scott Knaster (Apress, 2009).

There is even a light dusting of C# in the chapter on Unity3D. What?! C# in an iPhone book? I told you there is something for everyone here. The C# is very simple and mastery is not required to understand the chapter, but if you are interested, check out *Beginning C# 2008* by Christian Gross (Apress, 2007).

Astute iPad developers may notice that all of the sample code and projects in this book are generally built for the iPhone and iPod Touch devices. This is to make sure that we could cover as many devices as possible. All of the concepts and ideas covered here apply equally to the iPad, of course, and all the code runs perfectly well on that device.

What's in the Book

In Chapter 1, Danton Chin delves into concurrency on the iPhone to help speed up your interfaces and make your apps snappier. If you have some performance bottlenecks in your app, this chapter will be very useful.

Chapter 2 brings Claus Höfele showing you how to use some desktop tools to streamline your game content pipelines. He shows you a specific example from his own extensive game developer experience, but the concepts he elucidates are applicable to many type of apps.

In Chapter 3, Ben Kazez recounts some of the lessons learned and design choices made in developing the very popular Flight Track app. He sheds some light on the process of finding and utilizing external data providers. With so much data available to your applications these days, the concepts shown here will be very helpful.

Saul Mora reminds that testing is important in Chapter 4. He shows how to use unit testing to greatly improve your code stability and help speed up your iPhone development processes.

If you were curious how computers can recognize human faces, then Chapter 5 where Leon Palm's takes on computer vision will quench that thirst. Leon introduces you to the exciting world of computer vision and shows you how to integrate the very powerful OpenCV libraries into your applications. If you are thinking of doing some Augmented Reality in your apps, this chapter will be invaluable.

If you have ever tried to render fonts in OpenGL then you know it is a complex beast. Scott Penberthy breaks it down in Chapter 6. Scott provides some tools and direction that make custom font rendering so easy that you won't go back to boring system fonts ever again.

In Chapter 7, Ben Britten Smith dips his toes into the Unity3D game engine and shows you how to leverage that middleware to build some very complex 3D games very quickly.

If 3D isn't your thing, head to Chapter 8 where Chuck Smith gives you a great introduction to 2D game development with the very popular framework: Cocos2d. Chuck shows you everything you need to know to get started slinging sprites around like the pros.

In Chapter 9, David Smith gives some insight into his popular Audiobooks app, and shows you how to handle lengthy audio content in his sample code. Properly dealing with large audio files is a complicated task, but David makes it so easy.

In the final chapter, Chapter 10, Arne de Vries and Joost van de Wijgerd team up to tell you about their experiences integrating push notifications into their popular eBuddy application.

iPhone and iPad development have come a long way in the short years since the SDK became available. Even working on iPhone projects every day, I still have a hard time keeping up with all of the new features and APIs available to us as iPhone developers. This book is such a great resource you will want to keep it close at hand when you embark on your next iPhone project.

Ben Britten Smith

Danton Chin

Company: *iPhone Developer Journal*
(http://iphonedeveloperjournal.com/)

Location: *Pelham, NY*

Former Life as a Developer: *I have programmed with both procedural and object-oriented languages on hardware ranging from mini-computers, workstations, personal computer systems, and mobile devices. I started to program in BASIC and C. In 1993, I was looking for a better way of designing and developing systems and came across NeXTStep. The night I was ready to place my order for my own NeXT workstation, NeXT announced that they were out of the hardware business. Four NeXTStep conferences and two years later it was over. Later that year, the alpha version of Java was released and over the following years I was able to watch and use a new computer language as it was born, evolved, and grew. Along the way, I got my first experience with mobile application development using J2ME (now Java ME) for Palm PDA devices. I have also developed with Actionscript and MXML, and worked with relational databases and application servers. I have worked in the financial services sector for banks and brokerage firms as well as energy, radio station, and newspaper companies.*

Life as an iPhone Developer: *Doing iPhone development has led me to speak at the 360iDev iPhone Developer Conferences (http://www.360iDev.com/) in San Jose (http://www.360idev.com/about/san-jose-2009) and Denver (http://www.360idev.com/about/denver-2009), and at meetings of the NY iPhone Software Developers Meetup Group (http://www.meetup.com/newyork-iphone-developers/calendar/11630710/). I also started the iPhone Developer Journal blog and continue to do freelance iPhone development. I am currently working on an application for a newspaper company that should be in the App Store by the time this book is in print.*

App on the App Store:

- *PBN (Providence Business News)*

What's in This Chapter: This chapter looks at concurrency solutions that are available on iPhone and iPad devices. A real-world poorly performing application is developed. Then possible approaches to a concurrent solution are discussed. A working solution using operation queues and operation objects is developed. Finally, a solution is developed using operation queues, operation objects, and blocks. The main thesis is that using a concurrent solution that makes use of operation queues, operation objects, and blocks is an optimal way of writing your application today to reduce the complexity of developing a solution with concurrency and to take advantage of changes in the iPhone OS and underlying hardware tomorrow.

Key Technologies:

- *Concurrency*
- *NSOperationQueue*
- *NSOperation*
- *NSInvocationOperation*
- *Blocks*

Chapter 1

Using Concurrency to Improve the Responsiveness of iPhone and iPad Applications

You do not have to have a lot of experience developing iPhone applications before you begin to realize that you may need to fetch data from a server on the Internet or that you have a CPU intensive calculation that freezes your application and prevents your user from interacting with the user interface of your application. On any platform with any computer language, the standard way of dealing with such issues is to perform these tasks in the background allowing your application's user interface to remain responsive to a user's interaction with your application. Fortunately, iPhone OS, like its much bigger sibling Mac OS X, provides a rich array of concurrency solutions for developers needing to use them. However, as you will see the concurrency solutions vary quite a bit in terms of their degree of complexity, level of abstraction, and scalability. This chapter is a brief survey of the concurrency solutions available and you will develop solutions with some of them. There is a definite point of view that I've developed by working with the iPhone SDK and trying to divine the path that Apple might take in the future that hopefully will come across. After all, whether the application is for an iPod Touch, iPhone, or an iPad it isn't cool if the application is sluggish!

Prepare for Concurrency

It had been quite a while since I had attended a conference where Steve Jobs would normally be expected to appear and attendees would go home with their cube-shaped box of books and software for the latest version of the NeXTStep operating system. When NeXT faded away many hopes were dashed, but what is happening with Mac desktop, laptop, iPhone, iPod Touch, and iPad devices is far, far sweeter! Therefore, it was almost but not quite déjà vu as I sat in the audience at Apple's World Wide Developers Conference in 2009. As I listened, a point of view started to develop. Bertran Serlet and Bud Tribble were starting off the conference after the keynote with an overview of all the sessions (Session 700 WWDC Sessions Kickoff). Two new technologies being introduced in Snow Leopard—Grand Central Dispatch (GCD) and OpenCL (Open Computing Language)—stuck out. Grand Central Dispatch is a technology that has several facets: changes to the Mac OS X kernel; a language extension to Objective-C, C, and C++ called Blocks; and new APIs to take advantage of GCD using blocks, queues, and operation objects. OpenCL specifies OpenCL C, which is used to rewrite the calculation intensive portions of an application into C-like functions called OpenCL kernels. The OpenCL kernels are compiled at run-time for the target GPUs for execution. It was hard not to think that this was pretty amazing.

It was the "Seeker" demo (13:46 minutes into the presentation) that drove it home. Seeker is an interactive, 3D solar system simulator developed by Software Bisque (http://www.bisque.com/) for exploring our solar system. In the demo given by Richard S. Wright (co-author of the OpenGL SuperBible) the Seeker program calculates the position of satellites in orbit around the Earth using hundreds of calculations per frame per satellite and is able to perform the display at about 23 fps. Adding the display of space junk objects to the display of satellites brought the total number of objects in orbit around the Earth to over 12,000 maxing out the CPU and bringing the display rate down to 5 fps. Turning GCD on distributed the computations over all the cores and brought the framerate up to 30 fps! Then, GCD and OpenCL were used to display the position of over 400,000 asteroids in addition to the satellites and junk objects achieving a framerate of 30 fps. It was some demo!

At WWDC and in the months afterwards, I speculated and talked about whether GCD or some of its components, such as blocks and OpenCL, would someday become an integral part of iPhone OS in my presentations at conferences. As a follower of Apple and Apple-related news (see Table 1–1), I was aware of Apple's acquisition of P.A. Semi, a semiconductor design firm, in April 2008 and Imagination Technologies' desire to hire OpenCL engineers in December 2008 as reported by the media.

Table 1–1. *Apple and Apple-related News Items that May Impact Concurrency*

Date	News Item
2008	
April	Acquisition of P. A. Semi by Apple.
December	Imagination Technologies job openings for OpenCL engineers.
2009	
June	■ WWDC Apple announces GCD and OpenCL for Snow Leopard. ■ iPhone 3GS released.
July	Plausible Labs releases PLBlocks for Mac OS X 10.5+ and iPhone OS 2.2+.
September	■ Snow Leopard released. ■ ARM announces availability of dual core Cortex-9 ARM reference implementation.
2010	
January	■ Imagination Technologies announces the availability of the PowerVR SGX545 mobile GPU which provides full support for OpenGL 3.2 and OpenCL 1.0. ■ Apple announces the iPad powered by a 1 GHz Apple A4 SOC.
February	Plausible Labs PLBlocks 1.1 Beta with support for Mac OS X 10.5+ and iPhone OS 2.2+ including 3.2.
April	iPhone OS 3.2 and iPad released.

The availability of a third-party implementation of blocks for iPhone OS led me to wonder not *whether,* but *when* an official implementation from Apple would be available. In addition, the availability of reference implementations of dual core ARM chips, OpenCL implementations in the latest version of Imagination Technologies' PowerVR mobile GPU chips, the availability of the iPad and iPhone SDK 3.2 by April 3 all continue to point the way to the possibility that a multicore iPhone could be available around the WWDC 2010 timeframe. If there is a multicore iPhone device then we'll need enhancements to the operating system and the Cocoa Touch classes to harness the power of those cores using GCD and blocks. With rumors of multitasking coming to the next version of the iPhone operating system there may be sweeping changes ahead. We'll all know for sure once the successor to iPhone OS 3.2 is released under an NDA.

All this was speculation then and it still is. What then is an appropriate strategy for concurrency that will take advantage of multiple cores if and when they arrive? What I realized at WWDC was that using operation objects would be that strategy as long as it met the needs of my application. And, if multicore iPhones never arrive have we lost anything by using operation objects? No, especially if it helps to reduce complexity in your application. I think it would be really sweet and exciting to have Apple's implementation of GCD, blocks, and OpenCL on the iPhone at some point in the future—possibly in the next version of the iPhone and iPhone OS at WWDC 2010! But concurrent solutions exist already so let's look at a possible use case without using concurrency and see how various concurrent solutions can increase user satisfaction and perhaps ease development efforts.

Non-Responsive User Interfaces

Almost any long-running operation can make the user interface sluggish and unresponsive. Some examples of operations that can impact the responsiveness of your user interface are loading images or data over the Internet to be displayed in your application; manipulating images or data; parsing XML or RSS; performing a complex mathematical calculation such as finding *n* prime numbers, calculating pi to *m* decimal places, or calculating Euler's constant *e* to *p* decimal places. In addition, there are situations where a concurrent solution is typically used such as sorting a socket server as well as countless other situations. As a point of discussion for looking at concurrent solutions, you will develop a simplistic application to view the images that have made it into Flickr's top 500 *interestingness* list for the most recent day. Schematically, your Interestingness app will make RESTful HTTP requests to Flickr servers and receive a response in JavaScript Object Notation (JSON) a lightweight data format for transferring data in name—value pairs (see Figure 1–1). The images will be displayed using a UITableView managed by a UITableViewController. Interestingness is a ranking assigned to each photo using a secret algorithm patented by Flickr based on a number of factors including the number of users who added the photo to a list of favorites, origin of the clickthroughs, user assigned tags, comments, relationship between the uploader of the image and those who comment on the image, and other secret factors. Flickr's `flickr.interestingness.getList` API is used to retrieve this list and does not require user authentication—only an API key. The roadmap that you will follow to build the first version of the Interestingness app will be:

- Build the user interface.

- Add a JSON parsing framework to the application.

- Compose a RESTful request to fetch a list of interestingness images.

- Use the RESTful request and the JSON framework to parse the response.

- Implement the UITableViewDataSource Protocol Methods to display the results.

Let's get started!

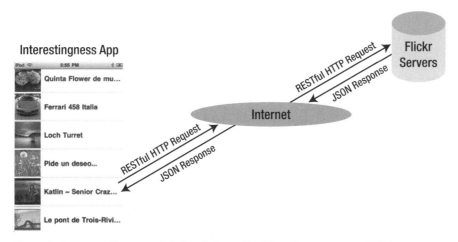

Figure 1–1. *Request/Response data flow between the Interestingness app and Flicker servers*

NOTE: The projects were all built using both iPhone OS 3.1.3 and Xcode 3.2.1 and iPhone OS 3.2 and Xcode 3.2.2 on Snow Leopard.

Building the Interestingness User Interface

The application as you'll build it does not check if the network is available nor does it provide any user feedback on the progress of fetching data over a network connection. Of course, a shipping application should do both. The Reachability APIs that are a part of the SystemConfiguration.framework will allow you to check for network availability while progress indicators are a part of the standard user interface components. These aspects have been left out to focus on concurrency. So start up Xcode and create a new project using the Window-based Application template. Name the application Interestingness to create the header and implementation files for the InterestingnessAppDelegate and the main window nib file. You do not need the main nib file in this simple application and it could even be deleted but you will just leave it.

TIP: For more details on creating iPhone applications, see the highly regarded book *Beginning iPhone 3 Development: Exploring the iPhone SDK*, by Jeff Lamarche and David Mark (Apress, 2009).

Next CTRL-Click on the Classes folder to add a new file, click on Cocoa Touch class templates, and choose the UIViewController subclass template making sure that the Options checkbox for UITableViewController is checked. Click the Next button and name the subclass InterestingnessTableViewController. Make sure that the checkbox to create the header file is checked then click the Finish button (see Figure 1–2).

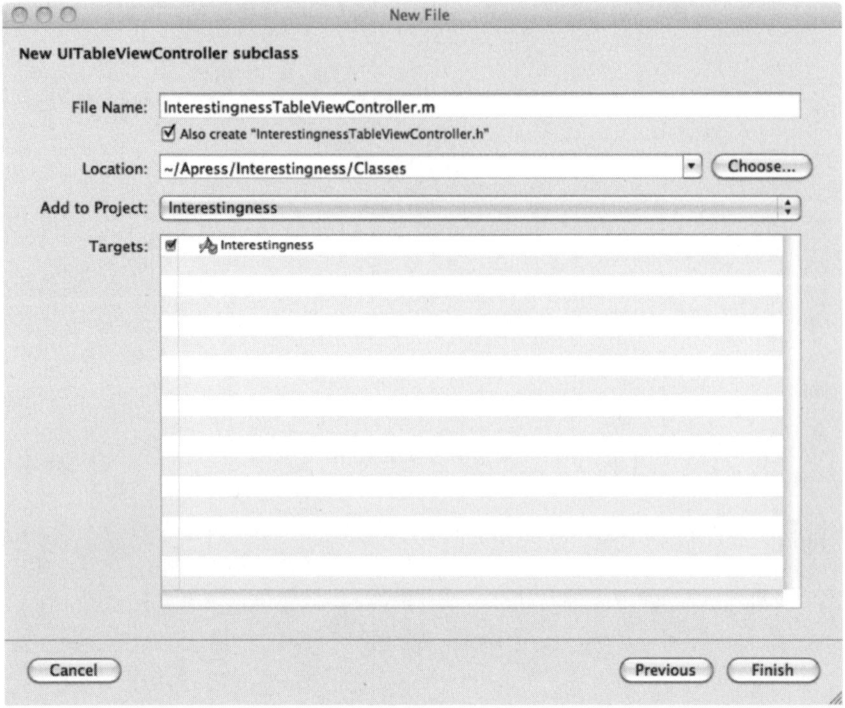

Figure 1–2. *Subclassing UITableViewController*

In the application delegate header file, you forward declare InterestingnessTableViewController and declare the variable for an instance of this subclass and name it tableViewController so that the declaration of the application delegate class appears as in Listing 1–1.

Listing 1–1. *InterestingnessAppDelegate Header fFle*

```
#import <UIKit/UIKit.h>

@class InterestingnessTableViewController;

@interface InterestingnessAppDelegate : NSObject <UIApplicationDelegate> {
        UIWindow *window;
        InterestingnessTableViewController *tableViewController;
}

@property (nonatomic, retain) IBOutlet UIWindow *window;

@end
```

On the implementation side of the application delegate import the header file for the InterestingnessTableViewController and in the applicationDidFinishLaunching method, allocate and initialize an instance of our table view controller, set the frame for the view controller, add the table view controller's view as a subview of the window, and for good memory management practice release the tableViewController in the dealloc method as in Listing 1–2.

Listing 1–2. *InterestingnessAppDelegate Implementation File*

```
#import "InterestingnessAppDelegate.h"
#import "InterestingnessTableViewController.h"

@implementation InterestingnessAppDelegate

@synthesize window;


- (void)applicationDidFinishLaunching:(UIApplication *)application {

        tableViewController = [[InterestingnessTableViewController alloc]
                                    initWithStyle:UITableViewStylePlain];

        [[tableViewController view] setFrame:[[UIScreen mainScreen] applicationFrame]];

        [window addSubview:[tableViewController view]];

    [window makeKeyAndVisible];
}


- (void)dealloc {
        [tableViewController release];
    [window release];
    [super dealloc];
}


@end
```

Note that you are programmatically creating your table view controller and that you are
not using a nib file in which a table view is defined with a data source and a delegate. In
this case, the UITableViewController by default sets the data source and the delegate
to self. Out of the box, the subclass provides stubs for two of the required methods of
the UITableViewDataSource Protocol—tableView:cellForRowAtIndexPath: and
tableView:numberOfRowsInSection:—and one of the optional methods
numberOfSectionsInTableView:. In addition, the subclass provides a stub implemention
of only one of the optional methods— tableView:didSelectRowAtIndexPath:—of the
UITableViewDelegate Protocol which you do not need to implement in this case since
the Interestingness app will not be providing a detail view for the selected row. Since
you are creating the table view controller programmatically uncomment the
initWithStyle: method. At this point, that is the only change in the implementation of
InterestingnessTableViewController. So go ahead and build and run this in the
Simulator to make sure that everything works. You currently have a responsive but
empty table view!

NOTE: The Interestingness project up to this point is in the folder Interestingness-Version1.

Adding A JSON Parsing Framework to the Interestingness App

As was mentioned earlier the Interestingness app will receive a response to an HTTP request in JSON format (see Figure 1–1). In order to use the data, the reponse will be parsed using a JSON parser. JSON has become increasingly popular as a data exchange format and parsers are available for just about every computer language. The next step then is to download and add a JSON parsing framework to your project. The framework used in this project is the json-framework which can be downloaded from Google's Code repository at `http://code.google.com/p/json-framework/` (see the "Resources" section). Download and expand the disk image. Drag the JSON folder to the `Interestingness` project and drop it on the project or into your favorite folder (such as Classes). Be sure to check the checkbox to copy the items to the destination folder (Figure 1–3). You can also CTRL-Click to add an existing folder and its contents to the project making sure to select the option to copy the items to the destination folder. Now importing `JSON.h` will provide access to the methods that make up the json-framework.

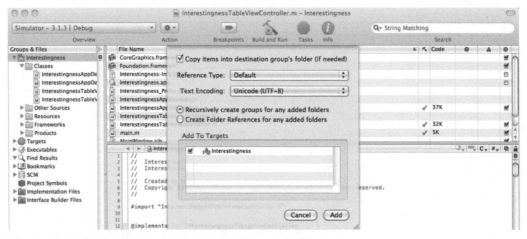

Figure 1–3. *Adding the JSON classes to the Interestingness project*

Composing a RESTful Request for a List of Interestingness Images

To fetch the images from the Flickr `interestingness` API make a RESTful request to Flickr for a list of these images. The information needed to build a URL for the individual images is extracted from the list to build a URL for an individual image. A Flickr API request consists of four components—a service endpoint, a method name, an API key, and a list of required and optional parameters for the method:

- *Service Endpoint*: Flickr accommodates requests and provides responses via three formats: REST, XML-RPC, and SOAP. Flickr also provides responses using JSON and PHP. You will be making RESTful requests using HTTP GET for which the service endpoint is http://api.flickr.com/services/rest/.

- *Method name*: Flickr provides authenticated and nonauthenticated access to the photos and the extended data attributes around the photos that are uploaded to their site. Most of the APIs require authentication in addition to an API key. You will use a nonauthenticated, "public" API named flickr.interestingness.getList to get a list of the most interesting photos.

- *Flickr API key*: If you have a Flickr API key you will need it in order to download images for your project. If you do not have a Flickr API key, head over to Flickr (http://www.flickr.com/services/apps/create /apply/) to create an API key for which you will need a Yahoo account.

- *Method parameters*: As parameters you will need to provide:

  - per_page (optional): The number of photos to return per page.

  - format (optional): Specify that the response be in JSON format. Additionally, you just want the raw JSON output without the enclosing function wrapper so that as part of the request one of the parameters of the request will be nojasoncallback=1.

Your Flickr request will appear as follows:

```
http://api.flickr.com/services/rest/?method=flickr.interestingness↩
.getList&api_key=%@&tags=&per_page=%d&format=json&nojasoncallback=1
```

with two values to be filled in, the API key and the number of photos per page, which will be done when you create the NSString.

Now to make the changes to the Interestingness application so it fetches and displays the images change InterestingnessTableViewController.h as follows:

```
#import <UIKit/UIKit.h>

@interface InterestingnessTableViewController : UITableViewController {

        NSMutableArray *imageTitles;
        NSMutableArray *imageURLs;
}
-(void)loadInterestingnessList;

@end
```

This declares two mutable arrays to store the image names and URLs and a method to load the list of interestingness images from Flickr.

Next, you will need to change the implementation. Begin by importing JSON.h, defining your Flickr API key, modifying the `initWithStyle:` method to initialize the two mutable arrays, and uncomment the `viewWillAppear:` method so that you can add the call to `self` to load the list of images:

```
#import "InterestingnessTableViewController.h"

#import "JSON.h"

#define API_KEY @"INSERT YOUR FLICKR API KEY HERE"

@implementation InterestingnessTableViewController


- (id)initWithStyle:(UITableViewStyle)style {
    if (self = [super initWithStyle:style]) {
            imageTitles = [[NSMutableArray alloc] init];
            imageURLs  = [[NSMutableArray alloc] init];
}
    return self;
}

- (void)viewWillAppear:(BOOL)animated {
        [super viewWillAppear:animated];
        [self loadInterestingnessList];
}
```

Now is as good a time as any to remember to release the mutable arrays in the `dealloc` method so that you don't leak memory.

```
- (void)dealloc {
        [imageTitles release];
        [imageURLs release];
    [super dealloc];
}
```

Using the RESTful Request and the JSON Parser to Parse the Response

Now implement the `loadInterestingnessList` method:

```
-(void)loadInterestingnessList
{

    NSString *urlString = [NSString stringWithFormat:@"http://api.flickr.com/services↵
/rest/?method=flickr.interestingness.getList&api_key=%@&extras=description&tags=↵
&per_page=%d&format=json&nojsoncallback=1", API_KEY, 500];

    NSURL *url = [NSURL URLWithString:urlString];

    NSError *error = nil;

    NSString *jsonResultString    = [NSString stringWithContentsOfURL:url
                                        encoding:NSUTF8StringEncoding
                                                        error:&error];
```

```objc
NSDictionary *results = [jsonResultString JSONValue];

NSArray *imagesArray = [[results objectForKey:@"photos"] objectForKey:@"photo"];

for (NSDictionary *image in imagesArray) {

    // build the url to the image

    if ([image objectForKey:@"id"] != [NSNull null]) {
        NSString *imageURLString = [NSString
            stringWithFormat:@"http://farm%@.static.flickr.com/%@/%@_%@_s.jpg",
                                        [image objectForKey:@"farm"],
                                        [image objectForKey:@"server"],
                                        [image objectForKey:@"id"],
                                        [image objectForKey:@"secret"]];

        [imageURLs addObject:[NSURL URLWithString:imageURLString]];

        // get the image title

        NSString *imageTitle = [image objectForKey:@"title"];

        [imageTitles addObject:([imageTitle length] > 0 ? imageTitle ↵
: @"Untitled")];

    }

  }
}
```

Here you build the URL string using NSString's class method `stringWithFormat:` to provide the API key and the number of images you want to retrieve per page. Then you retrieve the URL with NSString's convenience method `stringWithContentsOfURL:encoding:error` and store the result in `jsonResultString`. You then use the json-framework to return the NSDictionary represented by the string and retrieve the array of dictionary objects representing the images using the key "photo". Next, iterate through the array of dictionary objects (the info for each image) using the keys farm, server, id, and secret to retrieve the corresponding value in order to build a URL for the image and add the URL to your mutable array of URLs in the instance variable `imageURLs`. Your final steps in this method are to retrieve the title for the image and store either the title if the length is greater than zero or "Untitled" in your mutable array of titles `imageTitles`.

NOTE: More details on how to build a URL for an individual photo can be found at `http://www.flickr.com/services/api/misc.urls.html`.

Implementing the UITableViewDataSource Protocol Methods to Display the Results

Next, you need to modify the UITableViewDataSource methods numberOfSectionsInTableView:, tableView:numberOfRowsInSection:, and tableView:cellForRowAtIndexPath: to fetch and display the images in our table. Since your user interface is very basic there will only be one section in the table view and the numberOfSectionsInTableView: method returns the following:

```
-(NSInteger)numberOfSectionsInTableView:(UITableView *)tableView
{
        return 1;
}
```

Next change the tableView:numberOfRowsInSection: method to return the number of elements in the imageURLs array:

```
- (NSInteger)tableView:(UITableView *)tableView numberOfRowsInSection↵
:(NSInteger)section {
    return [imageURLs count];
}
```

Finally, change the tableView:cellForRowAtIndexPath: method to set the text of the label to the title of the image, fetch the image using NSData's class method dataWithContentsOfURL, and finally set the cell's imageView to the image that was just downloaded:

```
- (UITableViewCell *)tableView:(UITableView *)tableView cellForRowAtIndexPath↵
:(NSIndexPath *)indexPath {

    static NSString *CellIdentifier = @"Cell";

    UITableViewCell *cell = [tableView dequeueReusableCellWithIdentifier↵
:CellIdentifier];
    if (cell == nil) {
        cell = [[[UITableViewCell alloc] initWithStyle:UITableViewCellStyleDefault↵
 reuseIdentifier:CellIdentifier] autorelease];
    }

    // set the title

        [[cell textLabel] setText:[imageTitles objectAtIndex:[indexPath row]]];

        // fetch the image

        NSData *data = [NSData dataWithContentsOfURL:[imageURLs objectAtIndex↵
:[indexPath row]]];

        // set the cell's image

        [[cell imageView] setImage:[UIImage imageWithData:data]];

    return cell;
}
```

NOTE: The project up to this point is in the folder Interestingness-Version2.

Now it is time to test the Interestingness application on a device. Select the Interestingness target, CTRL-Click, select Info, and then select the Properties tab and set the Identifier to one that matches your provisioning profile that has been set up with your iPhone Developer Certificate. Then set the Active SDK to Device – 3.1.3 | Debug and build and run. The application can be installed and tested in the Simulator but performance of the application in the Simulator does not resemble the performance of the application on a real device. The Interestingness application should look like Figure 1–4 although the images and text will not be the same.

CAUTION: A splash screen will load immediately but it may take the application several seconds before the interestingness images appear.

TIP: If the application compiles but no images appear you may have forgotten to enter a valid Flickr API key so be sure to check that. Also, you must be a paid member of the iPhone Developer Program in order to install and test on an iPhone, iPod, or iPad device. See http://developer.apple.com/programs/iphone/develop.html.

Figure 1–4. *A screen shot of the Interestingness application*

Concurrency Landscape

Why is the application slow? Both Cocoa and iPhone Applications start life with one thread and a run loop. Basically, a run loop listens for events and passes them on to an appropriate handler. Once the handler finishes processing, the event control returns to the run loop which either processes the next event or puts the main thread to sleep until there is something to do. Your application is doing all of its work on the main thread preventing it from responding to any user interface events or any other event until your task has finished.

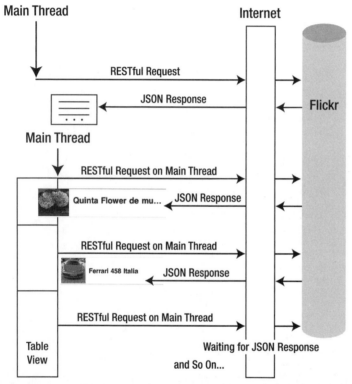

Figure 1–5. *The Interestingness app makes a RESTful request for the master list of images and then one RESTful request for each image for each exposed table view cell , all on the main thread in Version 2 of the app.*

Interestingness fetches data over the Internet at two points—once to fetch the list of Interestingness images and then one fetch for each image in each cell of the table view (see Figure 1–5). It does so synchronously, and until the data has been returned, no updates of the user interface can occur. Our application needs to perform such time consuming tasks in a background thread and not on the main thread. There are a lot of concurrent options available as you can see from Table 1–2. The concurrency solutions range from a high level of abstraction and a lower level of complexity to a low level of abstraction and a higher level of complexity. Depending upon the needs of your application one solution may be better than another. It may be almost obvious but it does not hurt to state that the best concurrency solution is the concurrency solution that has the highest level of abstraction that is consistent with your application needs. There are multiple benefits from doing so and in this case it applies particularly to the use of operation objects—it reduces complexity in your application (KISS), it may insulate your application from lower level changes, it may lay the groundwork for future changes in the operating system, and it may allow your application to take advantage of underlying hardware changes. Using the highest level of abstraction is consistent with the history and development of computers, programming languages, and programming methodologies.

Table 1–2. *Available Concurrency Solutions As of April 2010*

Level of Abstraction	Technology	Description	iPhone OS	Mac OS X	Complexity
High	Operation objects	NSOperation NSOperationQueue	Yes	10.5+	Low
	Grand Central Dispatch	Dispatch queues and blocks, etc.	No	10.6+	
	Cocoa Threads	NSThread NSObject	Yes	Yes	
	Asynchronous methods	Some classes have both synchronous and asynchronous methods, NSURLConnection, for example	Yes	Yes	
Low	POSIX Threads (pthreads)	C-based APIs and libraries for creating and managing threads	Yes	Yes	High

Considerations When Using Concurrent Solutions

There are some general considerations to be aware of when implementing any concurrent solution. A primary consideration is that generally UIKit classes are not thread safe unless the Apple documentation specifically states that it is. All updates to the user interface should occur on the main thread and not from a background thread. Another major concern that must be taken into account once an application has two or more threads is synchronizing access to shared data, especially mutable data. Altering shared data structures from more than one thread can lead to race conditions and deadlocks.

> **NOTE:** This is such an important point that it bears repeating: UIKit is not thread safe and all updates to the user interface should occur on the main thread. See Apple's Threading Programming Guide Appendix A: Thread Safety Summary for a compilation of thread safety issues across the frameworks.

For Cocoa Touch applications each thread must maintain its own autorelease pool. Although an autorelease pool is created for the application in main.m each new thread is responsible for creating its own autorelease pool. Creating the autorelease pool is the first thing that should take place in your thread's routine and the last thing the routine should do is to release the objects in the pool. The general outline looks like the following code:

```
-(void)main
{
        NSAutoreleasePool *localPool;

        @try {
                /*
                *    create an autorelease pool for objects released during
    a long running task
                */

                localPool = [[NSAutoreleasePool alloc] init];


                /*
                *    perform a long running task
                */
                ...

        }
        @catch (NSException * e) {
                NSLog(@"An exception was thrown %@", e);
        }
        @finally {
                /*
                * the @finally block is always executed whether an exception
    is thrown or not
                */

                [localPool release];

        }
}
```

If an autorelease pool is not created you will see messages in your console such as in Figure 1–6 and your application could eventually run out of memory and crash. In a loop that creates a lot of autoreleased objects, you will probably want to periodically release those objects in order to reduce the memory footprint of your application.

```
run
Running...
[Switching to thread 11779]
[Switching to thread 11779]
sharedlibrary apply-load-rules all
(gdb) continue
2010-03-25 23:13:11.663 Interestingness[463:3e03] *** _NSAutoreleaseNoPool(): Object 0x119db0
    of class __NSCFDate autoreleased with no pool in place - just leaking
Stack: (0x32ee9f83 0x32ebd973 0x32ebd93f 0x338ca851 0x3369 0x32ecbacd 0x32e79d15 0x3392f788)
```

Figure 1–6. *Console messages with no autorelease pool in place for a thread*

Concurrency with NSThread and NSObject

Since Objective-C is a superset of C one possible threading solution is to create and manage threads with the POSIX thread library a C-based API to the underlying Mach threads. Compared to the other possible options for concurrency in Table 1–2, POSIX threads are relatively low in terms of their level of abstraction and represent a higher degree of complexity. POSIX threads can be mixed with the Cocoa frameworks but you must ensure that Cocoa knows that your application is multithreaded. Use NSThread's class method +isMultithreaded to determine if your app is multithreaded. If it is not then spawning a thread and letting it exit is enough to let the application know that it is in multithreaded mode. Using POSIX threads may be a good solution for an application if you are using a C-based API already. Since it would represent a move towards more direct thread management rather than less it won't be examined further here.

Another solution that may solve an application's need for concurrency is to try to take advantage of the Apple APIs that have both synchronous and asynchronous methods. A good example is NSURLConnection with methods to initialize and set the delegate for the connection. The delegate at a minimum needs to implement the methods `connection:didReceiveResponse:`, `connection:didReceiveData:`, `connection:didFailWithError:`, and `connectionDidFinishLoading:`. Sometimes these asynchronous methods may be all your application needs.

At the next level up support for concurrency solutions starts right from the root object—NSObject. NSObject provides support for spawning a thread with the method `performSelectorInBackground:withObject:` that creates a detached thread using the named method as the entry routine for the new thread. NSObject also has methods to perform a method of the receiver on the current thread, to perform a method of the receiver on the main thread, and to perform a method of the receiver on a specified thread.

As a first step towards a concurrent solution in the Interestingness application, you will fetch the list of images from `flickr.interestingness.getList` in a background thread and parse the returned list in the main thread. NSObject's `performSelectorInBackground:withObject:` will be used to fetch the master list on a background thread while the `performSelectorOnMainThread:withObject:waitUntilDone:` method will be used to invoke the method on the main thread to parse the results (see Figure 1–7). You will break up the original `loadInterestingnessList` method into two parts: a `disaggregateInterestingnessList:` method which takes an NSDictionary parameter and returns void and a `fetchInterestingnessList` which takes no parameters and returns void.

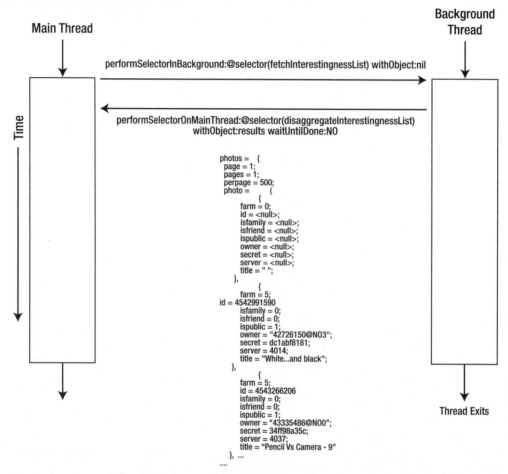

Figure 1–7. *Performing the RESTful request for the master list of interestingness images on a background thread for version 3 of the Interestingness app. A portion of the JSON results is displayed.*

Change the header file for the InterestingnessTableViewController so that it appears as follows:

```
#import <UIKit/UIKit.h>

@interface InterestingnessTableViewController : UITableViewController {

        NSMutableArray *imageTitles;
        NSMutableArray *imageURLs;
}

-(void)loadInterestingnessList;
-(void)fetchInterestingnessList;
-(void)disaggregateInterestingnessList:(NSDictionary *)results;

@end
```

Next change the implementation of the `InterestingnessTableViewController` as follows. First delete the implementation of the `loadInterestingnessList`. Then add the new method `fetchInterestingnessList`:

```
-(void)fetchInterestingnessList
{

        NSAutoreleasePool *localPool;

        @try {
                localPool = [[NSAutoreleasePool alloc] init];

                if ([NSThread isMainThread]) {
                        NSLog(@"fetchInterestingnessList is executing in the
 main thread");
                } else {
                        NSLog(@"fetchInterestingnessList is executing in a
 background thread");
                }

                NSString *urlString = [NSString
stringWithFormat:@"http://api.flickr.com/services
/rest/?method=flickr.interestingness.getList&api_key=%@&tags=&per_page=%d&format
=json&nojsoncallback=1", API_KEY, 500];

                NSURL *url = [NSURL URLWithString:urlString];

                NSError *error = nil;

                NSString *jsonResultString    = [NSString stringWithContentsOfURL
:url encoding:NSUTF8StringEncoding error:&error];

                NSDictionary *results = [jsonResultString JSONValue];

                [self performSelectorOnMainThread:@selector
(disaggregateInterestingnessList:) withObject:results waitUntilDone:NO];

        }
        @catch (NSException * exception) {
                // handle the error -- do not rethrow it
                NSLog(@"error %@", [exception reason]);
        }
        @finally {
                [localPool release];
        }


}
```

This method is the entry point for the background thread. The very first thing that you must do is to initialize an autorelease pool or you will leak memory. Then add a log statement to indicate whether the method is performing on the main thread or another thread. Then, perform your potentially long running task. When it is done the current thread is sent the message `performSelectorOnMainThread:withObject:waitUntilDone:` using `disaggregateInterestingnessList:` as the selector and passing it the

NSDictionary results object and indicate that you do not want this background thread to block until the main thread finishes executing the selector that was specified.

Now add the disaggregateInterestingnessList: method with the NSDictionary results parameter:

```
-(void)disaggregateInterestingnessList:(NSDictionary *)results
{
    if ([NSThread isMainThread]) {
        NSLog(@"disaggregateInterestingnessList is executing in the main thread");
    } else {
        NSLog(@"disaggregateInterestingnessList is executing in a background thread");
    }

    NSArray *imagesArray = [[results objectForKey:@"photos"] objectForKey:@"photo"];

    for (NSDictionary *image in imagesArray) {
        // build the url to the image
        if ([image objectForKey:@"id"] != [NSNull null]) {
            NSString *imageURLString =
        [NSString stringWithFormat:@"http://farm%@.static.flickr.com/%@/%@_%@_s.jpg",
                                    [image objectForKey:@"farm"],
                                    [image objectForKey:@"server"],
                                    [image objectForKey:@"id"],
                                    [image objectForKey:@"secret"]];

        [imageURLs addObject:[NSURL URLWithString:imageURLString]];

        // get the image title

        NSString *imageTitle = [image objectForKey:@"title"];

        [imageTitles addObject:([imageTitle length] > 0 ? imageTitle↩
  : @"Untitled")];

        }

    }

        [[self tableView] reloadData];
}
```

There are only a few changes here. The first is that it logs which thread the method is running on and there is an addition of the message to the table view to reload the data for the table. Finally, change the viewWillAppear: method to kick off the fetchInterestingnessList method on a background thread.

```
- (void)viewWillAppear:(BOOL)animated {
        [super viewWillAppear:animated];

        [self loadInterestingnessList];

        [self performSelectorInBackground:@selector(fetchInterestingnessList)↩
  withObject:nil];

}
```

NOTE: This version of the project is in the folder Interestingness-Version3.

Build and run it on a device. There is a slight improvement in the performance of the user interface in that the initial empty table view appears more quickly but after the images for each cell of the table start to appear the performance is sluggish at best. For a real performance boost the individual images need to be loaded on a background thread. The NSThread class method detachNewThreadSelector:toTarget:withObject: could be used to spawn a new detached thread as follows:

```
[NSThread detachNewThreadSelector:@selector(fetchImage:) toTarget:self withObject:url];
```

where fetchImage: is a new method implemented on the current object and passing it the url object for the image. Alternatively, a new NSThread object (see Figure 1–8) could be initialized and started:

```
NSThread *fetchThread = [[NSThread alloc] initWithTarget:self
                                         selector:@selector(fetchImage:)
                              object:url];
[fetchThread start];
```

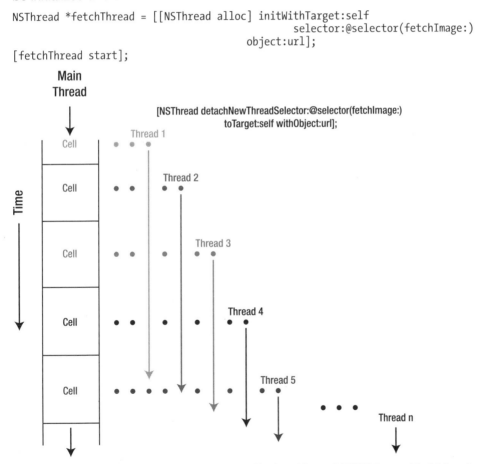

Figure 1–8. *A possible solution would be to spawn off a thread for each RESTful request to fetch an image.*

You could create an NSDictionary object to track and cache each image object using the image url as a key and determine whether you need to spawn a new thread to fetch the image. Even so, if you carry either of these alternatives to their logical conclusion, the following questions emerge: How many threads do you spawn? What is the optimal number of threads to spawn? It would be easy to see that you could end up in a situation where the application spawns enough threads to bring your application to a grinding halt. But wait, isn't there a solution for that?

Concurrency with Operation Objects

Need work done on a background thread? Think operation objects! Why use operation objects? There are some very good reasons to use operation objects. Operation objects are a high-level abstraction for threading which reduces the complexity and level of difficulty in developing a multithreaded application. That's a great reason right there! Secondly, it will position your application to take advantage of multiple cores should they become available on future iPhone and iPad devices with no effort on your part. Another great reason!

Operation objects have been available on Mac OS X since Leopard. It is a high level of abstraction approach to concurrency. Instead of thinking about creating and managing threads an operation queue manages that and the scheduling of the execution of the tasks submitted to it. Using operation objects allows you to focus on the task itself; the unit of work that is needed by your application and represented by an NSOperation object. In order to use operation objects there are only three classes that you need to become familiar with: NSOperationQueue, NSOperation, and NSInvocationOperation (Figure 1–9). NSOperationQueue and the abstract class NSOperation both inherit from NSObject while NSInvocationOperation is a subclass of NSOperation. NSBlockOperation is not available as a part of the standard iPhone OS distribution.

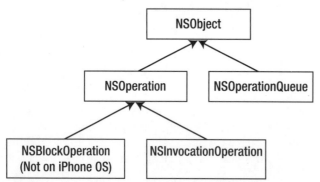

Figure 1–9. *Operation Objects class hierarchy as of April 2010*

NSOperationQueue

An NSOperationQueue instance manages the operations or work units added to the queue and works dynamically with the operating system to determine the optimal number of concurrent operations as a function of the number of cores available in the system and the overall load on the system at a given moment. A new instance of an NSOperationQueue is created just like any other Cocoa object:

```
NSOperationQueue *workQueue = [[NSOperationQueue alloc] init];
```

After the queue has been initialized the maximum number of concurrent operations—maxConcurrentOperationCount—is set to the constant NSOperationQueueDefaultMaxConcurrentOperationCount to allow the NSOperationQueue to determine how many operations can run concurrently. NSOperationQueue is key-value coding (KVC) and key-value observing (KVO) compliant and the properties maxConcurrentOperationCount and operations can be observed. To create a serial queue and only allow one operation to execute at a time set maxConcurrentOperationCount to 1:

```
[workQueue setMaxConcurrentOperationCount:1];
```

> **NOTE:** For more on key-value coding and key-value observing see Apple's Introduction to Key—Value Observing Programming Guide listed in the "Resources" section.

To set the maxConcurrentOperationCount back to its default value, use the constant NSOperationQueueDefaultMaxConcurrentOperationCount.

Operation queues can be suspended and restarted using the method setSuspended:YES to suspend and NO to restart the queue. Suspending or restarting a queue suspends the scheduling or restarts the scheduling of operations. Suspending a queue does not suspend the execution of currently running operations. Executing operations are allowed to run until they finish or are cancelled.

To add operations to the queue use the method addOperation: as in:

```
[workQueue addOperation:workOperation];
```

There is *no* corresponding removeOperation: method. All of the operations in a queue can be cancelled by sending the queue a cancelAllOperations message but there is no message that can be sent to the queue to cancel an individual operation in an operation queue. But you can send an individual operation object a cancel message:

```
[workOperation cancel];
```

All operations that are dependent on workOperation finishing receive notification that the dependency has been satisfied. A cancelled operation is still considered to be "finished". So if there are operations that depend on the operation that had been cancelled it would appear to have finished normally. If an operation is cancelled then it may be desirable to cancel all operations particularly if a subsequent operation is dependent upon a result of the operation. Cancelling all operations then would be more common then canceling individual operations. Note that it is up to the operation object to check to see that it has been cancelled and stop executing (this will be discussed in greater detail in the following section).

NSOperation and NSInvocationOperation

Operation objects encapsulate the data and the methods that belong to a task. If an application has a time-consuming task that would benefit from being executed in a background thread then there are two approaches to modeling that task, either subclass NSOperation to define a custom operation object or use an instance of NSInvocationOperation. NSOperation is an abstract class and must be subclassed in order to be used while NSInvocationOperation is a concrete subclass of NSOperation. Both are KVO compliant. The properties that can be observed are the following:

- isCancelled
- isConcurrent
- isExecuting
- isFinished
- isReady
- dependencies
- queuePriority

Operation objects also have characteristics that can affect their execution order, namely dependencies and priorities. Dependencies are used to serialize the execution of operation objects and are used to make the execution of an operation object be dependent upon another operation object. The methods addDependency: and removeDependency: are used to set and remove an operation's dependencies. Creating circular dependencies can lead to a situation in which the operations are deadlocked since an operation object will not run until all of its dependent operation objects have finished executing. As was noted earlier, a cancelled operation is considered to have finished executing. It is a recommended practice that an operation object's dependencies be set before it is added to a queue since a dependency added after may not prevent the operation object from running.

Operation objects can have priorities that range from the following:

NSOperationQueuePriorityVeryHigh	8
NSOperationQueuePriorityHigh	4
NSOperationQueuePriorityNormal	0
NSOperationQueuePriorityLow	−4
NSOperationQueuePriorityVeryLow	−8

and are set using the `setQueuePriority:` method. For operations in a queue the order of execution is determined first by the *readiness* of the operations followed by their *relative priority* levels. An operation is ready if all its dependencies have been met. As shown in Figure 1–10 a low priority operation that is ready will run before a high priority operation that is not ready.

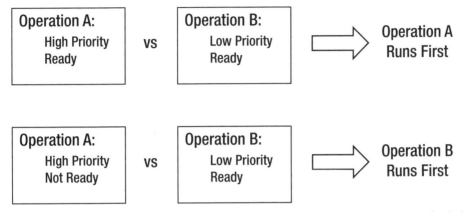

Figure 1–10. *Execution order of operations is determined first by their readiness then by their relative priorities.*

NSInvocationOperation—Quick and Easy

Depending upon your application needs using an NSInvocationOperation is a viable alternative when the task is already segregated in a method in an existing class of your application. Using an `NSInvocationOperation` object is the easiest way to define an operation object to be added to an operation queue for execution and eliminates creating custom operation objects. The operation object created by an `NSInvocationOperation` is a non-concurrent operation. To use an `NSInvocationOperation` object create and initialize a new instance by passing to the initialization method the target which defines the selector and the parameter object if any. A typical initialization would look like this:

```
NSInvocationOperation *myOperation =
[[[NSInvocationOperation alloc] initWithTarget:self
                                selector:@selector(doWorkMethod:)
                                    object:myData] autorelease];
```

Subclassing NSOperation

If an `NSInvocationOperation` does not meet the needs of your application then the alternative is to subclass `NSOperation`. There are two types of subclasses of NSOperation—a nonconcurrent operation and a concurrent operation. In a nonconcurrent operation (which is the default for operation objects) the operation's task is performed synchronously. As such, the operation object subclass itself does not create a new thread on which to execute the task and the `isConcurrent` method returns NO. On the other hand, a concurrent operation executes asynchronously; the operation object subclass creates a new thread to perform the task or calls an asynchronous method to execute a task and the isConcurrent method returns YES. In a nonconcurrent operation submitted to an operation queue, the operation queue will manage concurrency for the operation and will create a new thread in which to run the operation. The result is still asynchronous execution of the nonconcurrent operation.

You'll only be creating nonconcurrent subclasses of NSOperation. Creating a concurrent subclass of NSOperation is much more work in which the start, main, isExecuting, isFinished, and isConcurrent methods must be overridden. A nonconcurrent subclass must at a minimum implement an init method to create a known state for the long-running task, a main method to perform the long-running task, and a dealloc method to clean up any memory allocated by the operation object. The main method must create an autorelease pool and must try to respond to cancellation events. Responding to cancellation is entirely voluntary. To determine whether the operation has been cancelled, use the isCancelled method and if it returns YES free up memory and exit immediately. The isCancelled method should be called:

- Before any work is performed

- At the beginning of an iteration loop and within the body of a long iteration

- Anywhere you can

The implementation of the selector that performs the work in an NSInvocationOperation should also respond to cancellations.

Building HelloOperationQueues—a Toy Application

To make some of these ideas more concrete we'll develop a toy application to add and remove operations from a queue as pictured in Figure 1–11.

So fire up Xcode and choose as your template a view-based application. Name the new project HelloOperationQueues. The default declaration and implementation of the application delegate for HelloOperationQueues is all you need in your toy application. However, in the header file for HelloOperationQueuesViewController you'll declare outlets for the two labels that you will need to use to update the user interface—one for the operation count output and one for the operation work message. You also need to declare the operation queue that you will be using. You'll declare one action for the button presses and another method addOp: that will be used to add our work units to the operation queue. Then you'll also declare the custom subclasses of NSOperation that you will be adding to the queue. The completed HelloOperationQueuesViewController header file will look like this:

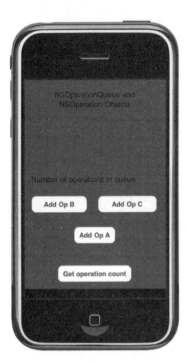

Figure 1–11. *Adding operations to a queue*

```objc
#import <UIKit/UIKit.h>

@class JobUnit;

@interface HelloOperationQueuesViewController : UIViewController {

        UILabel *operationCountOutput;
        UILabel *operationOutput;

        NSOperationQueue *workQueue;

        JobUnit                 *jobA;
        JobUnit                 *jobB;
        JobUnit                 *jobC;

}

@property(nonatomic, retain)IBOutlet UILabel *operationCountOutput;
@property(nonatomic, retain)IBOutlet UILabel *operationOutput;

-(IBAction)buttonPressed:(id)sender;
-(void)addOp:(JobUnit *)job;

@end
```

Building the User Interface for HelloOperationQueues

Save it and open up the `HelloOperationsViewController.xib` file in Interface Builder to build the user interface. If the window with a title of View is not already open double-click the View icon in the nib file's main window. Click on the view and ⌘-1 to bring up the View Attributes. Then, click on the background color well to change the background color to blue. Enter ⌘-shift-L to bring up the Library palette of components and drag a UILabel to the top of the View window. Change the size of the label so that vertically there is enough room for two lines of text and extend the width of the label to the outer edges. Change the text of the label to read "NSOperationQueue and NSOperationObjects".

Next, change the layout so that the text is centered and the number of lines is set to 2. Drag another UILabel from the Library palette and place it below the existing label. This second label will be used to display messages from the operations. Clear the text and set the layout so that the text is centered and the number of lines is 4. Extend the height to accommodate four lines of text and extend the width of this second label to the outer edges of the window. To connect the outlet for this label click on the *File's Owner* icon and control drag from the *File's Owner* icon to the label, let go, and select the `operationOutput` outlet. Now add two more labels on the same line. Set the text on the left label to hold the static text "Number of operations in queue", for the label immediately to the right clear the text. Then to connect the outlet for this label click on the Files' Owner icon and control drag to the label, let go, and select the `operationCountOuput` outlet as in Figure 1–12.

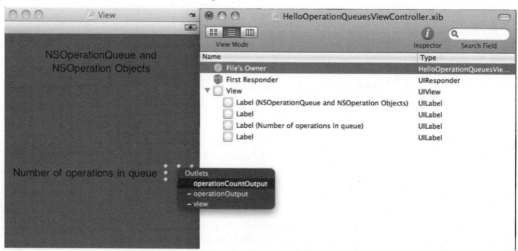

Figure 1–12. *The four UILabels added to the view with the last remaining outlet for operationCountOutput about to be selected.*

Now add four Round Rect Buttons to the View laying them out, as shown in Figure 1–13.

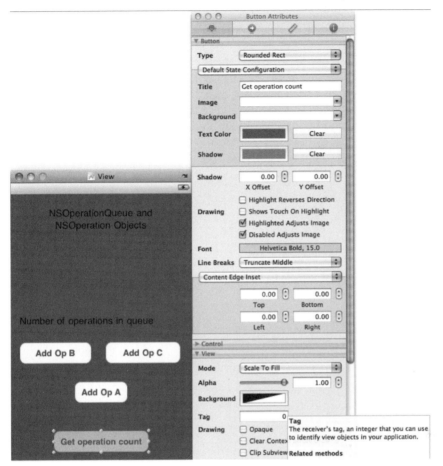

Figure 1–13. *Layout of the four buttons. The tag number for the "Get operation count" button is about to be set to zero.*

You will be using the tag property (an integer) of each button to identify which button was pressed to perform the appropriate action. Set the button's tag number to zero for "Get operation count", to one for "Add Op A", to two for "Add Op B", and to three for "Add Op C" in each button's attribute inspector window. Now control drag from each button to the *File's Owner* icon and select the buttonPressed: event, or you can control-click on a button and in the gray panel that pops up drag from the Touch Up Inside event to the *File's Owner* icon and select the buttonPressed: event. Save the nib file and close Interface Builder.

Creating Work Units by Subclassing NSOperation

Your operations will be a nonconcurrent subclass of NSOperation. In Xcode, click on the Classes folder and control-click to add a new file. Choose the Objective-C template and name the class JobUnit. Be sure to check the checkbox to create the header file as well. In the header file for JobUnit change the superclass of JobUnit to be NSOperation, declare a property for workMsg, and declare an initialization and a main method as follows:

```
#import <Foundation/Foundation.h>

@interface JobUnit : NSOperation  {
        NSString *workMsg;

}

@property (nonatomic, retain) NSString *workMsg;

-(id)initWithMsg:(NSString *)msg dependency:(id)obj;
-(void)main;

@end
```

Now change the implementation for JobUnit:

```
#import "JobUnit.h"

@implementation JobUnit
@synthesize workMsg;

-(id)initWithMsg:(NSString *)msg dependency:(id)obj
{
        if ( self = [super init]) {
                [self setWorkMsg:msg];

                if (obj != nil) {
                        //
                        [self addDependency:obj];
                }
        }
        return self;
}

-(void)main
{
        /*
         *              create an autorelease pool for objects released
         *                        during a long running task
         */

        NSAutoreleasePool *localPool;

        @try {

                localPool = [[NSAutoreleasePool alloc] init];
```

```
        /*
         *        check if operation has been cancelled
         */

        if ([self isCancelled]) return;

        /*
         *                perform a long running task
         */

        NSLog(@"performing work for %@", [self workMsg]);
    }
    @catch (NSException * e) {
            // handle the exception but do not rethrow the exception
    }
    @finally {
            [localPool release];
    }
}

-(void)dealloc
{
        [workMsg release];
        [super dealloc];
}

@end
```

The implementation of JobUnit uses initWithMsg:dependency: to initialize the object.
You'll use this to initialize operation objects with a different work message and a
dependent operation object if any. The main method implementation contains the
minimum that a main method must do: within an @try–@catch–@finally block you create
an autorelease pool, use the isCancelled method to see if the operation has been
cancelled, and since the @finally block is always executed release the autorelease pool
in the @finally block.

Implementing HelloOperationQueues

For the implementation of the controller you'll start by importing the header file for
JobUnit.h at the top of the HelloOperationQueuesViewController.m and then
synthesizing your two outlets as follows:

```
#import "HelloOperationQueuesViewController.h"
#import "JobUnit.h"

@implementation HelloOperationQueuesViewController

@synthesize operationCountOutput, operationOutput;
```

Change the viewDidLoad: method to allocate and initialize the operation queue
workQueue. Each of the work units JobA, JobB, and JobC are allocated and initialized
with a custom work message and a dependent operation object is set. JobA has no

dependencies. JobB is dependent upon JobA running while JobC is dependent on JobB running. For each work unit, you have added `self` as an observer of the KVO property `isFinished`. When a work unit has finished executing in the operation queue, you will be notified. Since operation queues are also KVO compliant, you have added `self` as an observer of the KVO property operations.

```
- (void)viewDidLoad {
    [super viewDidLoad];

        /*
         *             create the NSOperationQueue
         */

        workQueue = [[NSOperationQueue alloc] init];
        [workQueue setMaxConcurrentOperationCount:1];

        /*
         *             create the NSOperation objects
         */

        jobA = [[JobUnit alloc] initWithMsg:@"Welcome " dependency:nil];
        [jobA addObserver:self forKeyPath:@"isFinished" options↵
:NSKeyValueObservingOptionNew context:nil];

        jobB = [[JobUnit alloc] initWithMsg:@"to " dependency:jobA];
        [jobB addObserver:self forKeyPath:@"isFinished" options↵
:NSKeyValueObservingOptionNew context:nil];

        jobC = [[JobUnit alloc] initWithMsg:@"NSOperationQueues!" dependency:jobB];
        [jobC addObserver:self forKeyPath:@"isFinished" options↵
:NSKeyValueObservingOptionNew context:nil];

        [workQueue addObserver:self forKeyPath:@"operations" options↵
:NSKeyValueObservingOptionNew context:nil];


}
```

In order to capture the KVO notifications, you must implement the observeValueForKeyPath:ofObject:change:context: as follows. The first two parameters are the KVO property and the object that triggered the notification while the last two contain a dictionary with details of the change and the context that was used when you registered to observe the KVO property. You will be using the first two properties to determine which property and the object that changed (for more on Key Value Observing see the Apple documentation section in "Resources").

```
-(void)observeValueForKeyPath:(NSString *)keyPath ofObject:(id)object
                         change:(NSDictionary *)change context:(void *)context
{

        if ([keyPath isEqual:@"isFinished"])
        {
                // operation finished
                [operationOutput setText:[NSString
                             stringWithFormat:@"%@%@",
```

```
                                                [operationOutput text], [object↵
workMsg]]];
        }

        if ([keyPath isEqual:@"operations"]) {
                // number of operations changed
                [operationCountOutput setText:[NSString
                                stringWithFormat:@"%d",
                                        [[workQueue operations] count]]];
        }

}
```

The button presses have all been set to call the `buttonPressed:` action method. In the implementation of the `buttonPressed:` method, use the tag number that you previously set to a unique number for each button, and you are using that property to determine which button was pressed. To add the job to the operation queue, send yourself the `addOp:` message with the appropriate job as the single parameter. The addition of each operation to the operation queue is enclosed in a @try—@catch block. If there is an error, an alert is presented with the reason. Don't forget to release the operations and the queue in the `dealloc` method as follows:

```
-(IBAction)buttonPressed:(id)sender
{

        switch ([sender tag]) {
                case 0:
                        /*
                         * get operation count button pressed
                         */
                        {
                                NSArray *opArray = [workQueue operations];

                                [operationCountOutput setText:[NSString↵
stringWithFormat:@"%d", [opArray count]]];

                        }
                        break;
                case 1:
                        /*
                         *       Add JobA button pressed
                         */
                        [self addOp:jobA];
                        break;
                case 2:
                        /*
                         *       Add JobB button pressed
                         */
                        [self addOp:jobB];
                        break;
                case 3:
                        /*
                         *       Add JobC button pressed
                         */
                        [self addOp:jobC];
                        break;
```

```
        default:
                break;
    }
}

-(void)addOp:(JobUnit *)job
{
    UIAlertView *alert;

    @try {
        [workQueue addOperation:job];
    }
    @catch (NSException * exception) {

        alert = [[UIAlertView alloc] initWithTitle:@"NSOperationQueue Error:"
                            message:[exception reason]
                            delegate:nil
                cancelButtonTitle:@"OK"
                otherButtonTitles:nil];
        [alert show];
        [alert release];
    }

}

- (void)dealloc {
    [jobA    release];
    [jobB    release];
    [jobC    release];
    [workQueue    release];
    [super dealloc];
}
```

Build and run it. When all the operations have finished executing you'll see the screen on the left side of Figure 1–14. Trying to add an operation that has finished executing will display the alert shown on the right. Operation objects are one shot deals.

> **NOTE:** Use this application to experiment with priorities, multiple queues, and setting the maxConcurrentOperationCount to the default value.

Figure 1–14. *Adding operation objects to an operation queue and the result of adding an operation to a queue after it has finished executing.*

Changing the Interestingness App to Use NSOperationQueues

Now that you know how operation queues and objects work and interact with each other, you are ready to change the Interestingness application to use operation objects. You will use an NSInvocationOperation to retrieve the list of images from flickr.interestingness.getList (see Figure 1–15) and then a subclass of NSOperation to retrieve the individual images for the table view (see Figure 1–16).

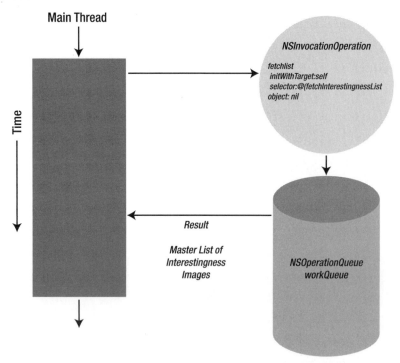

Figure 1–15. *Using NSInvocationOperation to retrieve the master list of interestingness images returned in result*

You'll start with the changes to use an NSInvocationOperation using version three of the project as you last left it or use the project in the folder Interestingness-Version4-Start. First, change the header file for InterestingnessTableViewController to include a declaration for the NSOperationQueue that will be used to execute the operations as follows:

```
NSOperationQueue        *workQueue;
```

Then, in the implementation file you need to change the initWithStyle: method to initialize the operation queue:

```
workQueue = [[NSOperationQueue alloc] init];
[workQueue setMaxConcurrentOperationCount:1];
```

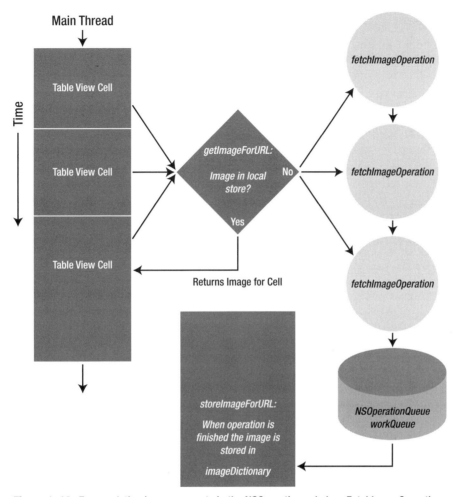

Figure 1–16. *Encapsulating image requests in the NSOperation subclass FetchImageOperation*

Implementing the NSInvocationOperation to Fetch the List of interestingness images

All of the work for the initialization of the NSInvocationOperation will occur in the viewWillAppear: method. Initialize the NSInvocationOperation object by passing self for the target, fetchInterestingnessList as the selector, and nil for the object since the method doesn't take a parameter. Once the operation has been added to the operation queue, you can release it or you will leak memory. Remove the call to the method performSelectorInBackground:withObject: and the viewWillAppear: method should look as follows:

```
- (void)viewWillAppear:(BOOL)animated {
    [super viewWillAppear:animated];

    // allocate and initialize the invocation operation
```

```
    NSInvocationOperation *fetchList =
[[NSInvocationOperation alloc] initWithTarget:self
                                     selector:@selector(fetchInterestingnessList)
                                       object:nil];

    // add it to the queue

    [workQueue addOperation:fetchList];

    // release the invocation operation

    [fetchList release];

}
```

The fetchInterestingnessList method needs no changes. Just as in the previous version, the method will fetch the list of interestingness images and then it will perform the disaggregateInterestingnessList: method with the results object on the main thread. Build it and run it on your device. Of course, there is no difference in performance since you have just substituted a different mechanism for performing the task using an NSOperationQueue and an NSInvocationOperation instead of using NSObject's performSelectorInBackground:withObject: method.

Implementing FetchImageOperation a Subclass of NSOperation

It will take a little more work to fetch the individual interestingness images asynchronously (refer back to Figure 1–16). Currently, these images are loaded synchronously using the url for the image when the image for the cell's imageView is set. One way to make this occur asynchronously is to use a method to check a data store to determine whether the image is present. If it is not present, store the url for the image and kick off a background fetch of the image using an NSOperation object. When the NSOperation object finishes fetching the image in the background the operation object will use the performSelectorOnMainThread:withObject:waitUntilDone: method to invoke a method on the main thread to update the data store with the image. In the InterestingnessTableViewController, you'll implement a method named getImageForURL: to check for the image and to kick off the fetch if needed. Then you'll implement a method named storeImageForURL: that will be used by the custom subclass of NSOperation to update the data store on the main thread.

To start, you'll create a nonconcurrent subclass of NSOperation to perform the loading of the images in the background. Click on the Classes folder and control-click to add a new file choosing the Objective-C template and name the class FetchImageOperation. Be sure that the checkbox to create the header file is selected. Change the superclass of FetchImageOperation to NSOperation instead of NSObject, declare a variable of type NSURL named imageURL, and declare a custom initialization method for the class named initWithImageURL:target:targetMethod that takes as parameters an NSURL, an object, and a selector as follows:

```
#import <Foundation/Foundation.h>

@interface FetchImageOperation : NSOperation {

        NSURL *imageURL;
        id         targetObject;
        SEL        targetMethod;

}

-(id)initWithImageURL:(NSURL *)url target:(id)targClass↵
 targetMethod:(SEL)targClassMethod;

@end
```

On the implementation side for `FetchImageOperation` the initialization method will retain and keep a reference to the url of the image to download. The other two parameters are the object on which you'll send the update message to and the selector that you want to perform. The main method is where all the work occurs. You set up the requisite autorelease pool and immediately check if the operation has been cancelled. Then NSData's `initWithContentsOfURL:` method is used to download the image data and create a `UIImage` with the data. In order to return two objects—the image and the url to the image—back to the main thread use an instance of an `NSDictionary` with the keys @"image" and @"url" to store the image and the url, respectively. Finally, the operation object uses the `performSelectorOnMainThread:withObject:waitUntilDone:` method to pass the results back to the `targetObject` or main thread. The `FetchImageOperation` implementation should look like so:

```
#import "FetchImageOperation.h"

@implementation FetchImageOperation

-(id)initWithImageURL:(NSURL *)url target:(id)targClass↵
 targetMethod:(SEL)targClassMethod
{
        if (self = [super init]) {
                imageURL = [url retain];
                targetObject = targClass;
                targetMethod = targClassMethod;
        }
        return self;
}

-(void)main
{
    NSAutoreleasePool *localPool;

    @try {
        // create the autorelease pool
        localPool  = [[NSAutoreleasePool alloc] init];

        // see if we have been cancelled

        if ([self isCancelled]) return;
```

```
    // fetch the image

    NSData   *imageData = [[NSData alloc] initWithContentsOfURL:imageURL];

    // create the image from the image data

    UIImage *image     = [[UIImage alloc] initWithData:imageData];

    // store the image and url in a dictionary to return

    NSDictionary *result =
            [[NSDictionary alloc]
                    initWithObjectsAndKeys:image, @"image", imageURL, @"url", nil];

    // send it back

    [targetObject performSelectorOnMainThread:targetMethod
                                   withObject:result
                                waitUntilDone:NO];

        [imageData release];
        [image release];
        [result release];
    }
    @catch (NSException * exception) {
        // log exception
        NSLog(@"Exception: %@", [exception reason]);
    }
    @finally {
        [localPool release];
    }
}

-(void)dealloc
{
        [imageURL release];
        [super dealloc];
}
@end
```

Implementing the getImageForURL: and storeImageForURL: Methods

Among the last changes that need to be implemented is the implementation of the
getImageForURL: and the storeImageForURL: methods in the
InterestingnessTableViewController. The getImageForURL: method will be called in the
tableView:cellForRowAtIndexPath method when the tableView needs to set the image
and the title for the cell while storeImageForURL: is called by a custom subclass of
NSOperation—FetchImageOperation—when it has finished fetching an image.

Start with the changes to the header file for the InterestingnessTableViewController by
making the additions in bold:

```
#import <UIKit/UIKit.h>
```

```
@interface InterestingnessTableViewController : UITableViewController {

        NSMutableArray          *imageTitles;
        NSMutableArray          *imageURLs;
        NSOperationQueue        *workQueue;
        NSMutableDictionary     *imageDictionary;
}
-(void)fetchInterestingnessList;
-(void)disaggregateInterestingnessList:(NSDictionary *)results;

-(UIImage *)getImageForURL:(NSURL *)url;
-(void)storeImageForURL:(NSDictionary *)result;

@end
```

Then, in the implementation file for the InterestingnessTableViewController begin by importing the header file for FetchImageOperation.h:

```
#import "FetchImageOperation.h"
```

Now initialize the mutable dictionary that will be used to store the fetched images in the initWithStyle: method:

```
imageDictionary = [[NSMutableDictionary alloc] init];
```

Next, in the tableView:cellForRowAtIndexPath method remove the synchronous loading of the image and set the image for the cell by calling getImageForURL: as follows:

```
        NSData *data = [NSData dataWithContentsOfURL:[imageURLs
                                      objectAtIndex:[indexPath row]]];

        // set the cell's image

        change this [[cell imageView] setImage:[UIImage imageWithData:data]]; to

        [[cell imageView] setImage:[self getImageForURL:[imageURLs
                                         objectAtIndex:[indexPath row]]]];
```

The implementation of the getImageForURL: method will get the object from the mutable dictionary using the NSURL object as the key. If the object is nil, an NSString object is added to the dictionary using the key and a new FetchImageOperation is initialized with the url for the image; using storeImageForURL: as the method that you want invoked on self when the operation is finished. The FetchImageOperation is then added to the queue and released so that you don't have a memory leak. Finally, if the object is not nil and it is an image object then it is returned to be used to set as the image to be set on the cell's imageView otherwise the object is set to nil. The implementation should appear as follows:

```
#pragma mark -
#pragma mark    Methods for Loading Remote Images using NSOperation

-(UIImage *)getImageForURL:(NSURL *)url
{
    /*
     * called by tableView:cellForRowAtIndexPath to get the image
```

```
     *             from the imageDictionary for the row
     * If the image is not in the row kick off a FetchImageOperation
     *             to get the image
     */

    id object = [imageDictionary objectForKey:url];

    if (object == nil) {

        // we don't have an image yet so store a temporary NSString object for the url

        [imageDictionary setObject:@"F" forKey:url];

        /*
         *       create a FetchImageOperation
         */

        FetchImageOperation *fetchImageOp =
                    [[FetchImageOperation alloc] initWithImageURL:url
                                                 target:self
                        targetMethod:@selector(storeImageForURL:) ];

        // add it to the queue

        [workQueue addOperation:fetchImageOp];

        // release it

        [fetchImageOp release];
    } else {
        // we have an object but need to determine what kind of object

        if (![object isKindOfClass:[UIImage class]]) {
                // object is not an image so set the object to nil
                object = nil;
        }
    }

    return object;


}
```

The implementation of storeImageForURL: is straightforward. The immutable dictionary that is returned by the FetchImageOperation is used to update the mutable imageDictionary. Then the tableView is sent a message to reload the data:

```
-(void)storeImageForURL:(NSDictionary *)result
{
        /*
         * method called by FetchImageOperation to store the image
         */

        // get the url object using the key @"url" from the dictionary
        // get the image object using the key @"image" from the dictionary
```

```
    NSURL   *url = [result objectForKey:@"url"];

    UIImage *image = [result objectForKey:@"image"];

    // store the image

    [imageDictionary setObject:image forKey:url];

    // tell the table to reload the data

    [[self tableView] reloadData];
}
```

You are done with all the required changes. Build it and run it on a device. You've enhanced your unresponsive application and made it much more responsive! Oh by the way, there's just one more thing!

NOTE: This version of the Interestingness project is in the folder Interestingness-Version4.

Concurrency with Operation Objects and Blocks

Grand Central Dispatch, blocks, and OpenCL are only available on Snow Leopard. GCD was implemented to move the job of managing, scheduling, distributing, and executing threads over multiple cores from the hands of application developers to the operating system. A key part of the implementation of GCD on Mac OS X is the language extension to Objective-C, C, and C++ called blocks. Blocks is not available for iPhone OS as a part of Apple's standard distribution of iPhone OS 3.1.2 and 3.2. However, a third-party implementation of blocks has been made available by Plausible Labs since July of 2009 for Leopard, Snow Leopard, and iPhone OS 2.2+. A new 1.1 beta 3 was released in March 2010 for Leopard and Snow Leopard that is compatible with the iPad OS. Plausible Labs has verified that both the 1.0 and 1.1 beta versions work with the iPad OS.

Based on the availability of reference implementations of multicore chips for mobile devices, industry competitive pressures, and the number of changes that Apple has made to over one hundred APIs on Snow Leopard to use blocks it is my guess that blocks, Grand Central Dispatch, and maybe even OpenCL may be available in the near future as a standard distribution from Apple for iPhone OS. In the meantime, why wait? Applications can be using operation objects and blocks now to be in the best position to take advantage of underlying hardware and operating system changes with little or no changes to the application once those enhancements occur. Who's using it in shipping apps? Plausible Labs of course and Cocos2d has added support for blocks using the PLBlocks framework. That should be some incentive to learn about blocks. You'll take a brief tour of blocks and then you'll put it to use.

Why use blocks? On Snow Leopard blocks are used in callbacks, to perform an operation on all items in a collection, to compare two objects when sorting the contents of an array, and to enclose a unit of work in a queue to mention a few uses. To place operation queues (see Table 1–2) in perspective there are two broad groups of queues in GCD: dispatch queues and operation queues. Dispatch queues are a part of GCD and the C runtime and are a C-based mechanism for executing tasks. Dispatch queues always execute tasks in a first-in, first-out order and use blocks to encapsulate the unit of work. There are three kinds of dispatch queues: serial, concurrent, and the main dispatch queue. Serial dispatch queues execute one task at a time while concurrent dispatch queues start as many tasks as it can and do not wait for the other tasks to complete before starting a new task. Serial dispatch queues are created and managed by you and you can create as many serial queues as needed (within the constraints of the system). Concurrent queues on the other hand are system queues—three are made available to each application—and for this reason are called global dispatch queues. The last type of dispatch queue, the main dispatch queue, works with the application's main thread to execute tasks. The operation queue that you have been using, NSOperationQueue, is the Cocoa equivalent of concurrent dispatch queues with the characteristics that have already been discussed. On Snow Leopard NSOperationQueue is implemented on top of GCD so that one could say it is an even higher level of abstraction than GCD. Another broad difference is the existence of NSBlockOperation on Snow Leopard (see Figure 1–9). On Snow Leopard NSBlockOperation is a concrete subclass of NSOperation and is used as a wrapper for one or more block objects around a block of code to be executed. You will be using an analogous version of NSBlockOperation to add a block of work to an NSOperationQueue.

Blocks

Blocks are similar to closures in other computer languages such as Scheme, Lisp, SmallTalk, and Ruby. Blocks can be explicitly declared using a syntax similar to C function pointers but use a caret instead of an asterisk. Unlike C function pointers which use the * operator to mark the beginning of a C function pointer blocks use the caret ^ operator to start the declaration of a block variable or a block literal. For example, the declaration of a block named cubeIt that will return the cube of a number would be written as shown in the following illustrations.

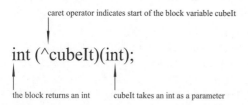

caret operator indicates start of the block variable cubeIt

int (^cubeIt)(int);

the block returns an int   cubeIt takes an int as a parameter

The block literal definition can be defined and assigned to the block variable.

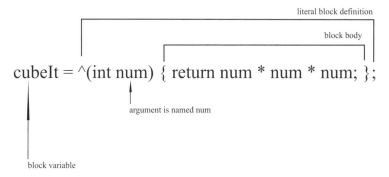

This can also be done on one line as follows:

```
int (^cubeIt)(int) = ^(int num) { return num * num * num; };
```

Since cubeIt was declared as a variable cubeIt can be used just like any function and the following log statement would print 64:

```
NSLog(@"%d", cubeIt(4));
```

Alternatively, blocks can also be defined as a type definition using the C language typedef feature. The cubeIt block above could have been defined as:

```
typedef int (^cubeIt)(int);

cubeIt cube = ^(int num){
        return num*num*num;
};
```

And subsequently, the cubeIt block could be used as:

```
NSLog(@"The cube of 5 is %d", cube(5));
```

Blocks can also be defined inline anonymously and can be passed as parameters in a method. When blocks are passed as parameters they use an abstract declarator form syntax:

```
(returnDataType  (^) ( parameterType1, parameterType2, …))blockName
```

Blocks capture const versions of variables that have been defined within the same scope as the block that can be used in the body of the block. If there is a need to change the variable within the block body, then the variable can be declared with the new storage modifier __block which would then allow the variable to be modified within the block.

Blocks start life on the stack as opposed to the heap and can be copied to the heap if needed. All blocks are Objective-C objects even when they are used in a C program. In an Objective-C environment blocks will respond to –copy and –release. Whew, that's a whirlwind tour of blocks!

Adding the PLBlocks Framework

Think this is academic? Not on your life! With this basic idea of what Blocks are let's apply this to our project and we'll begin with installation. To install PLBlocks download a distribution from http://code.google.com/p/plblocks/. Double click the compressed disk image to unarchive it. The expanded disk image includes a folder for the iPhone Runtime, a folder for the Mac OS X Runtime, and the Plausible Blocks SDK package. The package installs the custom compilers to be used with Xcode while the runtime frameworks must be included with your project. Exit Xcode and then double click the Plausible Blocks SDK package to install it. Click on the image of the hard drive to install it to the default location Developer or choose the folder for the location where Xcode is installed.

> **NOTE:** The applications were built using the PLBlocks 1.0 for Snow Leopard build and tested on a 3.1.3 device.

Start Xcode and open the project as you last left it or start with the Interestingness project in the folder Interestingness-Version5-Start. Add the PLBlocks.framework by dragging it to the Frameworks folder of the Interestingness project and dropping it or by choosing Add Existing Framework and navigating to the folder with the PLBlocks.framework and selecting it as in Figure 1–17. Be sure to check the box to copy the items. The next step is to set the PLBlocks compiler as the compiler for the project. Click on the target for the project and click ⌘-I or click on the Info button. In the Compiler Version section select GCC 4.2 (Plausible Blocks) as the compiler as in Figure 1–18. Now you're ready to use Blocks. Enter the following Block statements in the viewWillAppear: method in the implementation of InterestingnessTableViewController:

```
int mFactor = 2;

int numberToCube = 4;

int (^cubeIt)(int);

cubeIt = ^(int num)  { return num * num * num;  };

NSLog(@"The cube of %d is %d", numberToCube, cubeIt(numberToCube));

int (^cubeItTimesAFactor)(int) = ^(int num) {  return cubeIt(num) * mFactor;  };
NSLog(@"The cube of %d multiplied by a factor of %d is %d",
                        numberToCube, mFactor, cubeItTimesAFactor(4));
```

> **CAUTION:** Make sure that the compiler version appears *exactly* as in Figure 1–18 otherwise the project wll not compile.

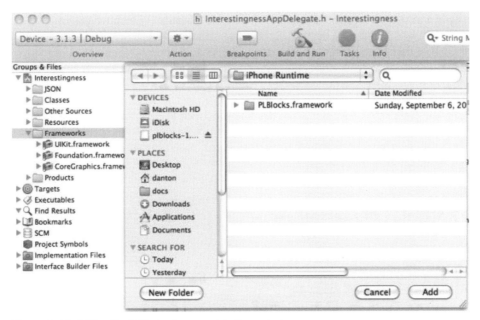

Figure 1–17. *Adding the PLBlocks.framework to the project*

Figure 1–18. *Set the compiler for the project to GCC 4.2 (Plausible Blocks).*

The statements define two block examples. The first declaration is a standard `int` variable named `mFactor` with a value of 2. The next statement declares a block variable named `cubeIt` that takes an `int` as a parameter. Then you define a block literal expression and assign it to the block variable `cubeIt`. The second block example declares the block variable `cubeItTimesAFactor` and declares the block literal that is assigned to it all in one statement. The block declaration in this example illustrates how blocks have access to variables defined in the same scope; in this case, another block variable and an integer. Since you declared `cubeIt` and `cubeItTimesAFactor` as block variables you can call them just like any other function. The NSLog statements do that and print the results. Build and run application and the results should appear in the console as:

```
2010-04-01 14:02:33.207 Interestingness[2425:207] The cube of 4 is 64
2010-04-01 14:02:33.230 Interestingness[2425:207] The cube of 4 multiplied by a
 factor of 2 is 128
```

Changing the Interestingness Application to Use NSOperationQueues and Blocks

Now you know that PLBlocks has been set up correctly. To see what blocks can do you'll change the Interestingness application to use Blocks and NSOperationQueues. You'll change the `getImageForURL:` method in the `InterestingnessTableViewController` implementation to use a PLBlockOperation—an operation with block support—to add an operation to our operation queue. First, you need to add a modified version of Plausible Labs' extensions (see Resources) to `NSOperationQueue` contained in the `NSOperationBlock` sample project. Add a new Group folder named Blocks to the Interestingness project. Then control-click on the folder to add existing files and select the files `NSOperationQueue+PLBlocks.h` and `.m` from the folder named Interestingness-Version5-PLBlockExtensions that are part of the project files for this chapter as in Figure 1–19. Be sure that the checkbox to copy the files is selected and click the Add button to add the files to the project. Then import the header file `NSOperationQueue+PLBlocks.h` and remove the import for `FetchImageOperation.h` at the top of the InterestingnessTableViewController implementation file as follows:

```
#import "InterestingnessTableViewController.h"
#import "FetchImageOperation.h"
#import "NSOperationQueue+PLBlocks.h"
```

Change the `getImageForURL:` method:

```
-(UIImage *)getImageForURL:(NSURL *)url
{
    /*
     * called by tableView:cellForRowAtIndexPath to get the image
     *          from the imageDictionary for the row
     * If the image is not in the row kick off a FetchImageOperation
     *          to get the image
     */
        id object = [imageDictionary objectForKey:url];
        if (object == nil) {
                // we don't have an image yet so store a temporary NSString object
```

```
        // for the url
                    [imageDictionary setObject:@"F" forKey:url];
                    /*
                     * create a block operation
                     */
                    PLBlockOperation *fetchImageOp = [PLBlockOperation↩
    blockOperationWithBlock:^{
                        NSAutoreleasePool *localPool;
                        @try {
                            localPool = [[NSAutoreleasePool alloc] init];
                            // fetch the image
                            NSData *imageData = [[NSData alloc] initWithContentsOfURL:url];
                            // create the image from the image data
                            UIImage *image      = [[UIImage alloc] initWithData:imageData];
                            // store the image and url in a dictionary to return
                            NSDictionary *result = [[NSDictionary alloc]
                                    initWithObjectsAndKeys:image,@"image",url,@"url",nil];
                            [self performSelectorOnMainThread:@selector(storeImageForURL:)
                                                        withObject:result
                                        waitUntilDone:NO];
                            [imageData release];
                            [image release];
                            [result release];
                        }
                        @catch (NSException * e) {
                            NSLog(@"error in block operation");
                        }
                        @finally {
                            [localPool release];
                        }
                    }];
            } else {
                // we have an object but need to determine what kind of object
                if (![object isKindOfClass:[UIImage class]]) {
                    // object is not an image so set the object to nil
                    object = nil;
                }
            }
            return object;
    }
```

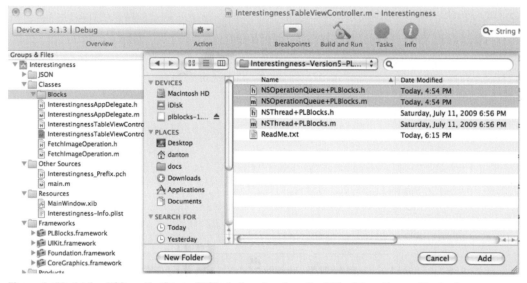

Figure 1–19. *Adding NSOperationQueue+PLBlocks.h and .m from the folder Interestingess-Version5-PLBlockExtensions folder to the Interestingness project.*

In the getImageForURL: method instead of allocating and initializing an instance of the subclass of NSOperation that you created—FetchImageOperation — to do the work of fetching the image you use a PLBlockOperation. A PLBlockOperation is a subclass of NSOperation that is a block operation and is an analogous version of Snow Leopard's NSBlockOperation. The blockOperationWithBlock: class method returns an NSOperation object with the provided block of statements. In the block, you create an autorelease pool, do all the work to fetch the image, and then execute the storeImageForURL: method on the main thread. When you are done with the objects imageData, image, result you release them. There is no need to release the block operation since the class method returns an autoreleased object. The local autorelease pool is released in the finally clause of the @try—@catch—@finally block.

> **NOTE:** This version of the project is in the folder Interestingness-Version5.

Build and run this version of the Interestingness application. While you will not notice any performance gains in the application there have been tremendous gains in terms of increased locality and clarity of the code. Because of blocks you are able to locate all of the statements near where they are used. Using blocks you were able to eliminate two files needed to declare and implement a subclass of NSOperation. All of the code that is needed to do the work is right there where you need to use it and not in another class. One of the truly great advantages of using blocks is this ability to create units of work that can then be executed where you need them with far less code; code that is easier to write, and code that is more precise.

Converting the Interestingness App to Use an Official Version of Blocks and NSBlockOperation from Apple

When an official version of blocks from Apple becomes available it should be quite simple to convert the Interestingness app with blocks to use the official version of blocks and NSBlockOperation from Apple on an iPhone or iPodTouch device. Since iPhone OS 4.0 for iPad devices will not be available until the fall 2010, as announced at the iPhone OS 4.0 media event, it is not clear whether the steps will work in the interim. The steps that would be required are the following:

- Remove the PLBlocks.framework.

- Remove the PLBlocks header and implementation files NSOperationQueue+PLBlocks.h and .m.

- Change the compiler for the project from GCC 4.2(Plausible Blocks) to GCC 4.2.

- In the implementation file for the InterestingnessTableViewController remove the import statement for NSOperationQueue+PLBlocks.h.

- In the getImageForURL: method change PLBlockOperation to NSBlockOperation as follows:

```
...
/*
 *      create a block operation
 */

NSBlockOperation *fetchImageOp = NSBlockOperation blockOperationWithBlock:^{
...
```

- Save and recompile.

Summary

This chapter covers a lot of ground in just a few pages. Just about every subtopic on concurrency can be expanded upon. You started by developing a sluggish application that performed a task that many applications need to perform and that is well understood—downloading data from the web. Using this starter application, you then looked at possible concurrency solutions and then honed in on operation objects. Using operation objects, you developed a fully asynchronous solution that eliminated any sluggishness in the application. Using operation objects to achieve concurrency when it is a good fit for the application gives the best chance of taking advantage of multiple cores on an iPhone device if and when it happens. On the software side, another reason for using operation objects is to position the concurrency solution in your application to take advantage of GCD and blocks when they are introduced for iPhone OS. Whether that happens is anyone's guess, but as I have been saying in conference presentations last year and here, I believe there is a very strong likelihood that it will. Finally, you looked at blocks on the iPhone even though it is not an official offering from Apple and saw how appealing it is to use operation objects and blocks. You also saw how easy it would be to convert the application to use an official version of blocks from Apple. I hope you'll be able to put some of this to practice in your own applications for the iPhone family of devices, and if not then certainly to try out some of the APIs available on Snow Leopard. Lastly, I certainly hope I have raised your interest in operation objects and blocks. Happy coding and have fun playing with your blocks! After all, we are all kids at heart!

Resources

The resources listed here are not exhaustive. The authoritative resources of course are the Apple documentation, sample code, and videos. While the Apple documentation are a tremendous resource it is often like drinking water from a fire hose. I always like to read about the same topic from different points of view to gain further understanding and clarity.

Apple and Apple-related News

- Future iPhones to wield OpenCL acceleration: http://www.appleinsider.com/articles/08/12/20/future_iphones_to_wield_opencl_acceleration.html

- Imagination Technologies reveals future iPhone GPU candidate: http://www.appleinsider.com/articles/10/01/08/imagination_technologies_announces_successor_to_iphone_3gs_gpu.html

- ARM Announces 2GHz Capable Cortex-A9 Dual Core Processor Implementation: http://www.arm.com/about/newsroom/25922.php

Apple Documentation

- Threading Programming Guide: http://developer.apple.com/iphone/library/documentation/Cocoa/Conceptual/Multithreading/Introduction/Introduction.html

- Concurrency Programming Guide: http://developer.apple.com/iphone/library/documentation/General/Conceptual/ConcurrencyProgrammingGuide/Introduction/Introduction.html

- Introduction to Key—Value Observing Programming Guide: http://developer.apple.com/iphone/library/documentation/Cocoa/Conceptual/KeyValueObserving/KeyValueObserving.html

- WWDC 2009 Videos

Blocks and Grand Central Dispatch

- Grand Central Dispatch Technology Brief:
  http://images.apple.com/euro/macosx/technology/docs/GrandCentra l_TB_brief_20090608.pdf

- Introducing Blocks and Grand Central Dispatch:
  https://developer.apple.com/mac/articles/cocoa/introblocksgcd.h tml

- Blocks Programming:
  http://developer.apple.com/mac/library/documentation/Cocoa/Conc eptual/Blocks/Articles/00_Introduction.html

- Blocks Specification:
  http://clang.llvm.org/docs/BlockLanguageSpec.txt

- Apple's Block presentation to the C Standards Working Group
  N1370:Apple's Extensions to C: http://www.open-std.org/jtc1/sc22/wg14/www/docs/n1370.pdf

- Plausible Labs Blog:
  http://www.plausiblelabs.com/blog/?tag=plblocks/

- PLBlocks download: http://code.google.com/p/plblocks/

- Blocks Examples: NSOperationQueue and UIActionSheet, Landon Fuller:
  http://landonf.bikemonkey.org/code/iphone/Using_Blocks_1.200907 04.html

- Landon Fuller/Plausible Labs extensions to NSOperationQueue and NSThread contained in block_samples:
  http://github.com/landonf/block_samples/tree/master/NSOperation Blocks

- Friday Q&A 2008-12-26: http://www.mikeash.com/pyblog/friday-qa-2008-12-26.html

- Friday Q&A 2009-08-14:Practical Blocks:
  http://www.mikeash.com/pyblog/friday-qa-2009-08-14-practical-blocks.html

- Blocks, Episode 1, Jim Dovey:
  http://quatermain.tumblr.com/post/135882428/blocks-episode-1

- Blocks, Episode 2: Life Cycles, Jim Dovey:
  http://quatermain.tumblr.com/post/138827791/blocks-episode-2-life-cycles

- Programming with C Blocks on Apple Devices, Joachim Bengtsson:
  http://thirdcog.eu/pwcblocks/

General

- Beginning iPhone 3 Development: Exploring the iPhone SDK, by Jeff LaMarche and Dave Mark, Apress, 2009.

JSON

- json-framework project page: `http://code.google.com/p/json-framework/`, which is currently version 2.2.3

- Introducing JSON: `http://www.json.org/`

POSIX Threads

Programming With POSIX Threads, by David R. Butenhhof, Addison-Wesley, 1997.

Claus Höfele

Company: www.claushoefele.com

Location: Sydney, Australia

Former Life as a Developer: Over the years, I have worked with various technologies and platforms such as the PlayStation 2 and 3, the Xbox 360, iPhone, Android, BlackBerry, Java Micro Edition, Symbian, i-mode, and lots of other proprietary stuff. I enjoy working on embedded systems and getting the most out of constrained memory and processing power.

In addition to being a software engineer, I'm the author of Mobile 3D Graphics: Learning 3D Graphics with the Java Micro Edition and many other publications about application development. I also serve as a member of the expert group for Java Specification Request 297: Mobile 3D Graphics API 2.0.

Life as an iPhone Developer: Professional game developer for video consoles. Currently developing my own game engine and tools for mobile games.

App on the App Store:

- Shark Feeding (working title)

What's in This Chapter:

- Starting an iPhone Game
- Why Write Your Own Tools?
- Creating a Flexible Content Pipeline
- Outline of the Example Code
- Exporting 3D Models
- Handling Textures
- Rendering the Converted Data on the iPhone

Key Technologies:

- *Maya, 3ds Max, Blender*
- *OpenGL ES*
- *FBX, PNG, PVRTC*

Chapter 2

Your Own Content Pipeline: Importing 3D Art Assets into Your iPhone Game

Before 3D models can be used in an iPhone game, they have to be converted into a format suitable for distribution and rendering. This process is particularly complex for 3D games which require specialized digital content creation tools to create art assets. The question is: how to export 3D models from software packages such as Maya, 3ds Max, and Blender and use them in an iPhone game?

Starting an iPhone Game

Developing games for video consoles and for the iPhone are polar opposites: On the one hand, dozens of people working for several years to wring the last drop of performance out of a platform. On the other hand, small teams creating innovative games in a few months. In many ways, programming iPhone games is a breath of fresh air for a seasoned game developer.

For this reason, I was looking forward to starting an iPhone project with two artist friends who also come from a commercial game development background. Having been involved in game development on video consoles for a while, we figured we had the skills to create something of our own for the iPhone.

Initially, we wanted to go for a zombie shooter in 3D with a story mode and dozens of levels. After a look at our time budget, however, we decided to start off with something a little less ambitious: a game involving sharks. Figure 2–1 shows a model from our upcoming game.

Figure 2–1. *One of the models for our shark game. Model courtesy of Dimitri Kanis.*

Despite the many game concepts we were discussing, they all had one feature in common: the games were to be realized with 3D polygon art—as opposed to 2D pixel art—because that reflected the games we had been working on so far.

3D games on the iPhone are a tricky proposition because the additional dimension makes content creation much more difficult and time consuming. In addition, 3D games often result in complex gameplay, which makes it more difficult to target a casual audience.

The way we've seen it so far is that these challenges allow our games to distinguish themselves from the sea of games offered in the App Store. If we can pull off a good 3D game, it might just afford us to earn our share of the iPhone market.

3D games have to score in the graphics department. So, I started to investigate the best way to render models in our game. Since I have been working on 3D games on consoles before, I found myself reflecting on my previous experience.

Why Write Your Own Tools?

Early on, I decided to aim for a high-performance render engine, as this will give my projects a leg up compared to games created with other engines. This decision had two consequences: one, my engine is programmed in C++ and two, I've started to create my own tools.

C++ allows me not only to structure the code in a modular way, but also to program to the bare metal when needed. In contrast to Objective-C, which I still use for APIs specific to the iPhone, C++ allows you fine-grained control over memory and performance trade offs. Using C++ in combination with OpenGL also makes it easy to port my engine, should I decide to create a game for a platform other than the iPhone.

Good render performance requires more than just the right choice of programming language. There's a lot of optimizations you can do to your game data to suit the target platform. Tools and engine code goes hand in hand because the output of the former is the input to the latter.

The idea is to write tools that optimize game data offline, on a desktop computer, where computational power is not an issue. The render engine on the iPhone, on the other hand, should be as simple as possible. In the best case, the engine would just pass data through to OpenGL, without any additional steps involved.

The process of transforming your data into an efficient game format isn't without its problems. The additional step required before you can use a new asset in your game takes time and adds complexity. Fortunately, the number of art assets used in iPhone games is fairly low, so it never takes more than a few minutes to process the data. (That's in contrast to console games, where I have seen this step take several days because of the high number of art assets involved.)

Another disadvantage is that it takes a lot of time to write tools. If you are like me, you'd rather spend your time writing code for a fancy graphics effect. However, having my own tools allows me to innovate on technology. For example, I could optimize my game data for a new hardware platform or take advantage of a new graphics effect that requires the game data in a special way fairly quickly.

Creating a Flexible Content Pipeline

Having decided on creating my own tools and engine, I set out to design a content pipeline that can achieve my goals of optimized game data.

The Tools Problem

The first idea I had was to write an exporter for a content creation tool. Blender, for example, can be extended with scripts written in Python. Autodesk's Maya and 3ds Max also have SDKs to allow you to extend these applications. Figure 2–2 shows the shark model in 3ds Max, where it was created.

Figure 2–2. *Screenshot of shark model in Autodesk 3ds Max. Model courtesy of Dimitri Kanis.*

The problem is that the exporter for one software package would be a completely separate development effort from the exporter for another one—each exporter requiring time to learn all the quirks of a particular application and make it compatible with the engine.

Big game studios often solve this problem by requiring people to use one particular tool set. Given that, as an independent game developer, I need to rely on the good will of artists to work with me, I could foresee problems if I did the same. Each artist has his or her own preferences when it comes to modeling tools and it's difficult to convince them to use a different software package, just because your tools can only handle one particular application.

The next idea I had was to use a file format that's widely supported by applications but simple enough to use in my games. Wavefront's OBJ file format (http://en.wikipedia.org/wiki/Obj) is such a format: it's a text based file format that's easy to parse and you'll find plenty of code on the internet that helps you get started.

This sounded like a good idea until I thought about the optimizations I wanted to implement. OBJ uses floating-point numbers to represent all data. What if I wanted to use a different number representation instead to save memory? (Single precision floating-point numbers use 4 bytes of memory for each datum whereas sometimes you can get away with using a 16-bit integer type that only uses 2 bytes.) What if you needed additional information to render the mesh more efficiently in the engine? (For example, by adding information about the memory layout of a mesh's geometry.)

Basically, if I used a format that I can't or don't want to change, I'd always be restricted in what I could do in my engine. At the same time, I don't want to write dozens of exporters either. The solution to this dilemma is to separate the file format used for exporting models from the file format used on the iPhone.

Data Exchange vs. In-Game File Formats

To satisfy all the requirements I had for my engine, I came up with the content pipeline depicted in Figure 2–3.

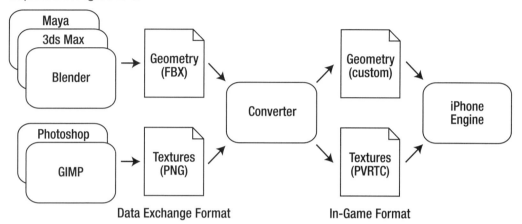

Figure 2–3. *Content pipeline with distinction between data exchange and in-game format.*

The important feature in this design is the distinction between a data exchange and an in-game file format. Whereas the data exchange format is used to unify the output of many different content creation tools, the in-game format is designed for my engine running on a particular platform. A converter transforms the data from one format into the other.

I've chosen FBX as the data exchange format for 3D model data. FBX—named after a product that used to be called Filmbox—is a file format owned by Autodesk, which uses it to provide interoperability between its content creation tools. This makes FBX well supported in all of Autodesk's products. Despite the fact that FBX is proprietary, a number of other companies and organizations have implemented FBX support. For example, both Blender and Cheetah have FBX exporters built-in.

An alternative to FBX would be Collada (http://en.wikipedia.org/wiki/Collada), an open file format that is managed by Khronos, the same organization that handles the OpenGL specification. In the end, however, I decided to use FBX because I found the exporters that support this file format very robust and well supported. Also, Autodesk provides a ready-to-use library to read FBX files, which simplifies the creation of tools.

FBX data is stored in a way so all parts of a model can still be edited when transferred from one application into another. This increases the files size, but also means that FBX is a good starting point for optimizations, because valuable information about the original data set is retained.

Similar to the way I'm using FBX as the format for mesh geometry, Portable Network Graphics (PNG) serves as format for image data. PNG is a good choice, in my opinion, because it's lossless, so you can modify PNG files without degrading the quality of the image. Also, it's widely supported by graphics editing tools such as Photoshop and GIMP.

The information from the FBX and PNG files is used in my converter to create the in-game versions of the content. At this stage of the pipeline, the converter applies transformations to make the data compatible with my engine, such as unit and data type conversions, but also optimizations for efficient rendering on the iPhone. The main design goal of the converter was to keep the engine simple and have all optimization logic that can be performed offline implemented in this tool.

The output of the converter is the file formats that are used in-game. For geometry data, I found that I needed to tweak the format every now and then to adapt it to new engine features. For this reason, the geometry format is specific to the engine and evolves in parallel.

In contrast to geometry, there aren't many different ways you would want to format textures. That's why in this case, I've opted for PowerVR Texture Compression (PVRTC), an optimized texture format that's natively supported by the iPhone hardware. PVRTC is a compressed texture format, which results in efficient memory usage while being easy to decode by the iPhone's GPU at the same time.

I find that the split between a data exchange format and an in-game format provides a lot of flexibility to change parts of the content pipeline without affecting the artists who create the models. When I implement a new optimization in the converter, for example, I simply re-run the tool on the original FBX and PNG files to produce new game data for the iPhone. This allows me to stay agile in development without requiring artists to re-export all the models.

Outline of the Example Code

The rest of this chapter will provide more details about the implementation of the converter and the handling of the mentioned file formats. Before jumping into a detailed discussion, I'd like to give an overview of the example code that comes with this chapter.

The example project includes the following directories:

- *assets:* Contains the shark model from Figures 2–1 and 2–2 as FBX and PNG files as well as the converted model data ready to be used on the iPhone.

- *converter:* An Xcode project to build the converter application. The converter is provided as a command line tool for Mac OS X and transforms the FBX and PNG files into the iPhone format.

- *lib:* Third-party libraries required for the converter application.

- *opengl:* an Xcode project for iPhone OS that displays the converted shark model.

- *src*: This folder contains the reusable part of the C++ code required to build the converter and read the converted model on the iPhone

You'll find most of the code discussed in this chapter in the src folder. If you don't want to open each file individually, simply open the Xcode projects in the converter and opengl directories, which reference the required files from the src folder. The converter and opengl folders themselves only contain the additional code required to create an executable application.

Exporting 3D Models

To start using the FBX technology, you can download the FBX SDK from Autodesk's web site (http://www.autodesk.com/fbx). For licensing reasons, the FBX SDK is not included in the sample project for this chapter (it's also a fairly large download). The FBX SDK contains pre-compiled libraries and includes files that allow you to read and write FBX files from C++ code.

On the same web site, you'll also find the latest versions of exporter plug-ins for Maya and 3ds Max as well as a tool to convert popular 3D mesh formats into FBX. Some modeling packages, such as Blender and Cheetah, have an FBX exporter already built in.

FBX actually defines two file formats: one is a text-based format (ASCII) and the other is binary. The main difference in features is that a binary FBX file can embed images, whereas a text-based FBX file has to store images in a separate file (don't forget to include those images when sending your models by email).

The FBX SDK handles both versions of the format transparently, but I usually store all my models in the text-based format because it makes it easier to examine the data if something goes wrong. Figure 2–4 shows how to select the file format in 3ds Max's FBX export dialog.

Figure 2–4. *FBX exporter dialog in 3ds Max with ASCII file format selected.*

Reading FBX files

For reading FBX files, I created a class called FbxResourceReader (see src/resource/fbx/FbxResourceReader.h and .cpp). This class contains three objects from the FBX SDK: one to manage FBX objects (an instance of KFbxSdkManager), one to hold the contents of a scene (KFbxScene), and another one to import files (KFbxImporter).

```
/** FBX file reader. */
class FbxResourceReader
{
public:

  /** Creates a new resource reader. */
  FbxResourceReader();

  /** Destructor. */
  ~FbxResourceReader();

  /**
```

```
 * Opens the given file and reads in the scene contents.
 * @param fileName file name.
 * @return true if the file was read successfully, false otherwise.
 */
bool open(const char* fileName);

/** Resets the current scene. */
void close();

//@{
/** Getter/setter. */
inline FBXFILESDK_NAMESPACE::KFbxSdkManager* getSdkManager();
inline FBXFILESDK_NAMESPACE::KFbxScene* getScene();
//@}

private:
  FBXFILESDK_NAMESPACE::KFbxSdkManager* m_SdkManager; ///< SDK manager for FBX API.
  FBXFILESDK_NAMESPACE::KFbxScene* m_Scene;           ///< Current scene.
  FBXFILESDK_NAMESPACE::KFbxImporter* m_Importer;     ///< Importer to load files.
};
```

All three FBX objects are needed to read in an FBX file and are created through calls↵
 to their Create() method:

```
FbxResourceReader::FbxResourceReader()
 : m_SdkManager(KFbxSdkManager::Create())
 , m_Scene(KFbxScene::Create(m_SdkManager, ""))
   , m_Importer(KFbxImporter::Create(m_SdkManager, ""))

{
}
```

When instantiating a class from the FBX SDK, KFbxSdkManager is passed in as a parameter. The SDK manager keeps tabs on all the objects that were created and handles the memory for those objects.

In the case of FbxResourceReader's constructor, the two objects created are KFbxImporter, which is used to read in FBX files, and KFbxScene, which will contain the models and other information from the FBX file contents.

With the required FBX objects created, you can load an FBX file as shown in FbxResourceReader::open():

```
bool FbxResourceReader::open(const char* fileName)
{
  close();

  // Initialize the importer with a file name.
  bool result = m_Importer->Initialize(fileName);
  if (result)
  {
    // Read in file contents.
    result = m_Importer->Import(m_Scene);
  }

  if (result)
  {
    // Convert coordinate system.
```

```
    KFbxAxisSystem fbxSceneAxisSystem = m_Scene->GetGlobalSettings().GetAxisSystem();
    KFbxAxisSystem fbxLocalAxisSystem(KFbxAxisSystem::YAxis,
      KFbxAxisSystem::ParityOdd, KFbxAxisSystem::RightHanded);
    if(fbxSceneAxisSystem != fbxLocalAxisSystem)
    {
      fbxLocalAxisSystem.ConvertScene(m_Scene);
    }

    // Convert units. "The equivalent number of centimeters
    // in the new system unit"
    const float centimetersPerUnit = 100.0f;
    KFbxSystemUnit fbxSceneSystemUnit = m_Scene->GetGlobalSettings().GetSystemUnit();
    if(fbxSceneSystemUnit.GetScaleFactor() != centimetersPerUnit)
    {
      KFbxSystemUnit fbxLocalSystemUnit(centimetersPerUnit);
      fbxLocalSystemUnit.ConvertScene(m_Scene);
    }
  }

  return result;
}
```

The FBX SDK comes with a number of handy utility functions that can save you a lot of time when writing a converter. In this case, I'm using KFbxAxisSystem to convert the coordinate system and KFbxSystemUnit to adjust the scale of the original geometry data.

OpenGL uses a right-handed coordinate system. In other words, if you use your right hand and stretch out thumb, index finger, and middle finger so they are orthogonal to each other, your thumb is the x axis, your index finger the y axis, and the middle finger the z axis. By convention, the y axis usually points up in world space, which means increasing the y coordinate of a model would move it towards the sky.

In comparison, Maya uses the same coordinate system as OpenGL, but both 3ds Max and Blender use a right-handed coordinate system with z as the up axis. The coordinate systems of these content creation tools is shown in Figure 2–5.

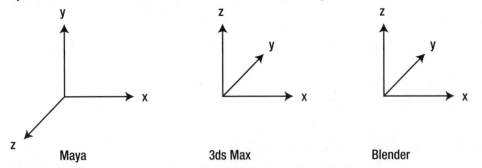

Figure 2–5. *Coordinate systems in Maya, 3ds Max, and Blender (front view).*

As long as you keep all data in the same coordinate system, it doesn't matter which system you use. However, as soon as you want to move or rotate an object in code or mix data from different tools, you need to know what convention was used. For this reason, I convert all geometry into the OpenGL convention. Similarly, I convert all units into meters so that all my models have the same scale.

It's important to know, however, that the FBX library doesn't modify the vertex positions, but instead modifies the scale and rotation parameters of the model. To render the model correctly, you will have to use the converted information rather than the information found in the content creation tool.

Traversing the Scene Contents

A scene (KFbxScene) is a container for all the contents of the FBX file, such as models, cameras, and lights. These scene objects are arranged in a hierarchical way. In other words, each scene object can have a number of child objects, which themselves can have children, and so on. An example hierarchy is shown in Figure 2–6.

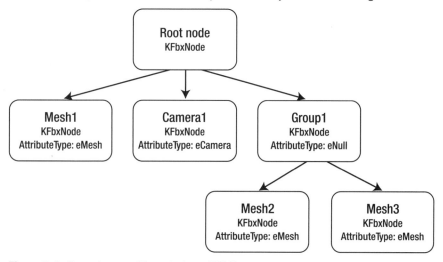

Figure 2–6. *Example scene hierarchy in an FBX file.*

To traverse this hierarchy, call KFbxScene::GetRootNode() to obtain the top-most node of the scene hierarchy and check if it has any children. If so, check all children for further children until you have recursively visited all scene nodes.

This code (implemented in converter/main.cpp) will call the function ConvertHierarchy() for every child of the root node:

```
FbxResourceReader fbxReader;
bool result = fbxReader.open(fileName);
if (result)
{
  // Traverse hierarchy of scene nodes.
  KFbxScene* scene = fbxReader.getScene();
  ...
  for(int i = 0; i < scene->GetRootNode()->GetChildCount(); i++)
  {
    ConvertHierarchy(..., scene->GetRootNode()->GetChild(i));
```

```
    }
  }
```

To also visit the children's children, you then call ConvertHierarchy() recursively.

```
void ConvertHierarchy(..., KFbxNode* fbxNode)
{
  if(fbxNode->GetNodeAttribute() != NULL)
  {
    ... do something with the scene node
  }

  // Recurse
  for(int i = 0; i < fbxNode->GetChildCount(); i++)
  {
    ConvertHierarchy(..., fbxNode->GetChild(i));
  }
}
```

Those two code snippets together allow you to get access to all scene nodes, which FBX represents as instances of KFbxNode.

Distinguishing between Different Types of Scene Nodes

An instance of KFbxNode represents a node in the scene hierarchy and contains properties that are generic for all types of nodes. For example, to get the position of a node, you would call

```
KFbxVector4 translation;
fbxNode->GetDefaultT(translation);
printf("x=%f y=%f z=%f\n",
  translation[0], translation[1], translation[2]);
```

Whether a node is a model, a camera, or another type of scene object, depends on the node attribute.

```
if(fbxNode->GetNodeAttribute() != NULL)
{
  const char* fbxNodeName = fbxNode->GetName();
  printf("Processing node '%s'\n", fbxNodeName);

  // Find out what type of node we are dealing with.
  KFbxNodeAttribute::EAttributeType attributeType =
    fbxNode->GetNodeAttribute()->GetAttributeType();
  switch (attributeType)
  {
    case KFbxNodeAttribute::eMESH:
    {
      // Convert mesh geometry.
      KFbxMesh* fbxMesh =
        static_cast<KFbxMesh*>(fbxNode->GetNodeAttribute());
      ...

      break;
```

```
        }
        // no default
    }
}
```

You can find out what type of node you are dealing with by calling GetNodeAttribute()->GetAttributeType() on a KFbxNode instance and comparing the returned value against a list of predefined values.

The only node type you're interested in here is KFbxNodeAttribute::eMESH, which corresponds to a mesh consisting of polygon data. (If the model in your content creation tool is a different type of mesh, for example a NURBS surface, you will have to convert it into a polygon mesh first.)

Once you know that the node is a mesh, you can cast the node attribute into a KFbxMesh:

```
KFbxMesh* fbxMesh =
    static_cast<KFbxMesh*>(fbxNode->GetNodeAttribute());
```

Whereas the KFbxNode instance contains generic node information, the KFbxMesh instance gives you access to the actual polygon data that makes up the model.

OpenGL Triangle Data

Because FBX is a file format designed for data interchange, it supports a number of different layouts for geometry data to match the native format of the original application. This allows FBX to be compatible with a range of content creation tools, but also complicates extracting data out of FBX objects.

For example, one application that exports FBX files might decide that a 3D model is best represented by quads with four vertex positions and one normal per quad. For rendering with OpenGL, on the other hand, you'll always want your data as triangles with each attribute (position, normal, texture coordinates) available per vertex. To save memory, the vertex data is usually indexed so that vertices that are used several times don't have to be stored more than once. This format is depicted in Figure 2–7.

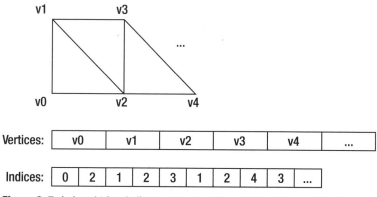

Figure 2–7. Indexed triangle list: each tuple of three indices forms a triangle.

As a code representation of the OpenGL vertex data, I created the class Geometry with the following members (see src/resource/Geometry.cpp):

```
/** Container for vertex data. */
class Geometry
{
public:

  /** Vertex declaration. */
  struct Vertex
  {
    float position[3];
    float normal[3];
    float uv0[2];
  };

  /** Index declaration. */
  typedef uint16_t Index;

  /** Type of primitives to render. */
  enum PrimitiveType
  {
    PT_TriangleList = 0,    ///< List of triangles.
    PT_LineList,            ///< List of lines.
    PT_PointList,           ///< List of points.
  };

  ...

private:

  std::vector<Vertex> m_Vertices;   ///< Vertices.
  std::vector<Index> m_Indices;     ///< Indices.
  unsigned m_VertexBufferId;        ///< OpenGL VBO ID.
  unsigned m_IndexBufferId;         ///< OpenGL VBO ID.
  size_t m_NumIndices;              ///< Number of indices to render.
  PrimitiveType m_PrimitiveType;    ///< Type of primitives to render.
};
```

The class Geometry is designed to be used both in the converter to hold the converted FBX data as well as on the iPhone when rendering the mesh. This makes sure that the converter produces a format that matches the data structures needed on the iPhone.

In the class, I added an array each for vertices and indices, which simply contains each set of data in a contiguous area of memory. The vertex layout defined by Geometry::Vertex is an interleaved format where positions, normals, and texture coordinates are written alternately.

Even though not implemented here, it's a good idea to support several vertex layouts specific to your needs (for example, a vertex layout without normals if you don't use lighting). The smaller the vertex data, the less time it will take to transfer the data to the GPU and the faster the rendering.

I also recommend you read Apple's OpenGL guide, which contains valuable information how the layout of your vertex data affects rendering performance:

http://developer.apple.com/iphone/library/documentation/3DDrawing/Conceptual/Op
enGLES_ProgrammingGuide/TechniquesforWorkingwithVertexData/TechniquesforWorking
withVertexData.html.

Converting FBX Models into Triangle Data

In a previous step, I've shown you how to traverse the scene hierarchy and distinguish
different node types (see ConvertHierarchy() in converter/main.cpp). The result was a
KFbxMesh instance when a polygon mesh was encountered. To make the FBX data useable
on the iPhone, however, you need the mesh converted into triangle data stored in Geometry.

The data conversion is the purpose of the following method (see
src/resource/fbx/FbxResourceConverter.cpp):

```
bool FbxResourceConverter::convert(KFbxMesh& fbxMeshIn,
  Geometry& geometry  ) const
{
  ASSERT_M(fbxMeshIn.GetNode() != NULL, "Invalid mesh.");
  ASSERT_M(fbxMeshIn.GetControlPoints() != NULL, "No position data.");
  ASSERT_M(fbxMeshIn.GetControlPointsCount() <= 65536, "Only 16 -bit indices
 supported.");

  // Reserve memory.
  vector<Geometry::Vertex>& vertices = geometry.getVertices();
  vector<Geometry::Index>& indices = geometry.getIndices();
  vertices.reserve(fbxMeshIn.GetControlPointsCount());
  indices.reserve(fbxMeshIn.GetPolygonCount() * 3);

  // Make sure all geometry is converted into triangles.
  KFbxMesh* newFbxMesh = NULL;
  if (!fbxMeshIn.IsTriangleMesh())
  {
    KFbxGeometryConverter geometryConverter(m_SdkManager);
    newFbxMesh = geometryConverter.TriangulateMesh(&fbxMeshIn);
  }
  const KFbxMesh& fbxMesh = newFbxMesh ? *newFbxMesh : fbxMeshIn;
  const int numTrianglesFbx = fbxMesh.GetPolygonCount();

  // Extract per-vertex data.
  FbxResourceUtils::processTriangles(fbxMesh, vertices, indices);
  ASSERT_M((int)indices.size() == numTrianglesFbx * 3,
    "Invalid number of indices.");

  if (newFbxMesh != NULL)
  {
    // Release temporary data.
    newFbxMesh->Destroy();
  }
  geometry.setPrimitiveType(Geometry::PT_TriangleList);
  geometry.setNumIndices(indices.size());

  return true;
}
```

At the beginning of FbxResourceConverter::convert(), I'm using another convenient feature of the FBX SDK: KFbxGeometryConverter can convert the input data into triangles. This makes sure that no quads or polygons with more than three vertices slip through. Quads are often used in content creation tools for convenience, but can't be rendered by OpenGL ES.

Once the mesh is converted into triangles, I'm passing the mesh to FbxResourceUtils::processTriangles() (see src/resource/fbx/FbxResourceUtils.cpp):

```
void FbxResourceUtils::processTriangles(const KFbxMesh& fbxMesh,
  vector<Geometry::Vertex>& vertices, vector<Geometry::Index>& indices)
{
  // Functor to help compare vertices.
  VertexPredicate vertexPredicate;
  vertexPredicate.epsilon = 0.001f;

  // Loop through triangles to extract a list of vertices with
  // per-vertex data. This normalizes the various ways in which FBX
  // stores mesh data.
  const int numTrianglesFbx = fbxMesh.GetPolygonCount();  for (int triangleIndex = 0;
triangleIndex < numTrianglesFbx;
    triangleIndex++)
  {
    for(int cornerIndex = 0; cornerIndex < 3; cornerIndex++)
    {
      // Vertex position
      KFbxVector4 position;
      FbxResourceUtils::getPolygonVertexPosition(fbxMesh, triangleIndex, cornerIndex,
position);
        vertexPredicate.currentVertex.position[0] = (float)position[0];
      vertexPredicate.currentVertex.position[1] = (float)position[1];
      vertexPredicate.currentVertex.position[2] = (float)position[2];

      KFbxVector4 normal;
      FbxResourceUtils::getPolygonVertexNormal(fbxMesh, triangleIndex, cornerIndex,
normal);
          vertexPredicate.currentVertex.normal[0] = (float)normal[0];
      vertexPredicate.currentVertex.normal[1] = (float)normal[1];
      vertexPredicate.currentVertex.normal[2] = (float)normal[2];

      // Vertex UV0
      KFbxVector2 uv0;
      FbxResourceUtils::getPolygonVertexUv(fbxMesh, 0, triangleIndex, cornerIndex, uv0);
          vertexPredicate.currentVertex.uv0[0] = (float)uv0[0];
      vertexPredicate.currentVertex.uv0[1] = (float)uv0[1];

      // Re-index vertices to remove duplicates.
      vector<Geometry::Vertex>::iterator existingVertex =
        find_if(vertices.begin(), vertices.end(), vertexPredicate);
      size_t index = existingVertex - vertices.begin();
      if (index == vertices.size()) // new vertex?
      {
        vertices.push_back(vertexPredicate.currentVertex);
      }
      indices.push_back(index);
    }
  }
}
```

This method loops through all the polygons in the FBX mesh and extracts the position, normal, and texture coordinates for each vertex. Because KFbxGeometryConverter triangulated the mesh, your code can be sure that it deals with triangles at this point.

To map from the FBX way of storing polygon data to per-vertex data, you created small conversion routines in FbxResourceUtils. For example, this function retrieves the position of a vertex:

```
void FbxResourceUtils::getPolygonVertexPosition(const
  KFbxMesh& fbxMesh, int polyIndex, int vertexIndex,
  KFbxVector4& position)
{
  int positionIndex =
    fbxMesh.GetPolygonVertex(polyIndex, vertexIndex);
  const KFbxVector4* fbxPositions = fbxMesh.GetControlPoints();
  position = fbxPositions[positionIndex];
}
```

Similar routines exist for normals and texture coordinates.

By this time, you would be finished with the conversion, if you didn't want the vertices to be indexed. To re-index the data, first store the current vertex temporarily in a variable of the type VertexPredicate (see src/resource/fbx/FbxResourceUtils.h).

```
/** Predicate to compare two vertices. */
struct VertexPredicate
{
  /** Returns true if two vertices are equal. */
  bool operator()(const Geometry::Vertex& other);

  Geometry::Vertex currentVertex;     ///< Current vertex.
  float epsilon;    ///< Difference that two floating-point values can
                    //   be apart, but still compare equal.
};
```

This structure serves two purposes: for one, it stores the current vertex that is being processed and for two, it has a method VertexPredicate::operator() to check if two vertices are equal (see src/resource/fbx/FbxResourceUtils.cpp).

```
bool FbxResourceUtils::VertexPredicate::operator()(
  const Geometry::Vertex& other)
{
  bool result =
    fabs(currentVertex.position[0] - other.position[0]) < epsilon &&
    fabs(currentVertex.position[1] - other.position[1]) < epsilon &&
    fabs(currentVertex.position[2] - other.position[2]) < epsilon;
  result &=
    fabs(currentVertex.normal[0] - other.normal[0]) < epsilon &&
    fabs(currentVertex.normal[1] - other.normal[1]) < epsilon &&
    fabs(currentVertex.normal[2] - other.normal[2]) < epsilon;
  result &=
    fabs(currentVertex.uv0[0] - other.uv0[0]) < epsilon &&
    fabs(currentVertex.uv0[1] - other.uv0[1]) < epsilon;
  return result;
}
```

This operator compares the vertex data with a tolerance stored in `epsilon`. This tolerance avoids problems with floating-point precision as well as snapping nearby vertices together to remove duplicates. Epsilon values must be large enough to find nearby vertices, but at the same time small enough to avoid collapsing vertices that shouldn't be merged. (In the sample code, I'm using 0.001, which works well for my meshes.)

The purpose of the VertexPredicate becomes clear when looking again at the last step of the vertex conversion in `FbxResourceUtils::processTriangles()`:

```
// Re-index vertices to remove duplicates.
vector<Geometry::Vertex>::iterator existingVertex =
  std::find_if(vertices.begin(), vertices.end(), vertexPredicate);
size_t index = existingVertex - vertices.begin();
if (index == vertices.size()) // new vertex?
{
  vertices.push_back(vertexPredicate.currentVertex);
}
indices.push_back(index);
```

In this code, I check if a vertex already exists in the vertex data by calling `std::find_if` with an instance of `VertexPredicate` that contains the current vertex. This loops through the existing vertices and compares each of them with the current vertex by calling `VertexPredicate::operator()`.

`find_if` either returns a pointer to the position of the matching array element or a pointer one past the last element of the array, if no matching vertex was found. This pointer is converted into an index number by subtracting a pointer to the beginning of the vertex array.

If the vertex doesn't exist yet, the index will be equal to the size of the vertex array. If so, I append the new vertex at the end, which creates a new element at the index position. If the vertex does exist, the index is already valid and no new vertex is required.

Either way, the index now points to the correct vertex element and can be added to the index array. This removes all duplicate vertices and creates the indices.

Converting Triangle Data into an In-Game Format

`FbxResourceConverter::convert()` resulted in two arrays: one with the vertices and one with the indices that describe the triangles of the geometry. This data is stored in an instance of "Geometry" and now needs to be written into a file that you can ship with your iPhone game.

As mentioned before, my goal is to implement all logic that can be handled offline in my tools, so that my engine can be as simple and fast as possible. For this reason, I decided to model the in-game format closely on the data layout I need for OpenGL ES.

A portion of one of my data files looks like this (you can find the entire file in the assets/converted/geometry folder):

```
// Sat Feb 27 09:25:40 2010
// Shark
geometry 0 740 2502
62.222061 -171.275208 14.209234
0.753058 0.017204 0 .657729
0.302249 0.610170

.. more vertices
0
1
2
2
3
0

...more indices
```

The first two lines are comments that allow me to see when the file was created and what the original FBX scene node was called.

After the comments, the line starting with "geometry" describes the data in the file. The numbers indicate the primitive type (0 stands for a list of triangles), the number of vertices, and the number of indices.

The geometry description is then followed by the vertex data. Each vertex consists of three lines, with one line each for position, normal, and texture coordinates. At the end of the file come the indices with each index in a separate line.

The file format is text based, so that you can generate and parse the data with the printf and scanf family of functions that are part of the C standard library. This makes the file format quick to implement and easy to debug because you can have a look at the file contents in a text editor.

Writing the data is accomplished with these lines of code (see src/resource/geometry/GeometryResourceWriter.cpp):

```cpp
bool GeometryResourceWriter::write(const Geometry& geometry,
  uint32_t resourceId, const char* comment)
{
  bool result = false;

  char dirName[sizeof(m_FileName) + 16];
  snprintf(dirName, sizeof(dirName), "%s/geometry", m_FileName);
  char fileName[sizeof(dirName) + 16];
  snprintf(fileName, sizeof(fileName), "%s/%08x", dirName, resourceId++);

  FILE* file = NULL;
  createDirectory(dirName);
  file = fopen(fileName, "w");
  result = (file != NULL);
  ASSERT_M(result, "Can't open file '%s'.", fileName);

  if (result)
  {
    char buffer[256];
```

```
  // Comment
  writeComment(file, buffer, sizeof(buffer), comment);

  // Geometry data
  snprintf(buffer, sizeof(buffer), "geometry %d %d %d\n",
    geometry.getPrimitiveType(), geometry.getVertices().size(),
    geometry.getIndices().size());
  fputs(buffer, file);

  // Vertices
  const vector<Geometry::Vertex>& vertices = geometry.getVertices();
  for (size_t i = 0; i < vertices.size(); i++)
  {
    const Geometry::Vertex& vertex = vertices[i];
    snprintf(buffer, sizeof(buffer), "%f %f %f\n",
      vertex.position[0], vertex.position[1], vertex.position[2]);
    fputs(buffer, file);
    snprintf(buffer, sizeof(buffer), "%f %f %f\n",
      vertex.normal[0], vertex.normal[1], vertex.normal[2]);
    fputs(buffer, file);
    snprintf(buffer, sizeof(buffer), "%f %f\n",
      vertex.uv0[0], vertex.uv0[1], vertex.uv0[2]);
    fputs(buffer, file);
  }

  // Indices
  const vector<Geometry::Index>& indices = geometry.getIndices();
  for (size_t i = 0; i < indices.size(); i++)
  {
    const Geometry::Index& index = indices[i];
    snprintf(buffer, sizeof(buffer), "%d\n", index);
    fputs(buffer, file);
  }

  fclose(file);
  result = true;
}

  return result;
}
```

On the other end, the iPhone app uses similar code to read in the geometry (see src/resource/geometry/GeometryResourceReader.cpp).

As you can see, the file format is fairly simple. However, it doesn't matter much what format you choose for your in-game files as long as you can change it quickly when needed. For example, I find the loading times in my game acceptable at the moment, but I could switch to a binary file format to improve performance if I wanted to. This change wouldn't require any modification to the original art assets (the FBX files). Instead, I would just run them again through my modified converter to benefit from shorter loading times.

Handling Textures

So far, I've only covered geometry data. Textures for 3D models require separate tools because the optimizations you can apply to images are completely different.

Image Compression vs. Texture Compression

Probably the most common image format used on the iPhone is the PNG format. PNG is a lossless format, but still compresses into small files for line art and images with sharp transitions such as text. JPEG, on the other hand, works best for photographic images where the lossy compression isn't noticeable and leads to good file size savings.

Image file formats, as their name implies, are designed to minimize storage space while retaining as much quality of the original image as possible. That's an important consideration for iPhone games because the download time of a game increases with its size. In addition, Apple limits the size of applications downloaded over mobile network connections. If your app exceeds this limit, buyers have to connect to a WLAN to download it, which prevents impulse purchases and thus is bad for your sales. However, file sizes are not the only thing you need to worry about. The memory used after loading the image on the device is important too.

For example, the texture for the shark in Figure 2–8 with dimensions of 256×256 pixels results in a PNG file that's 66 KB when exported from Photoshop. When using the image on the iPhone, however, the PNG file has to be decompressed and the same image will take up 192 KB in memory if you use an RGB format (256 * 256 * 3 bytes). The image will need to be transferred from memory to the GPU, costing valuable bandwidth on the electrical bus that connects the chips on the device. Especially for 3D art assets, the amount of run-time memory used by images and the associated bandwidth bottleneck adds up very quickly.

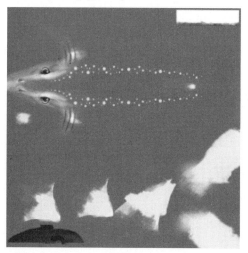

Figure 2–8. *Texture used for shark model.*

To address this problem, GPU manufacturers have introduced texture compression. The idea is that a texture is decompressed by the GPU, bypassing the CPU for any image decoding. This means the image can stay in a compressed format in memory up to the very end: when it's being used to color the 3D model.

Texture compression became popular with the introduction of the S3 Texture Compression format (S3TC, sometimes also called DXT or DXTC) into DirectX, but has also found its way into the iPhone with Imagination's PVRTC format. Imagination is the manufacturer of the GPU chips used in all iPhones to date.

Texture compression is designed to be easy to decode on GPU hardware. GPUs process pixels in parallel so they require random access to the texture data. That's why all widely used texture compression formats use a fixed compression ratio. The achievable compression is thus independent of the image contents. In contrast to PNG, which produces smaller file sizes the fewer colors you use.

PVRTC supports two modes: one which compresses the original data into 2 bits per pixel and one which results in 4 bits per pixel. For the example texture of 256×256 pixels, this results in 16 KB and 32 KB of memory usage. That's a massive saving compared to the original 192 KB, resulting in less memory usage and faster rendering.

Imagination's PVRTC Format

There's a downside, of course: PVRTC is a lossy compression format, resulting in a reduced quality compared to the original image.

The advantage of PVRTC is that you can trade quality against file size by increasing the texture resolution: if a 256×256 texture doesn't look good enough, try 512×512, and you are still only using 64 KB (2 bpp) or 128 KB (4bpp).

Apple's iPhone SDK comes with a command-line tool to convert images into the PVRTC format called texturetool. Alternatively, you can download Imagination's PowerVR SDK (http://www.imgtec.com/powervr/insider/powervr-sdk.asp), which includes PVRTexTool, which is similar to texturetool, but comes with a graphical user interface. (PVRTexTool runs on Mac OS, but requires installation of Mac OS's X Window System, which you'll find on the DVDs that come with your computer.) Figure 2–9 shows PVRTexTool with the original texture and the compressed version side-by-side.

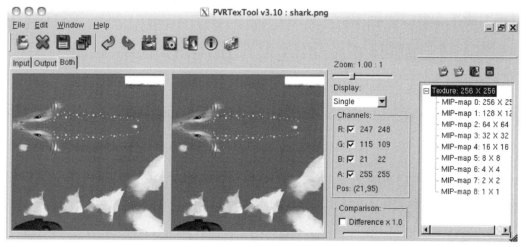

Figure 2–9. *PVRTexTool with uncompressed texture on the left and texture in PVRTC format on the right.*

There are a few requirements that using PVRTC textures on the iPhone imposes on your images:

- Height and width must be at least 8.

- The images must have a power-of-two width and height (8, 16, 32, etc). The iPhone 3G supports textures up to a size of 1024×1024.

- The images must be square (for example 256×256).

- Pixels at the border of texture elements should be surrounded by a 4 pixel wide outline, filled in with a color similar to the border pixel.

The size requirements are self-explanatory, but the border handling needs an explanation.

When decompressing a pixel, PVRTC takes adjacent blocks of pixels into account to create a kind of average color value. This allows it to avoid artifacts that could appear when encoding smooth color gradients. On the other hand, this technique will create problems when a pixel is surrounded by pixels that don't match its color, such as a black background. When the average color value is computed, the black is taken into account and causes a dark halo.

In the case of the texture in Figure 2–9, the gaps between texture elements (for example between the body of the shark and the fins) have been filled with a similar color to prevent this issue.

While it's easy to convert PNG files into PVRTC files, it's difficult to automatically adjust the images to all the peculiarities of the iPhone hardware. For this reason, I ask artists to provide images with all the requirements taken into account. Most artists are already well trained in the art of packing texture elements into power-of-two textures. The square size and border requirements are unusual, though, and you should discuss this early on with people new to the iPhone platform.

Reading PNG Images

It's theoretically possible to use PNG in your iPhone app and encode the image into a compressed texture format on the fly, but this process is too computationally expensive. Instead, the conversion process is done offline, when preparing the application, where no requirement for real-time processing exists.

To help reading PNG files in a Mac OS application, the converter tool uses libpng (http://www.libpng.org/pub/png/libpng.html) and zlib (http://www.zlib.net/) converter. libpng provides a C API to decode PNG images and uses zlib underneath. The advantage of using these open source libraries—in contrast to Mac OS specific frameworks—is that this makes my tools cross-platform.

Access to these libraries is wrapped in a class call PngResourceReader (see src/resource/png/PngResourceReader.h and .cpp), which is declared like this:

```
class PngResourceReader
{

public:

  /** Constructor. */
  PngResourceReader();

  /** Destructor. */
  ~PngResourceReader();

  /**
   * Opens the file with the given name for reading.
   * @param fileName file name.
   * @return true if successful; false otherwise.
   */
  bool open(const std::string& fileName);

  /**
   * Decodes a PNG image into RGB or RGBA format.
   * @param image resulting image.
   * @return true if successful; false otherwise.
   */
  bool read(Image& image);

  /** Closes the file and ends decoding. */
  void close();

private:

  FILE* m_File;    ///< File handle.
};
```

Decoding PNG images with libpng is fairly simple. At the core of PngResourceReader::read(), you'll find the following code:

```
bool PngResourceReader::read(Image& image)
{
    .
    .  // read the meta data
```

```
    int number_of_passes = png_set_interlace_handling(png_ptr);
    png_read_update_info(png_ptr, info_ptr);

    // Create Image
    color_type = info_ptr->color_type;
    Image::ImageFormat format;
    switch (color_type)
    {
    case PNG_COLOR_TYPE_RGB:
      format = Image::R8G8B8;
      break;
    case PNG_COLOR_TYPE_RGBA:
    default:
      format = Image::R8G8B8A8;
      break;
    }
    image.init(format, width, height);

    // Read image
    const png_bytep data = (png_bytep)image.getData();
    const size_t numChannels = image.getNumChannels();
    for (int pass = 0; pass < number_of_passes; pass++)
    {
      for (size_t y = 0; y < height; y++)
      {
        png_bytep row_ptr = &data[y * width * numChannels];
        png_read_rows(png_ptr, &row_ptr, NULL, 1);
      }
    }
    png_read_end(png_ptr, info_ptr);

    //... clean up
}
```

Image is a class that manages an image's memory and its attributes for me. The class has different format specifiers that determine how many color channels there are and how the image data is laid out in memory. Image::R8G8B8, for example, is RGB data whereas Image::R8G8B8A8 has an additional alpha channel (red, green, blue, and alpha pixels take up one byte each). These image formats map to the respective color types defined for PNG (PNG_COLOR_TYPE_RGB and PNG_COLOR_TYPE_RGBA).

RGB and RGBA formats are the most useful ones because PVRTC doesn't distinguish between greyscale and color images. Even if the PNG file doesn't contain image data in this format, You can force a PNG image to come out as either RGB or RGBA by applying input transformations when reading in the data with libpng:

```
    // Convert unusual formats into 8-bit RGB/RGBA format.
    if (color_type == PNG_COLOR_TYPE_PALETTE)
    {
      png_set_palette_to_rgb(png_ptr);
    }
    if (color_type == PNG_COLOR_TYPE_GRAY && bit_depth < 8)
    {
```

```
    png_set_gray_1_2_4_to_8(png_ptr);
}
if (png_get_valid(png_ptr, info_ptr, PNG_INFO_tRNS))
{
    png_set_tRNS_to_alpha(png_ptr);
}
if (bit_depth == 16)
{
    png_set_strip_16(png_ptr);
}
if (bit_depth < 8)
{
    png_set_packing(png_ptr);
}
if (color_type == PNG_COLOR_TYPE_GRAY ||
    color_type == PNG_COLOR_TYPE_GRAY_ALPHA)
{
    png_set_gray_to_rgb(png_ptr);
}
```

With this code in place, libpng will automatically convert all PNG image formats into either RGB or RGBA.

Converting Images into the PVRTC Format

To compress image data into the PVRTC format, Imagination's PowerVR SDK comes with a pre-compiled library called libPVRTexLib. This library expects the data in 32–bit RGBA format. If the PNG file doesn't have an alpha channel, I simply convert the RGB information into 32 bits and set the 8 bits for the alpha channel to 255.

Compressing the image is accomplished by these lines of code (see src/resource/pvrtc/PvrtcResourceWriter.cpp):

```
bool PvrtcResourceWriter::write(const Image& image)
{
  ASSERT_M(image.getFormat() == Image::R8G8B8A8,
    "Input image must be RGBA.");
  ASSERT_M(image.getHeight() == image.getWidth(),
    "Input image must be square.");
  ASSERT_M(image.getHeight() >= 32,
    "Input image must be at least 32x32 pixels.");

  bool result = true;
    PVRTRY
  {
    // 1. Wrap RGBA data in PVR structure.
  CPVRTexture originalTexture(image.getWidth(), image.getHeight(),
    0 /*num mipmaps*/, 1 /*num surfaces*/, false /*border*/,
    false /*twiddled*/, false /*cube map*/, false /*volume*/,
    false /*false mips*/, false /*has alpha*/,
      m_FlipVertically /*vertically flipped*/,
    eInt8StandardPixelType, 0.0f /*normal map*/, (uint8*)image.getData());

    // 2. Apply transformations
  CPVRTextureHeader processHeader(originalTexture.getHeader());
```

```
const size_t maxMipmaps = m_GenerateMipMaps ?
    ComputeMaxMipmaps(image.getWidth(), image.getHeight()) : 0;
processHeader.setMipMapCount(maxMipmaps);
PVRTextureUtilities* pvrTextureUtilities = PVRTextureUtilities::getPointer();
pvrTextureUtilities->ProcessRawPVR(originalTexture, processHeader);

    // 3. Compress to PVRTC
CPVRTexture compressedTexture(originalTexture.getHeader());
compressedTexture.setPixelType(
    m_TwoBppEnabled ? OGL_PVRTC2 : OGL_PVRTC4);
pvrTextureUtilities->CompressPVR(originalTexture, compressedTexture);
compressedTexture.setAlpha(m_AlphaModeEnabled);
compressedTexture.setTwiddled(true);
    compressedTexture.writeToFile(m_FileName);
}
PVRCATCH(exception)
{
    // Handle any exceptions here
    result = false;
}

    return result;
}
```

The conversion is a three step process:

1. Wrap the image data from the decoded PNG file in a CPVRTexture object, which is a type used by libPVRTexLib to handle textures. The parameters in the constructor describe the input format and must match the image contents.

2. Apply transformations with PVRTextureUtilities::ProcessRawPVR(). In my case, the purpose of this call is to generate mipmaps for the texture.

3. Compress texture and write out data into a file with the ending .pvr. (libPVRTexLib forces you to use this extension.)

When compressing the texture in the last step, it's important that you specify the correct output parameters. The pixel type determines whether the generated texture uses 2 bits per pixel (OGL_PVRTC2) or 4 bpp (OGL_PVRTC4). This is a quality/memory trade off that's easiest determined by compressing an image and having a look at the result on the iPhone.

The alpha setting specifies whether the texture features an alpha channel. The input to libPVRTexLib must be RGBA, but at this point, you can disable the alpha channel again if you don't need it.

"Twiddled" (sometimes also called "swizzled") refers to a non-linear memory layout. This means pixel values are not stored one after each other, but instead have been reordered to improve memory access locality. The GPU expects PVRTC textures in this format, so you have to enable this option.

Last, but not least, you should set setVerticallyFlipped() to true for OpenGL, or otherwise the texture will be displayed upside down.

Rendering the Converted Data on the iPhone

Now that you've learned how to convert FBX files into a custom in-game format and how to convert PNG files into PVRTC Textures, you are now at the point where you can take the converted data and render it on the iPhone.

Running the Converter Tool

As part of the source code that comes with this chapter, there's an Xcode project in the converter directory that wraps the code for converting FBX and PNG files in a command line tool for Mac OS. You'll also find shark.fbx and shark.png in the assets folder as sample input to the converter.

After building the application, you can start the conversion process by entering the following command line:

```
converter ../../../assets/converted ../../../assets/shark.png \
    ../../../assets/shark.fbx
```

The first argument is the target directory of the converted files, followed by the files to be converted. The converter automatically figures out what to do based on the file ending.

I've already added this command line to the Xcode project at converter/converter.xcodeproj, so you only need to build and run this project on Mac OS to convert the data.

Creating the iPhone Project

Afterwards, the converted files are in the assets/converted folder and need to be included in your iPhone project in which you want to render the model. To do this, right click on in the Groups & Files pane in your Xcode project. Then, add the files by selecting **Add ➤ Existing Files...**.

Again, I've already done those steps with the shark files and the resulting Xcode project is located at opengl/opengl.xcodeproj. Figure 2–10 shows this Xcode project.

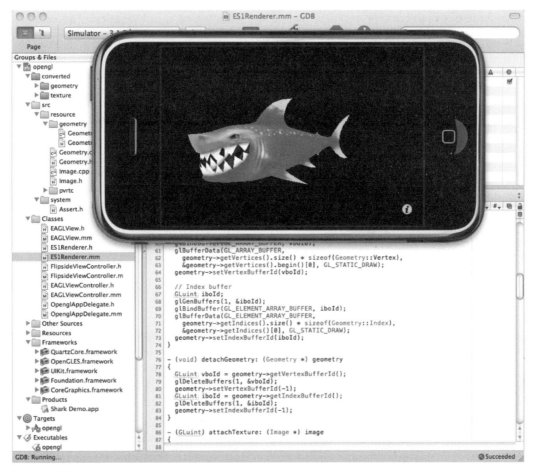

Figure 2–10. *The Xcode project to render the converted shark model*

The iPhone project is based on the OpenGL ES Application template that comes with Xcode; modified to use the custom geometry format and PVRTC textures. To get started, I suggest you have a look at opengl/Classes/EAGLView.mm to see how to read in the files and at ES1Renderer.mm to see how the model is rendered.

Summary

Writing your own tools can be a lengthy process, but a flexible content pipeline is well worth it because it allows you to optimize your data for the target platform and innovate on new engine features quickly.

The distinguishing feature of the content pipeline that I presented in this chapter is the separation between a data exchange and an in-game file format. The former is used to export data losslessly from content creation tools and the latter is designed to take advantage of the target platform and engine. A converter transforms the one format into the other and allows you to apply optimizations on the way.

Once the content pipeline is in place, it's straight-forward to add additional features. Here are some ideas, how you could optimize your data to increase render performance:

- Experiment whether your models benefit from an index buffer (glDrawElements()) or whether rendering is faster without indices (glDrawArrays()).

- Create strips out of the list of triangles coming from the FBX file to decrease the file size. You could use Nvidia's NvTriStrip library, for example (http://developer.nvidia.com/object/nvtristrip_library.html).

- Try reordering the vertex data to be in the same order as the indices. This improves cache coherency. Imagination's PowerVR SDK contains code to help you with this (have a look at PVRTTriStrip()).

- Implement settings in your converter to disable unused vertex attributes. For example, remove normals if you don't use lighting when rendering your models.

- Merge geometries from different files into one large triangle list. This benefits rendering because it reduces the number of draw calls. This requires that you also move all required textures into one file because you can't change textures in between render calls.

The way I go about optimizations in my games is that I implement the major game features first and then have a look where the performance bottlenecks are. The flexibility of my content pipeline allows me to add optimizations easily, even late in the project.

Ben Kazez

*Company: Mobiata
(http://www.mobiata.com)*

Location: Ann Arbor, Michigan

Former Life as a Developer: Built web applications in PHP, MySQL, JavaScript, and Mac applications in Objective-C/Cocoa. Designed user interfaces for desktop web apps, Mac desktop apps, and iPhone web apps.

Life as an iPhone Developer: Designed and built multilingual dictionary applications for Ultralingua. Currently heading up design and development at Mobiata, where we develop and maintain the best-selling FlightTrack, HotelPal, and TripDeck apps, and develop and manage mobile apps for major travel brands.

Apps on the App Store:

- *Ultralingua*

- *FlightTrack*

- *FlightTrack Pro*

- *HotelPal*

- *TripDeck*

- *StayHIP*

What's in This Chapter: This chapter describes how to develop effective data-driven iPhone applications, using real-world examples from FlightTrack, the best-selling travel app on the App Store.

Key Technologies:

- *• Third-Party XML APIs*

- *• Data-Driven UI Design*

- *• Design Patterns for Consuming Real-Time Data Sources*

- *• Data-Driven Cocoa App Architecture*

How FlightTrack Uses External Data Providers to Power This Best-Selling Travel App

The idea for FlightTrack was born, very appropriately, in an airport.

Picture one more weary traveler wandering the endless walkways of Minneapolis–St. Paul International Airport. This particular traveler is on his way home to visit family at the end of a relaxing summer spent baking cookies and hanging out with friends. He's flying Northwest Airlines through O'Hare International Airport. As usual, he's awkwardly pulling a boarding pass out of his computer backpack to remind himself of the flight number, gate, and departure time, and checking the current time on his watch before realizing that it was probably time to run.

Concerned that the gate might have changed, he squints at the flight information display monitors, hunting for the flight number printed on the boarding pass. Cancelled. The running was for naught. It was going to be a long day.

That weary traveler was me last September, as just one among the nearly one in four passengers every year who experiences flight delays, cancellations, or other so-called "flight irregularities."

Focusing initially on the annoyance of the paper boarding pass, I thought, "This could be better. There should be an iPhone app for this." Sure, I could type my flight info into the Notes app on the iPhone, but that didn't seem as sexy—and it wouldn't update as my flight information changed. Moreover, if the app was going to display real-time flight information updated minute-by-minute, why not include a map view that helped ease airport pickups and added a fun factor by showing exactly where any flight was on a map of the world? As a former Apple software engineer who had been looking for a fun side project, this seemed perfect. I began figuring out how to make it happen.

The chapter you are about to read is structured differently from most chapters in this book. Since FlightTrack is a live iPhone (and now iPad) app available on the App Store today, it's unfortunately not possible to list code samples directly from FlightTrack itself. However, I hope you'll enjoy the more conceptual nature of this chapter, in which I've attempted to take you through the process of choosing a data source, designing an effective user interface, and architecting the backend, using high-level concepts from the actual design and development of FlightTrack as a running example.

Choosing a Data Source

Most iPhone apps that are not driven by user-entered content are driven by external data sources. These data-driven applications are the bread and butter of iPhone apps for checking the weather, navigating streets or backwoods, traveling the globe, and many more. As a solo developer on this side project, I had no means of developing an original set of flight data—calling every airline every minute? Photographing flight info displays? It seemed impossible.

A simple online search was encouraging, though. At least half a dozen flight data providers appeared in a sea of similarly named services like FlightWise, FlightAware, FlightView, and FlightStats. No matter what the data-driven app, I found over the past year that a few basic techniques are helpful in evaluating data providers.

API Design

You'll be working with the provider's APIs, whether that means a barrage of XML tags or dense JSON code. For this decision, the engineer in you should speak loudly: How are the data fields named? How is the data structured? How many API calls does it take to do one "operation" in your application, whether that's refreshing the display or searching for new data? If it seems that the API design does not affect the user, take another look. As a mobile developer, you should be particularly concerned about the number of API calls, since per-request latency is a major issue on today's cellular data networks. If the API is returning formatted English text where it might otherwise return structured data, this could directly influence your user interface design possibilities. Consider the following XML snippets:

A

```
<WeatherForecast>
<day>Partly cloudy with a 30% chance of showers</day>
<day>Sunny</day>
<day>Partly cloudy with a 10% chance of showers</day>
</WeatherForecast>
```

B

```
<WeatherForecast>
<day showerChance="30" conditions="partlyCloudy"/>
<day showerChance="0" conditions="sunny"/>
<day showerChance="10" conditions="partlyCloudy"/>
</WeatherForecast>
```

Figure 3–1. *Apple's Weather app is developed from an API that's more like API B above. The data is heavily structured so that the developer has much more freedom in making user interface design choices (which temperatures to display, how to indicate sunny and partly cloudy, and so on).*

With API A, you'd better be planning on writing an English-only application that displays weather forecast data in a textual format. With API B, you'll have the freedom of displaying weather condition iconography (assuming a finite set of values for the "conditions" attribute), displaying the chance of showers in a larger font, localizing to any number of languages, and so on. It may take a bit more work if you're developing the simple display of weather forecast data in text, but the longer-term freedom will be worth it.

Data Coverage and Accuracy

Your application's usefulness will be judged largely on the coverage and accuracy of the data source you choose. Does the data source work in the United States only? Regardless of the countries covered, what is the coverage like within those countries (major cities, small towns, rural areas, etc.)? Breadth of coverage is excellent, but what about depth? Many data sets have both essential and less essential information: to return to FlightTrack, I knew gate and baggage claim information would be very helpful both to travelers and to their friends and colleagues making airport pickups.

Excellent coverage is only a plus, though, if given excellent accuracy as well. Not only is it important that the data be correct, but it must also be as close to real-time as possible. Your iPhone application will likely not retrieve data more often than every few minutes, so a data provider with untimely info will be particularly difficult to deal with.

Let the customer speak loudly for this decision. Think of your application in all its possible usage contexts, being used by all the types of users you can imagine.

Economics

Next, you'll need your business development hat. Most companies will not permit you to develop applications that use their data and make money from doing it. These data companies, like you, probably want to make money in order to continue improving their data and adding new features. A few application developers I've seen over the past months have decided to forego business terms and steal the data—not only illegal, but a terrible idea since it is in the data provider's interest to cut off that stream of data and disenfranchise you and your app users. A few of the actually acceptable arrangements you may find include the following.

Attribution

Some companies looking to extend their brand will simply require you to include a "Powered by X" footer in your application and give you their data for free. Generally, a win-win for the developer and data provider.

Subscription

Some data providers simply require a flat fee for using their data, whether that's monthly, quarterly, or yearly. For a typical application engineer without a business background, this will seem fairly risky, as you will need to ensure that you make at least a certain amount of revenue from the application each period. However, with fixed costs per time period, as your application downloads grow, your application only becomes more profitable. Not bad.

Transactional

Data companies looking to share in your success often use a transaction-based model wherein they meter your app's usage and charge you, the developer, per query. Think of this like your natural gas bill: If you use 25 cubic feet of natural gas in a given month, you'll pay a certain amount. If you use less the next month, you'll save on your next natural gas bill.

Though tying payments to usage seems attractive, it poses problems on the iPhone where, at least to date, an effective means of charging auto-renewing subscriptions has yet not been developed. If your customers pay you a fee for the application download, that fee will need to cover all future use of your application. Some users may delete the app (in which case you or your accountant is happy), but some users may use the app heavily for years, incurring large costs. Again, as a typical engineer without a business background, this may seem overly risky. Modeling various scenarios is the way to go, but beware—there will be lots of unknowns.

Revenue Share

If you're charging a purchase price for your app, why not simply pay your data provider a percentage of that and call it a day? This simple arrangement carries no risk for you as a developer, and requires no complicated accounting on the data provider's end. Users can pay once for your application and use it as much as they'd like. The data provider will likely have server costs to worry about as your application grows in popularity, but many providers will be willing to consider an arrangement like this if your application looks like it will be successful. For the provider, this model is still transactional—more queries means more server capacity and bandwidth—but a revenue share places the burden of risk on the provider rather than yourself.

On the downside, a revenue share may limit your flexibility to add more data sources in the future. The Apple developer royalty pie is only so large, and if you're giving 35% of revenue to one provider, 25% to another, 20% to another, you'll need to consider that there may not be much left for you to buy a Ferrari at the end of the year.

Trials

Most self-respecting data providers, whether providing dictionary data, destination guides, weather, or something altogether obscure and different will give you an evaluation account so you can try the data for yourself. This is the time to evaluate breadth of coverage, depth of coverage, accuracy, and API design so as to weigh these factors against the business terms that the providers can offer you. For FlightTrack, I quickly narrowed the field to two consumer-focused data providers. One company had superior accuracy and coverage (both breadth and depth) but required a transactional model. For me, that was too risky. I wasn't a venture-funded startup, I was a single developer looking for a great side project that would be fun to develop and engaging to users. That was a deal-breaker for me. I ended up choosing a different company that covered only the US and Canada and didn't include gate or terminal info, but had much less risky revenue-share terms that I could easily deal with.

Source-Driven User Interface Design

I quickly learned that each data provider supplied slightly different information—not only less or more accurate data, but also different levels of depth and descriptiveness. Some providers might, for example, list an aircraft type code ("777") rather than a full aircraft name (Boeing 777). More major differences such as lack of gate or baggage claim info can make for substantial differences from provider to provider. All of this means that designing a user interface for a data-driven application requires considerable attention to the data source: what depth of data is available, how descriptive the fields are, how normalized they are, and so on. Of course, the user is the true driving force, but the data source itself influences user interface design decisions considerably. This section guides the reader through the process of designing a user interface while keeping data source limitations and features in mind.

Challenges

Having secured a data provider, I next tackled the user interface design portion of the application. External data sources add user interface constraints not present in applications driven by user-generated content, such as games, to-do lists, and so forth. That's a challenge I love—human-computer interaction and graphical user interface design are fascinating to me, and the small screen of the iPhone coupled with external constraints ups the ante but keeps things fun.

Recall API A, which was previously shown. An API of this sort will severely limit the user interface design choices you can make when presenting the flight information, because the data is much less structured. For example, say you wanted to accompany each daily weather forecast with an image representing the weather for that day. In API A, this would require guessing at the weather forecast meaning by filtering for keywords ("cloudy," "x%," etc.), which is an extremely error-prone approach that API B avoids through more detailed data structuring. Perhaps you chose this source for other reasons, or perhaps this was the only source available for the type of data you needed to display. Regardless, you'll need to spend some time thinking about how to work with the limitations of the API in order to present useful data to users (see Figure 3–2).

Figure 3–2. *Depending on the flight, FlightTrack's flight detail screen may hide more data than it shows. The result is a user interface that is useful to travelers running through chaotic airport environments, even the most frequent road warrior .*

Another consideration that many developers overlook is simply how much data to display. A good API will give you a large, sometimes monstrous amount of data to work with. For FlightTrack, that meant an API that gave potentially nearly a dozen times for a flight departure or arrival: published gate time, scheduled gate time, estimated gate time, estimated runway (takeoff/landing) time, actual gate time, actual runway time, and so on. Only the most professional users will actually have any use for this kind of data breadth. In my case, a traveler rushing through the airport surely didn't need to know all these pieces in order to figure out when to arrive at gate G7. This led to the interface depicted in Figure 3–2. Of course, your app may have a very professional audience, but always keep in mind that what you leave out is almost more important than what you leave in.

Techniques from FlightTrack

User interface designs for FlightTrack started with user narratives. Though I never wrote out actual user stories, each decision was motivated at least in part by picturing travelers and other flight trackers in their element, tracking flights for various reasons. A traveler rushing through an airport terminal to catch a flight is likely looking for live, at-a-glance departure gate and time info, whereas a grandmother waiting to pick up her grandchildren from the airport is likely more interested in a live flight tracking map and arrival gate and time information. You may find it helpful to write out a few types of stories and annotate them based on what your data source provides: What pieces of data will most help the user at each point? What pieces will be somewhat helpful? Which will be extraneous? By keeping your users and data source in mind at all times, you'll find yourself developing an application that is not only more useful, but that you can actually implement once it comes time to parse data and turn it into an iPhone application.

The design process for FlightTrack then turned to visual interface design. I like to start with pencil sketches of user interfaces. Some start directly in Photoshop, and some developers start coding immediately (to the obvious detriment of the final product!). The tools aren't important; it's a matter of progressing from the most freeing medium (pencil and paper for me) to the most exacting (Photoshop, Illustrator, etc.). Original user interface sketches for Mobiata's latest application, TripDeck (created in conjunction with Mobiata engineer Jason Bornhorst), are shown in Figure 3–3.

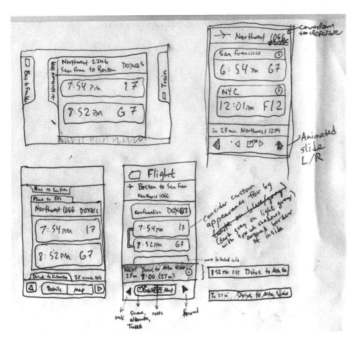

Figure 3–3. *Initial interface sketches for TripDeck. Note the barebones, wireframe style—the emphasis is on concepts, not execution.*

A full treatment of user interface design techniques is outside the scope of this chapter. However, you'll find many references to help you such as books, web sites, and any particularly forthright friends you might have.

Design Patterns for Data Source Consumption

Having settled on a user interface design, you'll next want to decide on the client-server interactions your app may use. FlightTrack requires live flight status information in order to give up-to-date, reliable, actionable information to travelers and their families, friends, and colleagues. Distributing this information to iPhones in a scalable way is a challenge, and two primary patterns for designing these interactions exist.

Direct-Client Consumption

In the simpler approach, each iPhone queries the remote data provider directly. This was the clear choice for FlightTrack's initial design: With only one data provider, it was incredibly simple to write an application that queried the provider directly. I wanted to avoid server costs and constraints on my end, so that if the application did well, I wouldn't need to become a server administrator and worry night and day about whether my server piece was operational. I preferred to leave that concern to the data provider, which ultimately was equipped with better expertise and equipment, as shown in Figure 3–4.

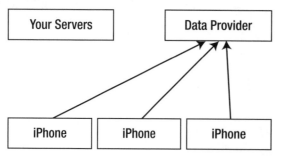

Figure 3–4. *Direct-client consumption requires no server infrastructure on the part of the developer.*

Server-Intermediary Consumption

A more flexible alternative does exist, however: Rather than having each iPhone contact the data provider directly, point each iPhone to a server application that you maintain (see Figure 3–5). That server application can then query the data provider directly. This approach, though it slightly increases latency and requires paying additional server costs, provides far superior flexibility. If your data provider goes out of business, you can point the server to a new provider. If you want to supplement your data with additional information from other sources, you can become a data aggregator without changing your iPhone app. Some data providers may even require this.

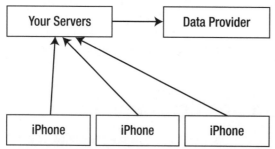

Figure 3–5. *Server-intermediary consumption requires added server infrastructure but lends enhanced flexibility in design and development.*

In the case of HotelPal, Mobiata's live hotel rate, availability, and booking application, our booking partner Travelocity required secure connections for booking requests to come from a single IP address. Though the server component required specialized knowledge to write (our engineer Daniel Lew saved the day here), and though maintaining the server has required ongoing expertise for the continuous uptime of HotelPal, this approach has been a boon for flexibility. We can update hotel data and even some aspects of the user interface presentation by tweaking the server rather than making application releases. We've even been able to improve overall usability by adjusting which providers we use for reverse address geocoding, or translating vague user-entered locations like "ann arbor mi" to latitudes and longitudes (see Figure 3–6).

Figure 3–6. *Users can type very freeform locations to search HotelPal for available rooms and rates. Adding this feature post-launch without necessitating an App Store update was made possible through server-intermediary consumption.*

Today, FlightTrack is actually a hybrid of these approaches. FlightTrack consumes data from three data sources, each specialized for various times of the flight and features of the application. This data source consumption happens directly from the application, to avoid server scalability issues that would increase server costs. However, FlightTrack Pro's push notifications of airport delays are generated by a server component that communicates directly with the data provider, to receive notifications of flight status changes as they happen.

Data-Driven Cocoa App Architecture

A full treatment of object-oriented application design patterns is clearly outside the scope of this chapter, but I wanted to highlight a few aspects that you may find helpful in developing your data-driven applications.

Data Model Design

The most important item to attend to in the design of your data object model is decoupling from the data source. You will surely find it all too easy to design a data model that perfectly fits the data source you have chosen, with all its design benefits and idiosyncrasies. But this is the best time in application development to consider the future: Your users may tell you that your data source is inaccurate, or your data source may go out of business. Whatever the case may be, you'll want the flexibility afforded by a data model design that's data-source agnostic, designed to accommodate any idiosyncrasies of your chosen source but not so well molded to it that any other data source would be a misfit. You'll find that time here is well spent.

The accompanying code sample demonstrates a data object model design for very simple weather data. The key point is that regardless of which API is chosen—API A or API B or one entirely different—this data structure ought to be able to represent the data effectively. In the case of API A, this may be a bit more difficult given the freeform nature of the fields, but the goal remains the same: a single data representation, regardless of the data source.

```
@interface MyWeatherForecast {
NSArray *_days;
}
// ...
@end

typedef enum _MyWeatherForecastCondition {
        MyWeatherForecastConditionCloudy,
        MyWeatherForecastConditionSunny,
        MyWeatherForecastConditionPartlyCloudy
} MyWeatherForecastCondition;

@interface MyWeatherForecastDay {
        float _showerChance;
        MyWeatherForecastCondition _condition;
}
// ...
@end
```

Connecting Data to UI

Having developed a beautiful, incredibly flexible data model, you'll face the problem of ensuring that the user interface is as up-to-date as possible. When the data source has updated data, your app's data will likely refresh through a timer (NSTimer will be your friend here), but then how will the user interface know that an update has taken place? In FlightTrack's case, it was one thing for our data provider to refresh, another thing for each application to pull in that updated data, but getting the data to the various view controllers that make up FlightTrack's interface could be surprisingly complex. Fortunately, a few design patterns will help you avoid any nightmarish spaghetti code.

Delegates

If you've developed an application that uses table views, you're already familiar with delegates: UITableView has delegate methods that allow you to customize various user interaction behaviors and receive notifications when users perform table-related actions, such as entering editing mode or attempting to rearrange a cell.

This same pattern can apply beautifully to data driven applications in which only one object needs to be notified of changes to a particular object. Simply add an instance variable to a data controller object, using Objective-C protocols to enforce the implementation of certain methods:

```
id <MyDelegateProtocol> _delegate;
@property (nonatomic, retain) id <MyDelegateProtocol> delegate;
```

You'll need to define the MyDelegateProtocol protocol, which is simply a list of methods that your delegate will need to implement:

```
@protocol MyDelegateProtocol
- (void)dataDidChange;
@end
```

Your data controller can simply call this method, if the delegate is set, and otherwise do nothing. In this way, the data source can let any user interface object know about changes to the data model, without the inflexibility of needing to know which particular user interface object is displaying its data.

Notifications

Delegates are simple and clean, but they don't scale well beyond a single data object. In a different model, your data source is updated by a controller class, which then sends out a notification of the change. Any user interface controller objects that need to stay up-to-date simply listen for notifications and update upon receiving them. This is where Apple's NSNotificationCenter comes in.

```
+ (id)defaultCenter;
- (void)addObserver:(id)notificationObserver selector:(SEL)notificationSelector↵
 name:(NSString *)notificationName object:(id)notificationSender;
- (void)postNotificationName:(NSString *)notificationName object:↵
(id)notificationSender userInfo:(NSDictionary *)userInfo;
- (void)removeObserver:(id)notificationObserver;
```

NSNotificationCenter lets each user interface controller object register for notifications by first retrieving the shared, "default" notification center object, and then by adding itself as an observer:

```
[[NSNotificationCenter defaultCenter] addObserver:self↵
 selector:@selector(dataDidChange:) name:MyAppDataDidChangeNotification object:nil];
```

This call registers the current object (self) to receive notifications called MyAppDataDidChangeNotification. I've left the optional object parameter nil in this sample; see NSNotificationCenter documentation for details on scoping notifications by object. In the data source, you define MyAppDataDidChangeNotification simply as a string:

```
#define MyAppDataDidChangeNotification @"MyAppDataDidChangeNotification"
```

Then, post notifications whenever data changes:

```
[[NSNotificationCenter defaultCenter] postNotificationName:↵
 MyAppDataDidChangeNotification object:self userInfo:nil];
```

This all automatically calls the appropriate methods in the observer classes, optionally passing additional information, stored in the userInfo NSDictionary parameter, to the observers of this notification. Bingo. Each object is up to date.

Setter Propagation

An alternate approach that combines the simplicity of delegates with the multiobserver power of notifications is one I'll term *setter propagation*. This model works particularly well with the hierarchies of UINavigationController objects that typically appear in navigation-based iPhone applications: The front screen of the app is replaced by a detail view ("pushed" into view), which is then replaced by a more detailed view, and so on. In this model, any data source changes will neatly cascade up the stack of navigation controllers without any need for notifications flying around to all objects at once. Here's how to do it:

1. Set up a delegate pattern with the top-most controller in your navigation stack. In FlightTrack's case, that meant that the application delegate (later moved to a flight data controller class, `FTFlightManager`) made queries to the flight data server and waited for their properly parsed responses.

2. Create a setter in your user interface controller. For `FlightTrack`, the top-level flight data controller set an `NSArray` property on `FTFlightListController`, the table view controller that displays the list of user flights.

3. Override the setter in your user interface controller to propagate the changes upward. FlightTrack's `FTFlightListController`'s `-setFlights:` method ensured that any currently displaying view controller was informed of the new flight info by a `-setFlight` method.

4. Repeat from step 2. Each view controller is responsible only for telling its "child" view controller about the data that that child needs to know about.

In this way, through only one delegate point of contact (step 1), your entire application user interface can be kept up to date.

Choosing an Approach

The approach you choose will depend on how complicated your application is, how many controllers are involved, and how they relate to one another. I've found that setter propagation is simple and natural, but in practice notifications can actually work better and be more flexible. You may want to start with notifications, since the cascading of setter propagation can be a tad more difficult to debug, but most of you should experiment and see what works best for you.

Release!

It's what all developers anticipate endlessly. Having settled on a data source, developed intuitive user interface designs that reflected the ways I thought users would interact with flight data, designed a data source consumption model and Cocoa app architecture, and then having actually implemented the nuts and bolts that hold everything together, it was time for some testing. I didn't have the luxury of a QA staff that we had at Apple—a team of smart folks who are pros at breaking code. I simply left my development machine, went to the couch, and started poking around as a user, uncovering a few bugs and noting them as I went.

I also recruited a few beta testers by posting messages to iPhone enthusiast forums. One beta tester was especially helpful, testing out numerous versions of FlightTrack and finding, on more than one occasion, major bugs that would have resulted in terrible reviews and a malfunctioning app.

After a few weekends and late weekday nights spent at Goodbye Blue Monday coffee shop, drinking cappuccinos and typing ever more furiously (caffeine can be a wonderful thing), FlightTrack made it to completion and I submitted it to the App Store in early November. After a lucky two-week review time, Apple approved the app and it went live!

Post release, I did encounter a few problems that tested decisions made throughout the process. Most importantly, it turned out that the initial data provider did not provide good coverage of pre-takeoff delays and cancellations, because the provider's clients were primarily limo drivers and other ground transportation agents who care more about arrivals. This, coupled with a colossal snow storm and airport closures nationwide on Thanksgiving weekend in November, meant my e-mail box was flooded with users who were upset that the app hadn't notified them of delays and cancellations. Moreover, users wanted gate info, international flight data, and so on. Other data sources had this data well covered but presented other limitations, such as only being able to search a few days in advance.

Through some clever feature implementation, and eventually by partnering with additional data providers, I was able to get around these issues. Talking frankly with the data source about coverage to make sure that I had the right expectations would have been helpful. The original data provider didn't have a bad product; it just wasn't that suitable for our use, and it would have avoided some tough telephone calls to find that out earlier.

FlightTrack Today

Today, FlightTrack is maintained by a team of engineers at Mobiata, including myself. Marshall Weir's server background means he maintains the push notification server, though he also writes plenty of new features into the app. Daniel Lew has contributed some major backend improvements (even an Android version), and Jason Bornhorst has developed features as well. The app now exists in a Pro version as well, which adds the push notifications and syncs with an online itinerary service. An in-app purchase makes the upgrade process seamless. We've attempted to present users with the best of all worlds—graphical flight maps from a provider that specializes in those, FlightStats flight data that covers the world with excellent depth, and flight schedule data that fills in scheduled airline flight information for up to 330 days in advance. It's taken a huge amount of hard work to get here, but in the end, it's the happy stories of users who were able to spend time with their kids at an airport restaurant rather than waiting at the gate for a delayed flight, or people reassured by knowing where their spouses are, that make it all worthwhile.

Saul Mora

Company: *Magical Panda Software, LLC*

Location: *Phoenix, Arizona*

Former Life as a Developer: Prior to jumping in head-first to the iPhone waters, Saul worked at IBM on Java applications, Intel on C# web applications, and then a Phoenix-area startup on Ruby on Rails web applications. Saul started his journey into Mac development when he bought his first MacBook Pro in late 2007. It's been a wild ride since then, and he wouldn't trade it for anything!

Life as an iPhone Developer: In between jobs as an independent iPhone developer and consultant, Saul has managed to squeeze in some time to publish a couple of apps on the store that he needed himself. Saul is an active member of the Phoenix-area developer community, with contributions at the Phoenix iPhone Developer user group and local Cocoaheads meetings. Saul spoke on the benefits of unit testing at the April 2010 360iDev iPhone developer conference in San Jose.

Apps on the App Store:

- **Freshpod**
- **Desert Code Camp Schedule**
- **DocBook (as a consultant)**

What's in This Chapter:

- **What is Unit Testing?**
- **What is it in Cocoa?**
- **Why do you need to test your code?**
- **How do you test your code (quickly)?**

Key Technologies:

- *XCode*

- *SenTest, GHUnit or Another Cocoa/Objective-C Unit Testing Framework*

- *OCMock*

Chapter 4

Write Better Code and Save Time with Unit Testing

Along my journey as a professional software engineer, I have encountered few developers eager to write code that exercises their code. In a typical structured environment, management is usually the least excited about developers writing unit tests because they assume it takes them away from actually writing production code. Some developers proudly proclaim that their code is perfect the first time, and will fly through the testing phase of development only to be shocked when their flawless creation of art and code has been returned, unapologetically, by some random QA guy.

You know this scenario: That random guy in QA is the iTunes AppStore approval process. While approval times have gotten better, wouldn't you like to know that when you submit an app for approval that you have run your app through a thorough battery of tests that you've handcrafted over the lifetime of the app's development? I feel much more confident giving an app to the AppStore approval gods, or a client, once it has passed my suite of unit tests. This doesn't mean I've caught every bug to be found. But it does mean that old bugs don't show up. It also means that the new features I add don't break existing code, and those simple assumptions that I had taken care of six months ago when I started working on the app are taken care of, once and for all.

With all the cool things to write (and read) about, why do something on, of all things, unit tests? Unit tests are boring. OpenGL, MapKit, or GameKit is where the hotness is with games, location-based applications and peer-to-peer connectivity, so who has time for unit testing? Besides, this code is never going onto a customer's device anyway, so why waste time on it in the first place?

The simple answer is that Unit Tests will return your time investment tenfold. It may not feel like it when you're writing tests and getting things set up, but every test you write will make your code more solid, flexible, reusable, documented, and easier to read. After a while, you will also start to notice that tested code will be written in smaller, more understandable chunks. Methods will be fairly concise and easily understandable.

One big advantage to testing your code is that you will rarely use the debugger. Why use the debugger to step through your code when you have something that verifies the method is returning the correct value automatically? It turns out that minimizing your time spent in the debugger will speed up the time it takes to complete your app with a higher level of quality. You just don't realize how much the debugger slows you down until you've essentially automated that process. So, if you think unit testing takes too much time, ask yourself how much time you spend in the debugger.

Unit Tests are something even Apple Engineers are starting to pick up. A blog post[1] by long time Apple Engineer, Bill Bumgarner explains at length why the Core Data team has unit tests around the Core Data framework, and how it has greatly improved the quality of the framework, the quality of the code, and allows new team members to make drastic changes while at the same time making the code simpler and easier to understand.

XCode has a unit testing library built-in called OCUnit. The OCUnit framework that comes with XCode is based off an old third-party framework called SenTest.[2] I have found that the built-in library has a few problems that make it more difficult to use:

- Setting up unit tests in XCode is difficult and error prone.

- Not all that useful since you can't debug the tests when necessary.

- Not terribly in vogue among other cocoa and iPhone Developers.

The built-in Unit Testing project works, however I find the experience to be difficult at best. By default (and with no easy way to change this behavior), unit tests are run every time you build your project. When tests pass or fail, they show up in the build results window. While that isn't so bad, the tests aren't necessarily debug-able from XCode. This is not quite useful, nor ideal. This ties your tests too close to your app.

Cocoa itself is actually an ideal framework for unit testing. Back when you were learning the basics of Cocoa, don't you remember something about the Model-View-Controller pattern, and how it was built into the framework? You use Views and ViewControllers all over your app, and if you use Core Data, you have implemented Models. Plain old Objective-C objects are Models as well. The MVC pattern lets you easily partition your app into components that are easier for testing and replacing.

Let's go over the basics of installing a Unit Testing framework that will get you started running unit tests against your iPhone Applications quickly and easily.

GHUnit, written by Gabriel Handford, is a newcomer to the Cocoa Unit Testing Framework space. GHUnit was written to address many of the shortcomings of the unit testing framework built into XCode, OCUnit. GHUnit (available on Github.com at

---

[1] http://www.friday.com/bbum/2005/09/24/unit-testing/

[2] http://www.sente.ch/software/ocunit/

http://github.com/gabriel/gh-unit) is an open source alternative to OCUnit and builds off the unit testing part of Google's Mac Toolkit. GHUnit is actively developed, and has several lofty goals, mostly filling in the gaps where the built-in tool lacks. The most notable, and perhaps useful, goal is:

- The ability to debug unit tests.

GHUnit also excels in other areas that OCUnit makes difficult, such as:

- A stand-alone unit test running app that runs on the simulator and, more importantly, on your devices.

- Being easier to install, correctly, the first time.

- Being easily run from the command line for regularly scheduled testing.

GHUnit provides a nifty unit testing harness. This harness does all the heavy lifting of scanning the compiled test library for subclasses of GHTestCase, reading those subclasses for all the test methods, running them, reporting broken tests—all in a helpful user interface that runs both on the iPhone simulator and your devices.

Let's install GHUnit into a default XCode Project. Be sure to download GHUnit from http://github.com/gabriel/gh-unit/downloads. You'll be using version 0.4.12 for iPhone OS 3.x for the remainder of this chapter. The GHUnit package file will contain several header (.h) files and a static library file, in addition to a couple of other contents that will be used to build and run your unit test project.

One important thing to keep in mind while installing GHUnit is the Configuration into which you are installing. A Configuration in XCode is a simple way to maintain a group of build settings for a particular part of your application's development and access them by a name. I normally keep tests in the Debug configuration, as this is the default selected configuration in any new XCode project, and they won't be accidentally included in the released application when using the Release configuration. However, there is no limit to which configurations your tests can be run.

First things first, you need to create a new project in XCode. I'll be working with a View Based Application Template, however, these steps will work with any application template. Let's name the project *MusicPlayer* (see Figure 4–1).

Figure 4–1. *Making a new view-based XCode project called MusicPlayer*

Next, you need to add a new build target, as shown in Figure 4–2. Control-click on the target item in the **Groups & Files** pane in XCode, and select "Add ➤ New Target...". Set the type as Application. Ignore the Unit Test Bundle here, as you're creating your own test suite. Then, click Next. Give your new Build Target a name, *MusicPlayerTests*. I typically use the convention "<ProjectName>Tests". This new build target will be a place where all the unit test code will be collected specifically for unit tests. This is how you will separate your application code from your unit test code.

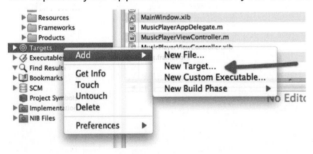

Figure 4–2. *Adding a new Build Target to your project*

The next step in creating a new build target is to include libraries and bundles required to build and run the target. If you do not already have the Target Info window open, Control-click on MusicPlayerTests target, and select "Get Info". Select the name of the other build target, MusicPlayer as seen in Figure 4–3. In the MusicPlayerTests General tab, click on the plus icon under the **Direct Dependencies** section shown in Figure 4–4. By adding this to the unit testing target, your shipping app will be built (based on normal compile rules) when you build your unit tests.

Figure 4–3. *Select the Direct Dependent library, MusicPlayer*

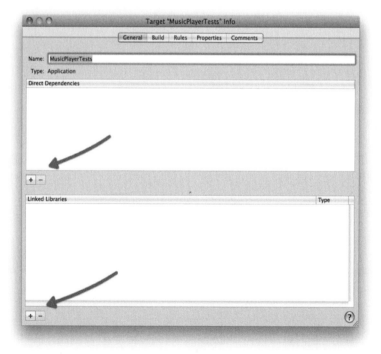

Figure 4–4. *To add the proper libraries to the Unit Testing target, you will need to click the Plus icons to display the available libraries.*

This essentially makes sure that when you run your unit tests, they are being run against the latest code you've written.

Next, click the Plus icon under the Linked Libraries section in the General tab. These are the runtime Frameworks that you need in order to run the unit test harness GHUnit provides (see Figure 4–5). The unit test harness is essentially the main UI Application that will run your tests, and show whether they have passed. Make sure to select the following, then click add:

- UIKit.framework

- Foundation.framework

- CoreGraphics.framework

Figure 4–5. *The minimum required libraries for GHUnit are CoreGraphics.framework, Foundation.framework, and UIKit.framework.*

There is one last step to configure in the Test Build target window before you can install your unit tests. Select the Build tab and you will see all the preprocessor, compiler, and linker options available for configuration. Let's get to the one option you need to alter, "Other Linker Flags" (see Figure 4–6). In the search bar, start typing "linker", and the option will be easily visible in the Linking section. Add the following parameters to this option:

```
-all_load -ObjC
```

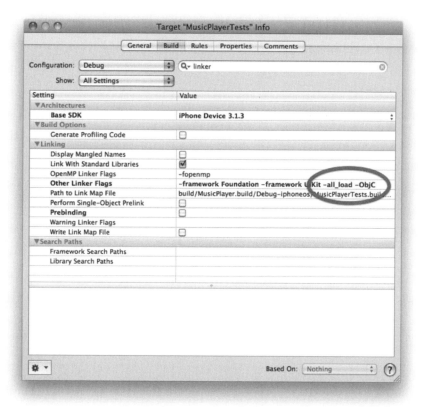

Figure 4–6. *Debug configuration linker flags in the Build tab for the MusicPlayerTests target*

Now, you have a new build target specifically for running your unit tests and unit testing harness; however, you still haven't included the GHUnit libraries yet. Before you do, let's set the Active Target to your new Unit Test Target. Do this by selecting the Project menu item, "Set Active Target ➤ <YourProject>Tests". In your case, you'll be selecting MusicPlayerTests. Only one build target can be the Active target at a time. A little green checkbox in the target list will indicate that your test target is indeed the Active Target.

Let's add the GHUnit Libraries, now that you have your unit test build target set up.

First, let's add a Tests folder to your project. I like to add an actual test folder in my code directory, and add that to XCode so that all my tests are in their own little area which is not part of the application code. This way, when you create new tests within XCode within the Tests folder, they will be created in this actual folder.

Next, grab the GHUnit Library you already downloaded, and copy it to the Tests folder you just created in XCode. The easiest way to do this is to drag the entire folder you downloaded into the folder structure of XCode. Make sure the little blue indicator appears as a sub item of the Tests folder in order for the destination to be in the Tests folder, as shown in Figure 4–7.

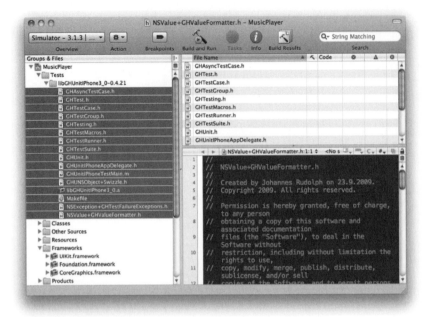

Figure 4–7. *The GHUnit folder in XCode will contain all the files required to compile and run the unit test harness for your unit tests*

In the "Add Files" Sheet that appears after dragging your folder into XCode, make sure that the MusicPlayer target is checked, while the MusicPlayerTests target is checked (see Figure 4–8). Doing this adds all the files into their proper places in your unit testing target by default. Now, your unit test project should be properly configured.

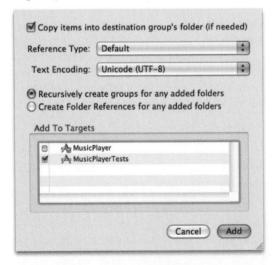

Figure 4–8. *When copying external files into your project, make sure you have the copy option selected, and select the MusicPlayerTests target.*

You're now ready to add actual unit tests to your project! Don't let this process scare you. It is only done once per project, and can be done in about five minutes.

You're going to start building unit tests for a simple app that will grab some items (MP3s, podcasts, or whatever else is there) from the built-in iPod library on a device, and insert those objects into a Core Data store[3]. Plus, you're going to have unit tests for all moving parts you write. First though, you have to learn how to write a unit test and how to run it.

With GHUnit, as well as OCUnit, you specify a test by implementing a new method in your GHTestCase subclass that begins with the word "test". So, all your tests are going to look like the following:

```
- (void) testSomething {}
```

After a while, you may notice that many tests look similar. That is, you are setting up your tests in a similar fashion for each test case. To help keep your tests clean and usable, GHUnit provides four wrapper methods in each test case:

- ■ `- (void) setUp;` —Called once before every unit test method in your GHTestCase.

- ■ `- (void) tearDown;` —Called once after every unit test method in your GHTestCase.

- ■ `- (void) setUpClass;` —Called once before all tests are run, and before the first time setUp is called.

- ■ `- (void) tearDownClass;` —Called once after all tests are run, and after the last tearDown is called.

Define one or more of these methods when you find your tests have some setup or teardown commonality.

The unit test harness will dynamically scan your test executable for all GHTestCase subclasses, and look for all methods whose names start with "test" within those classes. It will then run each method in the order it chooses (generally alphabetically by method name). For the iPhone, each test will appear in a section on its own based on the GHTestCase subclass in which it is defined.

Add a new NSObject class file to your Tests folder in XCode, and call it **PlaylistControllerTests.m**. Make sure the Unit Test Target is checked, and uncheck the Project Target so that the tests are only built when you build the test target. Since you created the test case class from a default NSObject template, you will need to make a couple of modifications to the file to transform it into a GHUnitTestCase:

At the top of the PlaylistControllerTests.h file, add

```
#import "GHUnit.h"
```

---

[3] This application will only run on iPhone OS 3.0 or higher, since the CoreData and MPMediaPlayer frameworks were only introduced in this version.

and, change the superclass of the class to

    GHTestCase

This new unit test class will contain all the test cases you are going to write. It should look like Figure 4–9.

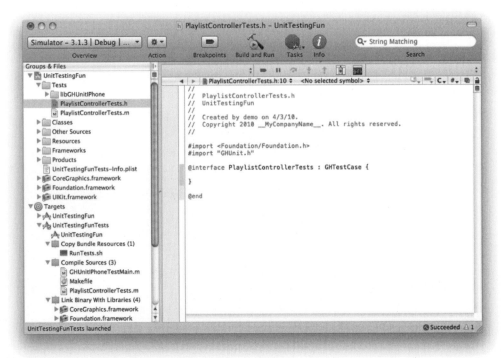

Figure 4–9. *Class definition of PlaylistControllerTests, your first test case*

In the PlaylistControllerTests.m file, you're going to add a simple test for sanity checking your install.

```
- (void) testFirstUnitTest
{
        GHAssertEquals(1, 2, @"If this works, the universe has contradicted itself");
}
```

One of the core aspects of unit testing is assert macros. After all, you are trying to verify that return values from methods are within your own specifications. GHUnit contains a set of predefined macros that help with comparing actual results with expected results in your test. The full list is on the GHUnit project page; however, the basic format of each macro is the first two parameters are what will be compared, while the third parameter is a description of why the particular result is expected, which will be displayed in the output window if the test were to fail.

Click Build and Run (or Command + Return) and you should see the iPhone simulator appear, with a new UI (this is packaged with GHUnit). The test named "testFirstUnitTest" is in black. Tap Run, and you should see the name of the test turn red, indicating that it has failed (see Figure 4–10). Hooray! (As of this writing, GHUnit support for the iPad and the iPad simulator was still being finalized.)

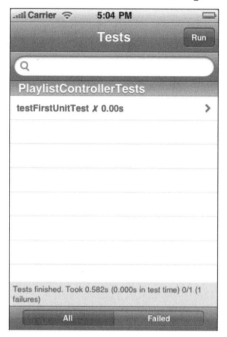

Figure 4–10. *The GHUnit unit test runner application on the iPhone simulator*

Now, you can easily fix this by changing the assertion to test that 1 is indeed equal to 1, but maybe you want to do something a little more complex.

Your application's goal is to create a list of PlaylistItem objects, based off the MPMediaItems you can get from the internal iPod Library, and save them into a CoreData store. Let's write one test that gets you going:

```
- (void) testCreatePlaylistItemFromMPMediaItem
{
        MPMediaItem *sampleItem = [[MPMediaItem alloc] init];
        PlaylistItem *testItem = [[PlaylistItem alloc] init];

        [testItem readMediaItem:sampleItem];

        GHAssertEquals(testItem.title, @"My Title", nil);
}
```

This seems like a simple test. However, since you're writing it before writing your application code, this forces you to do quite a few things even before you can compile your code, let alone run it. To be sure, the list of steps required to run your tests is identical to what you would need to do without tests, so the added value of tests here is that they guide in telling what needs to be done next.

The things that need to be done in order for this test to work are as follows:

- Import the MediaPlayer.framework library, and add it to the Link steps in both the unit test, and project targets.

- Create a PlaylistItem class.

- Add the preprocessor directive #import <MediaPlayer/MediaPlayer.h> to the PlaylistItem header, and your test case.

- Add the PlaylistItem.h header to your test case file.

- Create a readMediaItem method on your PlaylistItem class.

- Create a title Property on your PlaylistItem class.

That's a long list of things to be done since you wrote the test first. But these steps will always need to be taken regardless of whether you include tests in your application. The exercise of writing the test first only verified that these steps were, in fact, required for the application to work. This is indeed valuable information because you only want enough code and libraries for your app to work and nothing more.

After you complete the quick list of to-do's your non-compiling test just gave you, do simplest thing possible to make the unit test pass in the readMediaItem method, namely:

```
- (void) readMediaItem:(MPMediaItem *)mediaItem
{
        title = @"My Title";
}
```

What value is there in that, you ask? Well, since the test was failing before, if you run it now, you know it passes. The simple information that you know the test is running against actual application code is valuable information. Now, it's time to make the test fail again. But how? There is no way to set a title property on an instance of a MPMediaItem since it's a system provided, readonly object. Heck, this implementation isn't even using the mediaItem parameter, and the test still passes, something smells funny here.

Mock Objects

Quite simply, mock objects are a class of objects that stand in for the real thing. Think of a mannequin at the mall. Mannequins are essentially mock objects, since they fill in for the real object (a person instance). They don't replace the functionality of the real object, but do a good enough job (of displaying clothes) to let you understand how well the function works (how does the shirt look unfolded).

You may be wondering, "Why do I need a mock object? Shouldn't I be writing tests on REAL objects?" The answer to that is, you are. The mock mannequin has a definite purpose which is that a person isn't moving or getting bored. Mock objects make it easier to set up scenarios that occur in real applications, so in a sense they're even better than the real objects because of this control.

Take, for example, a typical Twitter app. Back in the early days of Twitter, the web service would display the "Fail Whale" quite often. But if you were to write a test that touched the actual network to test for a failed connection, it would probably not pass all the time. That's because the Twitter service, for all the Fail Whale stories, was up most of the time. In order to induce a Twitter connection problem in your app, you could unplug the network cable from your machine, turning off your Airport card or any number of other means for manually disconnecting the app for testing. With mock objects, however, you can simply command your Mock Twitter Connection to fail for one test, and you can then design the app to handle that one issue appropriately. This is the power of mock objects.

OCMock is a mock object framework for Objective-C. But why would you need a whole framework for mock objects? Shouldn't you be able to create these as new classes in your tests? While this is certainly possible, the reason you need a whole framework is because several aspects of creating mock objects from real objects (or rather, classes), and reacting to real objects are the same. All instances of mock objects created by OCMock behave the same way. That is, they will all keep track of the real expectations of your real objects, keep track of the methods that are or aren't called, and fail accordingly.

To get started with OCMock in your test project, download version 1.55 of the OCMock Framework[4]. Copy the OCMock.framework folder from your Downloads folder to your Tests folder, and make sure the Test target is checked, and not the main application build target. Also make sure at the top, that Copy Files is checked as well.

When you add OCMock to the MusicPlayerTests target, OCMock will automatically be added to the "Link Binary with Libraries" section of the MusicPlayerTests target. This alone won't get OCMock running the on the iPhone simulator. You will need to add a custom build step to copy the library to your unit test application bundle.

1. First, create a new Copy Files build phase in the Unit Test Project (see Figure 4–11).

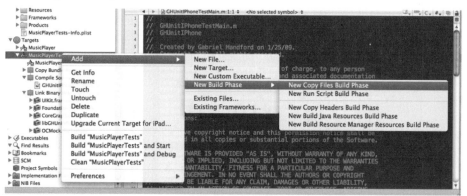

Figure 4–11. *Use the New Copy Build Phase option to copy the OCMock static library into your unit test application bundle to use mock objects in your unit tests.*

---

[4] http://www.mulle-kybernetik.com/software/OCMock/

2.   Set the destination to $(BUILT_PRODUCTS_DIR), as shown in Figure 4–12.

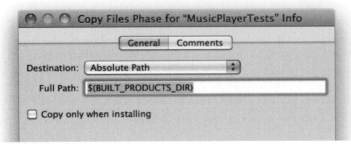

Figure 4–12. *Set this custom copy files phase to copy OCMock.framework to the Absolute Path of your unit test application bundle.*

3.   Drag the Copy Files phase to just before the link framework step in the build target (see Figure 4–13).

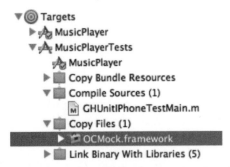

Figure 4–13. *Copy OCMock.framework to the unit test application bundle before linking. Otherwise, the link step will fail.*

4.   Drag the OCMock.framework item within XCode to this new phase. OCMock is now ready for use within your project.

To use OCMock in your unit test files, you must add the proper import statement to the top of your test case (.m) files:

```
#import <OCMock/OCMock.h>
```

Now that you have a mock object framework installed, you have the ability to write the following test:

```
- (void) testCreatePlaylistItemFromMPMediaItem
{
        MPMediaItem *sampleItem = [OCMockObject mockForClass:[MPMediaItem class]];
        [[[sampleItem expect] andReturn:@"My Title"] ↵
valueForProperty:MPMediaItemPropertyTitle];

        PlaylistItem *testItem = [[PlaylistItem alloc] init];

        [testItem readMediaItem:sampleItem];
```

```
        GHAssertEquals(testItem.title, @"My Title", nil);
        [sampleItem verify];
}
```

Notice a few things about this test:

- If you run it now, it will fail.

- You don't perform an alloc/init for a "real" MPMediaItem instance, instead, you're creating a mock instance.

- The mock instance is now expecting that you call a method named valueForProperty, with the explicit parameter MPMediaItemPropertyTitle.

- After the assertion passes, you must verify that the mock object met its expectations, which leads to the test failure in the unit test runner on the iPhone simulator.

Using a mock object here makes sense because, even in your real production code, you never actually create an instance of an MPMediaItem object. Instead, you perform a query using MPMediaQuery, which returns pre-allocated and initialized instances. Also, notice that while you are running a test app that references the MediaPlayer.framework, if you tried to run a normal app in the simulator, it will not work since there is no iPod application. The MediaPlayer framework requires the iPod application to function because an MPMediaItem is, under the covers, a proxy to an internal object reserved for direct use only by the internal iPhone applications. You have overcome this limitation by simply working around this fact with a mock object that looks and acts good enough for your code to keep running based on what you know about the (documented) Cocoa APIs. This is the core of why you need mock objects.

How can you make your test pass? Let's try the following:

```
- (void) readMediaItem:(MPMediaItem *)mediaItem
{
        title = [mediaItem valueForProperty:MPMediaItemPropertyTitle];
}
```

This is a simple, straightforward implementation. However, this makes your test pass. If you want to verify that this is indeed checking the parameter passed to the valueForProperty: method, you can change it to MPMediaItemPropertyGenre, and watch it fail on the next run. The fact that the test fails for anything other than what is expected is valuable information.

You might be thinking "Golly gee willikers, there's a whole lot of stuff to do just to get the first line of production code to pass just one test." And, "There's about five lines of code just to get one single line of application code written. I could have saved all those steps."

You're right, there's quite an investment not only in setup, but in authoring tests in the first place. However, let's think about how this will logically progress. Will the second test cost more to write? Not too much, since the setup is done, you can get to the next test fairly quickly. And the next one after that, and so on. After a little while, you can have a tested application that gives you quite a bit of useful information:

- If you broke something, you will know right away what broke and where.

- By knowing that all tests pass before you move on to the next one, you can easily build on that foundation.

In most tested code I've ever seen or written, the ratio of test code to actual code is around four to one. That is, about four lines of test code leads to one line of app code. The one method you tested is a single line of simplicity. However, your test is a perplexing six lines. This will often be the case in tests, since there is going to be some setup involved in creating test instances, verifying mocks, and asserting values are correct. Keep your test code clean and as well maintained as your app code. When it comes time to change up a test because an application-wide assumption changes, you'll find it easier to change.

Now that you have a fully functioning test environment, utilitize mock objects and are testing your code before you write it. Let's discuss some techniques on how to test certain parts of your application.

Objective-C categories are like puppies: they're fun, cute, and cuddly until they poop in your favorite shoes. Categories give you unlimited flexibility to extend any Objective-C class without subclassing it. This is great for adding that one method on NSString that you think should be there, without getting into the problems of subclasses or submitting a bug report, hoping Apple will see things your way. With great power, comes great responsibility. You must make sure that your new categories are working correctly, and not trampling over existing functionality. So, let's go over how you would test a category.

For this example, you're going to extend NSDate to have some simple to use methods such as[5]

```
(void) mp_isBefore:(NSDate *)otherDate;
(void) mp_isAfter:(NSDate *)otherDate;
(void) mp_isEqual:(NSDate *)otherDate;
```

First, you'll create a new GHTestCase class called NSDate+HelpersTests. I generally put categories in files named for the object I'm extending and append '+Helpers', or another descriptive name when necessary. Create a new test:

```
- (void) testNSDateImplementsIsBefore
{
        NSDate *testDate = [NSDate date];

        BOOL result = [testDate respondsToSelector:@selector(mp_isBefore:)];
```

---

[5] One convention to avoid category collisions in your code is to prefix your category names in the same vein that all Cocoa classes have a prefix convention of NS. mp_ is the designated convention for Magical Panda.

```
        GHAssertTrue(result, nil);
}
```

What are you doing here? You're checking that an instance of NSDate has your new category by checking if it respondsToSelector. If you run this test prior to actually implementing the basic category, this test will fail. That is good news since you can see a difference from before adding the category and then after. So, let's make the test pass:

- ■   Add a new file called NSDate+Helpers.(h m) and make sure both test and project build targets are selected.

- ■   Add the following category implementation:

```
//NSDate+Helpers.h
@interface NSDate (Helpers)

- (BOOL) mp_isBefore:(NSDate *)otherDate;

@end

//NSDate+Helpers.m
@implementation NSDate (Helpers)

- (BOOL) mp_isBefore:(NSDate *)otherDate
{
        return NO;
}

@end
```

Next, select Build and Run from the menu and the previous test should pass. You have now extended NSDate with a new method, mp_isBefore:(NSDate *)otherDate. Now, let's make sure mp_isBefore works as expected.

```
- (void) testSelfIsBeforeDistantPast
{
        NSDate *testDate = [NSDate date];

        BOOL result = [testDate mp_isBefore:[NSDate distantPast]];

        GHAssertFalse(result, nil);
}

- (void) testSelfIsBeforeDistantFuture
{
        NSDate *testDate = [NSDate date];

        BOOL result = [testDate mp_isBefore:[NSDate distantFuture]];

        GHAssertTrue(result, nil);
}
```

These two tests cover the simplest test cases I can think of to test next, namely what happens when you compare the current date (the result of [NSDate date]) with the largest and smallest date values available. Running these tests will result in one passing and one failing. That's because you gave mp_isBefore a default return value of NO, so for the first test, this result will be correct. Let's make isBefore something a little more useful:

```
- (BOOL) mp_isBefore:(NSDate *)otherDate
{
        return [self compare:otherDate] == NSOrderedDescending;
}
```

Now, if you run your unit tests with this implementation, both will fail. This is the incorrect constant you are comparing to. The correct constant should be NSOrderedAscending. Change that the right side of the comparison to NSOrderedAscending, and you have it passing tests again. You're on a roll. Let's see what happens when you compare the date to itself.

```
- (void) testSelfIsBeforeSelf
{
        NSDate *testDate = [NSDate date];

        BOOL result = [testDate mp_isBefore:testDate];

        GHAssertFalse(result, nil);
}
```

Let's step back and think about why this test is necessary. If two dates are equal, then they are not greater than or less than each other. The mp_isBefore operation will cannot return true for equal dates. This test is saying, in a sense, that today cannot come before today. While this may seem obvious, it is these types of foundational tests and assumptions that applications are built around. Nailing down these assumptions with tests will make it easier for you to find real errors faster.

However, there is a problem with this test as it is now: it already passes without adding code. It's more important that the test fails first, then passes to make sure that the code is actually being executed. Ideally, this shouldn't happen, as you want to add tests that fail first so you know they are working only against the new code. Practically speaking, it is fine if you manually make this test fail through the implementation of the method being tested. That is, you can make sure this test is checking the method correctly by breaking the method in its current working form to something that doesn't work, such as the following:

```
- (BOOL) mp_isBefore:(NSDate *)otherDate
{
        return [self compare:otherDate] == NSOrderedSame;
}
```

This same process and similar tests can be repeated for correctly tested implementations of mp_isAfter: and mp_isEqual: category methods.

However, let's try writing a test for isEqual, without your mp_ method prefix:

```
- (void) testNSDateImplementsIsEqual
{
        NSDate *testDate = [NSDate date];

        BOOL result = [testDate respondsToSelector:@selector(isEqual:)];
```

```
        GHAssertTrue(result, nil);
}
```

This test will pass since isEqual is a method on NSObject, and all objects will have a default implementation for isEqual. Since this test passes without your own implementation, you need to make a choice. You can do either of the following:

- Overwrite the implementation of isEqual for all NSDate instances in your application

- Choose another name for your category

Of course, since you are choosing to name your methods with the mp_ namespace, you won't be overriding built-in methods. The unit test you wrote reveals the implications of your design decisions right away, and leads to better method naming conventions for your categories. This should lead to less hair pulling in the future as you will be 100% sure that there isn't a category overriding functionality, as well as knowing that functionality works as expected when it is used.

Testing Your Core Data Models

Core Data is a convenient way to persist objects in your application. While it is an object storage mechanism, the underlying SQLite store gives you a better idea of how it stores its data. Using the fact that your app is backed by SQLite does not change the way you test your Core Data models.

There is a philosophy of MVC development that tries to emphasize the Skinny-Controller-Fat-Model paradigm. That is, your controllers (not your View Controllers) should be fairly lightweight code, while your Models should have most or all of your application logic. The reason being that Models are easier to test since they contain no UI. By having simple controllers, they are easier to test even though they will eventually require UI interactions; those are simple and less error prone to begin with. Another reason to have more isolated models is that your resulting code will be more portable should you decide that extending your app to the Mac platform is the next step.

While any NSObject is essentially a Model in Objective C, Core Data is a powerful way to build Models and persist instances of your Model objects. Core Data has a great built-in Entity Modeling tool that basically lets you configure your schema with entities, their attributes and relationships. In fact, this mechanism can be thought of as Interface Builder for your data model. Once your data model is defined in the Core Data Entity Modeling tool, it's fairly simple to persist these models to disk, and herein lies the problem.

Bringing unit testing into the picture, you can test many aspects of your data model, specifically the additional logic you place in each Entity or NSManagedObject subclass. In this way, unit testing your model classes is very similar to testing any other normal object. However, there are a couple of caveats in this approach.

First, in order to create an instance of an Entity in Core Data, it needs to be defined in an NSManagedObjectModel. The built-in Entity modeling tool in XCode defines that model for you. After you have a model, you have to create the entire Core Data stack. While each piece of the stack can exist independently, in order for your objects to work in a normal app, you should test your app with the stack you intend to use. How can you create tests using Core Data entities that are re-runable? All data is persisted to a Core Data store by performing save: on an NSManagedObjectContext. By not performing save:, you can avoid persistence, but you will also not be triggering the built-in core data validations on your data entities and their relationships. A better way is to perform save: and toss the persisted data. But that involves some messy cleanup routines. An even better way is if you used an idea built into the Objective C language itself, namely, saving to nil. Core Data has an InMemory store data type, which gets reset every time your test harness is run. This is the key to testing your core data models and taking advantage of the other handy attributes built into the Core Data framework.

Let's add to your music player application example, and design a Core Data model with Songs and Playlists (see Figure 4–14). A Song has a few standard attributes such as title, artist, and duration. A Playlist has many Songs and a Playlist can have a name that isn't necessarily unique. You'll not order the Songs in the Playlist for now.

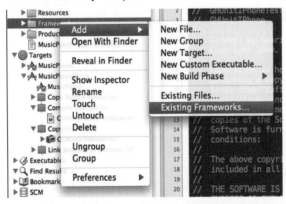

Figure 4–14. *To add one of the iPhone SDK Frameworks, choose Add ➤ Existing Frameworks...*

Where do you start testing this? There are a few specifications here, such as the relationship between a Song and a Playlist and the attributes that are present on Songs and Playlists. Let's start there.

Before you can start with Core Data, you have to add the CoreData.framework library into your project. Control+Click on the Frameworks folder, and select "Add Existing Frameworks...". From the list that appears, select CoreData.framework and click Add. Your project will now compile, link against, and run with the Core Data framework.

To create a Core Data entity model, from the File menu item, select New File. In the New File window select Resource in the left menu, and Data Model in the main file type (see Figure 4–15). Click Next, and name this new Data Model MusicPlayer.xcdatamodel.

Figure 4–15. *Create a new Core Data Model file using the standard New File menu item in XCode*

To follow along with the remainder of this example, you will find the following tools helpful: mogenerator, active record fetchers for Core Data:

- http://github.com/rentzsch/mogenerator
- http://code.magicalpanda.com/activerecord-for-core-data

The first tool, mogenerator, is a code generation tool that implements the Generation Gap pattern[6] made popular among Cocoa developers by Jonathon "Wolf" Rentzsch. Many seasoned developers will tell you they abhor generated code. In some cases, such as when using the Core Data Entity Modeling tool, generated code is necessary. The Generation Gap pattern specifies simple boundaries for working with generated code using the object oriented properties of classes, namely subclassing. mogenerator will generate four files for each Entity you define in your model, two machine specific files, and two human specific files. The idea is that all your custom model logic code will go into the human specific files. As you make changes to your Model, mogenerator will

---

[6] http://www.research.ibm.com/designpatterns/pubs/gg.html

update the machine specific files to keep your code in sync with the Model. Also included in the mogenerator tool is a plug-in for XCode so that this generation happens on every save of your Model file. mogenerator then essentially automates a process that is quite manual with the default XCode tools.

The second set of code is a simple helper library developed for use with custom NSManagedObjects (the core data entities in Core Data). This library makes it extremely simple to add Core Data to your application as well as to perform fetches on your Entity data. Core Data consists of several objects; however, two will be used most often, NSManagedObject and NSManagedObjectContext. The Active Record Fetching helpers have added the idea of a default NSManagedObjectContext instance. This default context will be used in the following examples. It's important to keep in mind that this default context is not part of Core Data, but the Active Record Fetching helpers.

Now, create two new test case files, one called SongTests, and the other called PlaylistTests. (Notice that you're going with the Test First approach here.)

Next, you're going to test your data model intentions, namely that a Playlist should have one or more Songs, as shown in Figure 4–16.

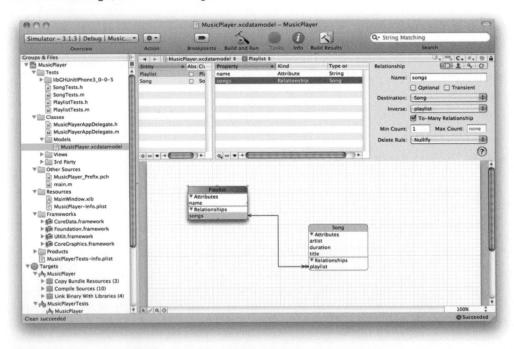

Figure 4–16. *A simple Core Data model with Playlist and Song entities defined.*

The first thing you want to create is a new Playlist. You're going to require that all Playlists have at least one Song and a name. You'll start this time with a data model, and write tests to solidify your assumptions. Create your Core Data model in XCode, and call it MusicPlayer.xcdatamodel. Once it's in your project, command + click on the MusicPlayer.xcdatamodel file and select Get Info. In the comment tab, enter "xmod".

This will tell the mogenerator tool to generate custom NSManagedObject subclasses. While it is perfectly acceptable to use Core Data with only NSManagedObject instances, managing the extra custom logic your entities will contain, it's best to have custom subclasses for the code to live in.

In order to test your Core Data model in your test cases, you need to set up the Core Data stack every time you run your tests. Not only that, but you need to make sure your Core Data Model will store its data using an In Memory store. Your friends at Magical Panda Software have put together several Core Data helper files that make including Core Data in your applications quick and easy. How easy? One line easy as follows:

```
- (void) setUpClass
{
        [ActiveRecordHelpers setupCoreDataStackWithInMemoryStore];
}
```

If you were to manually set up the Core Data stack of objects without this simple one-line helper, you'd very quickly get lost in the details of providing the support structure before you were even close to testing. First, you'd have to create and set up instances of an NSManagedObjectModel, NSPersistentStoreCoordinator, an NSPersistentStore and an NSManagedObjectContext. Configuring each of these is not trivial, and can be error prone if you've never dealt with Core Data prior to reading this chapter. This single line helper method contains two important features. The first is the obvious need to consolidate all the logic and boiler plate Core Data setup code for an In-Memory SQLite store. The second, and more important, is that this single line of code easily documents the intended environment the tests will need in order to run without all the mess.

The Active Record helpers used in the follow code are provided by the Active Record Fetching for Core Data library previously referenced. Be sure to add the proper import statement to get this one line of awesomeness:

```
#import "CoreData+ActiveRecordFetching.h"
```

You should also be studious and clean up after all the tests are run:

```
- (void) tearDownClass
{
        [ActiveRecordHelpers cleanUp];
}
```

Getting back to your data model, let's test what happens when you create a Playlist entity and try to save it without a song and without a name. Let's write the following test in a new test case called PlaylistTests, and let's check that the Playlist entity is only valid when you have at least one Song.

```
- (void) testPlaylistIsNotValid
{
        Playlist *testPlaylist = [Playlist newEntity];

        NSError *error = nil;
        [[NSManagedObjectContext defaultContext] save:&error];

        GHAssertNil(error, @"Shouldn't be any errors on save!");
}
```

Once you run this test, however, you find that the test fails (see Figure 4–17).

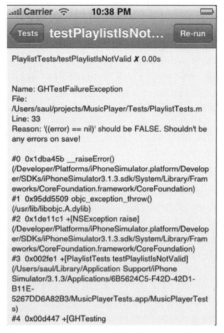

Figure 4–17. *Your test fails since the value you're testing is not nil.*

After a quick realization that an invalid Playlist entity should have errors when it saves, fix the assertion that error should be not nil:

```
- (void) testPlaylistIsNotValid
{
        Playlist *testPlaylist = [Playlist newEntity];

        NSError *error = nil;
        [[NSManagedObjectContext defaultContext] save:&error];

        GHAssertNotNil(error, @"Shouldn't be any errors on save!");
}
```

You can test further that the error contains two userInfo messages; however, the mere fact that there are errors is enough to validate that if you try to save a Playlist that doesn't have the required fields set, the code will generate an appropriate error.

This brings me to an important piece of testing philosophy I generally adhere to: Don't test the framework. To be sure, you are in fact testing that Core Data generates errors on save. However, the subtle difference here is that you are configuring a particular entity to validate in a certain way on save. Knowing that this happens only when you expect it is useful knowledge, and is not testing the low-level bits of the framework, but rather that our assumptions are configured correctly in your Core Data model.

Now, let's test that a playlist can calculate its total duration based on the duration of each song it contains. First, let's set up a new test that verifies that the duration method on the Playlist Entity will add two song durations together upon calculating the total duration of the Playlist:

```
- (void) testPlaylistCalculatesDurationBasedOnSongDuration
{
        Playlist *testPlaylist = [Playlist newEntity];
        Song *testSong1 = [Song newEntity];
        [testSong1 setTitle:@"Song 1"];
        [testSong1 setDurationValue:3];

        Song *testSong2 = [Song newEntity];
        [testSong2 setTitle:@"Song 2"];
        [testSong2 setDurationValue: 2];

        [testPlaylist addSongsObject:testSong1];
        [testPlaylist addSongsObject:testSong2];

        GHAssertEquals([testPlaylist duration], 5.0, nil);
}
```

Let's add a default implementation of the duration method in your custom Playlist entity:

```
- (NSTimeInterval) duration
{
        return 0.0;
}
```

Running this test with your obviously wrong implementation results in another test failure (see Figure 4–18).

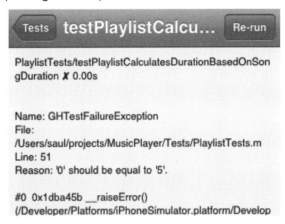

Figure 4–18. *The test failed since the return value of the duration method is 0. Your test expects the return value to be 5.*

Let's add the simplest implementation that comes to mind to get this test to pass, namely, loop through all the Songs, and sum all the durations together into one calculation:

```
- (NSTimeInterval) duration
{
        NSTimeInterval duration = 0.0;
```

```
for (Song *song in [[self songs] allObjects])
{
        duration += [song durationValue];
}

return duration;
}
```

Now your test passes, but this may not be the most optimal implementation. You can use the power of KeyValue coding to solve this calculation. However, now that you have a test to make sure that your outcome is what you expect, you can craft this code with confidence to something more optimal. Let's try this implementation:

```
- (NSTimeInterval) duration
{
        return [[self valueForKeyPath:@"songs.@sum.duration"] doubleValue];
}
```

Your code is cleaner and the test still passes. That is the power of Unit Testing.

Summary

You've now entered the world of unit tested code. There are many ways to get even more value for your unit tests, such as through a Continuous Integration environment. A Continuous Integration environment (usually a server or spare desktop) is simply a method to automatically compile your application and run your unit tests against this compiled app. Continuous Integration relies heavily on version control systems such as Mercurial, Git, or Subversion in order to checkout a copy of the code for itself. So, now if you configure your Continuous Integration system to your version control system, your application can be automatically checked for bugs as soon as you check in your code. The only requirement to kick off the process is to check in the code. There are several solutions that are compatible with XCode (and the command line tool, xcodebuild) such as Integrity, Cruisecontrol.rb, Hudson, and buildbot.

Automated Unit Testing is how the small shops can maintain their development productivity without the need for a huge QA department. More importantly, it's another tool you can use to improve the quality and simplify the design of your iPhone applications. Learning to write unit tests that are easy to read, not very brittle, and exercise your code well takes many hours of practice. It's almost like learning to code all over again. But, just as it was when you first learned to code, the more you practice, the better you become.

This chapter was a broad overview explaining how to start incorporating unit tests into your development cycle with a little less pain and effort than is required by the built-in tools. The examples and frameworks discussed here were chosen due to their real-world issues in testability. The questions asked throughout each example are typical of the questions I ask myself when I set about testing a new piece of code. These are a few of the solutions I've come up with thus far on my journey into unit testing in Cocoa. I hope these help you in your unit testing endeavors.

Leon Palm

Companies: Google and MagicSolver.com

Location: Washington, DC

Former Life as a Developer: Constantly creating and solving AI problems from an early age. Examples include poker bots, Real Time Strategy AIs that automatically learn to play any game and Augmented Reality interfaces. If it is an AI-Complete problem, he has probably tried solving it.

Life as an iPhone Developer: Co-founded MagicSolver.com with two other outstanding students at the University of Cambridge. Together they released Sudoku Magic which instantly solves Sudoku puzzles on newspapers from just a picture and FaceShift, a fun face detection and swapping app.

Apps on the App Store:

- *Sudoku Magic (+Lite version)*
- *Faceshift (+Lite version)*

What's in This Chapter: All the steps required to get the world's most powerful computer vision library up and running on your phone, as well as code to build a computer vision app that automatically blurs faces in images.

Key Technologies:

- *Compiling and Running OpenCV on the iPhone*
- *Loading Images from the Camera and Photo Library*
- *Converting Between the OpenCV and iPhone Image Formats*
- *Face Detection and Image Manipulation with OpenCV*

Chapter 5

Fun with Computer Vision: Face Recognition with OpenCV on the iPhone

My interest in Computer Vision began in October 2008 after having read a paper on optical Sudoku puzzle solving.[1] I was just beginning the final year of my Computer Science Tripos[2] at the University of Cambridge and I had to pick a final year project. The Sudoku solver seemed perfect. Unfortunately, I was not allowed to pursue that project due to it being too specific and hard to evaluate scientifically.

Instead, I would be developing a more general system to provide Augmented Reality playing interfaces for board game programs (see Figure 5–1). Augmented Reality provides a live view of a real-world environment whose elements are merged with virtual computer-generated imagery, creating a mixed reality. The project would be quantitatively evaluated by batch testing it with thousands of images of realistic computer-generated models. This approach would be far more challenging and technically impressive, giving me invaluable experience in Computer Vision. However, I still yearned to build an application to solve Sudoku puzzles with a single snap.

---

[1] An *Optical Sudoku Solver*. Martin Byröd. February 12, 2007.

[2] Cambridge parlance for "Bachelor's Degree."

Figure 5–1. *My finished final year project. With 100 lines of code and a cheap webcam, an open-source Checkers or Connect-4 library could now play against humans on a real board. The computer's move is rendered on top of the original image in real-time.*

One month later in early 2009, Oliver Lamming, a colleague of mine, mentioned that the CUE[3] business plan competition was coming up and asked if I had any ideas. We would be competing for a £1k prize and entry to the £5k final. I pulled out my iPhone and checked the calendar to see how many weeks we had to decide. Suddenly, the penny dropped and it all became clear: we would build a Sudoku solver for the iPhone and sell it on the App Store!

Oliver and I had the necessary technical skills, but no business savvy or marketing experience. We would need someone to fill that gap. The two of us began attending Enterprise Tuesdays, a popular series of talks for would-be entrepreneurs, held at the Engineering Department in Cambridge. After the main talks, there were networking sessions. It was in one of those sessions where we met Emmanuel Carraud, an MBA student with a decade of international marketing experience under his belt. Emmanuel got fired up about our idea and soon team iSolve was formed.

---

[3] Cambridge University Entrepreneurs. A society that provides training and advice to students on starting up a company.

After writing and submitting our executive summary and app development plan, iSolve won the £1k prize. This money was immediately invested into purchasing two Mac Minis so that we could begin developing the app. At the awards ceremony, we met some graduates who developed a similar application in the past and were also involved in Computer Vision research. They provided us with advice and expertise for the next round.

The £5k grand finale would involve a more detailed business plan, a live demo, and a pitch to future investors (Dragon's Den style, see Figure 5–2). To make things more difficult, the finale was just days before our final exams.[4] Despite a tough pitch and technical problems with the demo, we pulled through and seized the £5k prize. This led to the incorporation of our company MagicSolver.com Ltd.

Figure 5–2. *MagicSolver.com pitching to a panel of judges and investors at the CUE £5k Grand Finale.*

Since then, MagicSolver has developed and released a string of apps, each one more successful than the previous. Our team is still playing a role in the Cambridge Entrepreneur scene, having won other prizes. One of our main goals is to help build an iPhone developer community in Cambridge; therefore, we're always looking for the chance to give talks on iPhone development and Entrepreneurship. We also help budding iPhone developers by providing advice, Apple developer memberships and lending Mac hardware.

---

[4] For this reason, no other undergraduates competed through to the final.

For the remainder of this chapter, I will guide you step-by-step into downloading and compiling the world's most powerful Computer Vision library on your iPhone and building a fully functioning face detector app with it. I'll finish up with some advice on improving performance and further paths to be explored.

We've got a lot of ground to cover so let's get started!

What Is Computer Vision?

Computer Vision is the science of making machines see. It is a broad collection of disciplines rather than just a set of algorithms. It could be used to describe just about any process whose input or output consists of visual data. This data can be in the form of still images, infrared footage, or video, for example.

Computer Vision has been researched for over 40 years. However, it can still be said to be in its infancy. This is understandable as processing visual data requires a huge amount of computing power.

Take, for example, the old NTSC standard for video, with a resolution of 640×480 (just over 0.3 megapixels) and running at 30 frames per second. This corresponds to 9.2 million pixels per second. Using 8 bits to represent each color channel, you end up with 27.6 MB/s. For comparison, the human eye has around 120 million photoreceptors, or 400 times NTSC's resolution. Now that's a lot of data! Only recently have computers become powerful enough to perform more interesting visual processing tasks. Thanks to Moore's law, rapid advances have been made.

The goal of a Computer Vision algorithm is to build models from visual data, reducing enormous floods of pixel data to simpler representations of regions, contours, and properties. These representations are far easier to manipulate and usually less sensitive to noise. They can be further refined so that object detection and tracking, face recognition, pose estimation, scene segmentation, texture extraction, or image rectification can be performed. When these models are then used to modify the original visual data, the process is said to produce an Augmented Reality.

However, computing capacity isn't the only hurdle in the way of processing vision. The problems themselves are inherently hard. Some reasons are the following:

- Reconstructing a 3D scene from 2D data is mathematically impossible. There are infinitely many possible scene arrangements that could produce a given 2D image.

- Objects may appear to have different surface color and texture under different types of light.

- Two different people photographed with the same expression, pose and illumination will look much more similar than the same person in two shots where those parameters vary a lot.

- Objects change apparent shape as they rotate, may be occluded by other objects and their texture changes due to shadow positions and viewing angle. To make things worse, some objects are deformable, such as faces.

Despite these challenges, today's Computer Vision is already capable of incredible feats, and will become ever more present in devices and robots.

Phone-based barcode scanners and gaming consoles using cameras as a controller are a thing of the past. Enter today. Have you ever seen the movie *Minority Report*? Those scary iris scanners are a reality. There are systems being built that can quickly and automatically find a person's eyes and reliably scan their irises from 30 feet away as they walk by.

The mobile front has advanced rapidly as well; imagine pointing your phone at the Mona Lisa. Looking through your phone screen, her face has a 3D relief, as if she was popping out of the canvas. She is fully animated and telling you about how she was painted in a soft, lip-synched voice. This is all being done in real-time, even as you move the phone around the painting. I've seen technology capable of this on a real phone long ago.

Why Do Computer Vision on an iPhone?

Now is arguably the best time ever to be developing Computer Vision apps for mobile devices and the iPhone is arguably the best platform to do it in. Phones have just become capable of handling it, with the iPhone being one of the fastest and thus most capable phones available. Its screen is large enough for you to see the results. Being always connected, the iPhone could allow better use of Computer Vision apps by fetching prices from scanned barcodes, contact information extracted from images of business cards, or automatically tagging images from detected faces or fetching automated translations of foreign street signs.

The possibilities of mobile Computer Vision are endless. Cameras are the most powerful sensor on the iPhone. Yet, it is the least used sensor for directly interacting with apps. Out of your five senses, vision is the most important and frequently used and the world is built around it—from aesthetic design to advertising to education. Shouldn't phones take advantage of this to help us? There exists an endless stream of possible inventions. Finally, due to its novelty and lack of established libraries (until now!), there is very little competition for mobile Computer Vision/Augmented Reality providing huge payoffs for first movers. To seize this opportunity, one must act quickly so let's get started in the next section.

The rest of the chapter will provide you with the initial skeleton for building and using OpenCV on the iPhone. OpenCV is one of the world's most powerful Computer Vision libraries, having been used in many, many applications. Surveillance software, off-road robot vehicles that drive themselves, paintball sentry guns and optical Sudoku solvers are just some of its current uses.

Unfortunately, OpenCV was designed mainly for use with Windows/Linux and won't run on other platforms off the box. Thankfully with a little work on the Terminal you'll compile it for the iPhone OS. It is mainly targeted for the iPhone as it has a camera but it should also work on iPod Touch or any other iPhone OS device. You will then build a simple app that provides everything that you'll need to unleash the power of OpenCV on your device.

Your Project: Creating a Face Detector

You are about to build a face detector app from scratch then add a fun twist to it. Excited? Good! Being your first time, it is best to be prepared or it might be a little painful. Before getting started, make sure that you have the following:

- Some resemblance of familiarity with command-line interfaces: You have to be able to find the terminal app so you can launch it and know how to navigate the directory structure.

- Used Xcode and Interface Builder before: I'll make this a very gentle ride to cater to most, but you should roughly know your way around. If not, go do some tutorials. It will only take a moment.

- The iPhone SDK 3.0+ installed. It would be hard to build apps otherwise!

- Internet access, allowing you to download OpenCV. This almost goes without saying in today's hyper-connected world.

> **NOTE:** Typing code from a book is rather dull. To keep it short, I've left out safety procedures such as checking for null pointers after loading a resource. Be sure to add these if you plan to release your app. Check out the documentation and samples included with OpenCV for examples of such checks. If you really don't like typing, you could always cheat and download the complete source code for this chapter at the code download area of the Apress web site at www.apress.com.

Setting Up OpenCV

This first section will guide you through the process of downloading, configuring, and compiling OpenCV, so that it can be used with the ARM processor found in the iPhone and iPod Touch.

1. Open up the terminal. I assume you'll be using bash, so make sure to switch to it if needed or look up equivalent commands if you like being difficult.

2. Make sure your computer is connected to the Internet and that the iPhone SDK 3.0+ is installed.

3. The following commands will download and compile OpenCV with the correct settings for the iPhone OS 3.0+ and then build universal static libraries that run on both the Intel-based simulator and the ARM-based device.

First, let's create a working directory.

```
$ mkdir OpenCV; cd OpenCV
```

Use CURL to fetch the OpenCV 1.1 package SourceForge. The following command should be in a single line, but the URL was too long for this book. The "L" flag performs the request upon redirect (SourceForge first needs to give us a mirror). The "O" is so the response is written to a file rather than blurting out binary data all over the terminal, which would be most rude.

```
$ curl -LO http://downloads.sourceforge.net/project/opencvlibrary/opencv-
unix/1.1pre1/opencv-1.1pre1.tar.gz
```

```
The downloaded file is compressed, so we extract it with tar.
$ tar xvfz opencv-1.1pre1.tar.gz
```

> **NOTE:** This is not the latest version of OpenCV, but it is far easier to compile for the iPhone than v2.0. Once you're feeling more confident, check the web for instructions and scripts for compiling OpenCV 2.0+ on the device.

Any good programmer likes to avoid repeated work, so let's set some variables to save some typing further on.

First, let's set some compiler flags to remove features incompatible with the iPhone OS such as video windows and webcam support.

```
$ CFLAGS="--disable-apps --disable-dependency-tracking --disable-shared \
$ --without-carbon --without-gtk --without-imageio --without-python \
$ --without-quicktime --without-swig"
```

DEV is just shorthand for the developer directory. BIN serves a similar purpose.

```
$ DEV="/Developer/Platforms/iPhoneOS.platform/Developer/"
$ BIN="${DEV}usr/bin/"
```

To keep things tidy, create directories to separate the compiled files for the device and simulator. opencvlib will hold all the files needed to use OpenCV in an Xcode project.

> **NOTE:** The next three commands depend on your version of OS X. If you're running a 64-bit OS X version such as Snow Leopard+, you'll want to use "x86_64" instead of "i686" for the next three.

```
$ mkdir armv6 i686 opencvlib
$ cd i686
```

The following command will set the compiler for the i686 (Intel x86) architecture. The compiled code will be used by the simulator which runs on your Intel-based Mac.

```
$ ../opencv-1.1.0/configure $CFLAGS --host=i686-apple-darwin9 CXXFLAGS="-arch i686"
```

If you were running on a 64-bit operating system, the three previous commands would instead be the following:

```
$ mkdir armv6 x86_64 opencvlib
$ cd x86_64
$ ../opencv-1.1.0/configure $CFLAGS --host= x86_64-apple-darwin9 CXXFLAGS="-arch x86_64"
```

With the configuration in place, it's time to compile. This may take several minutes...

```
$ make
```

Now you do the same for the armV6 (iPhone) architecture.

```
$ cd ../armv6
```

The configuration command for the ARM platform is a little bigger!

```
$ ../opencv-1.1.0/configure $CFLAGS --host=arm-apple-darwin9 \
$ CXX="${BIN}arm-apple-darwin9-g++-4.0.1" \
$ CXXFLAGS="-arch armv6 -isysroot ${DEV}SDKs/iPhoneOS3.0.sdk" CXXCPP="${BIN}cpp"
```

Next, it is time to compile again. Go make a coffee, we're just warming up!

```
$ make
```

Now merge the compiled code for the two platforms using lipo, a program that creates universal (multi-architecture) files. The five resulting universal library files can be used by either the device or simulator without the need to swap them.

```
$ cd ../opencvlib
$ for LIB in libcv.a libcxcore.a libcvaux.a libml.a libhighgui.a
$ do lipo -create `find .. -name $LIB` -output $LIB
$ done
```

In order to access functions in these libraries, you'll need the header files containing the function declarations. These files are found under cv/include, cvaux/include, cxcore/include, ml/include, and otherlibs/highgui.
To save you from looking around and copying them manually, use the following hacky command to copy all the necessary .h and .hpp files to the opencvlib directory automaticaly. Essentially, it looks for certain header filename patterns (grep), but excludes some unnecessary matches (egrep –v) and copies the results.

```
$ cp `find ../opencv-1.1.0 | grep '\.[h]p*$' | egrep -v 'tests|swig|/_|\/apps'` ./
```

You're all set. The opencvlib directory has all that you need to start using OpenCV on your iPhone. Just drop it in your project folder when you need it! I always keep a copy of this folder around so I can quickly copy it into new projects. Whew! You are done here so feel free to close the terminal.

> **TIP:** The opencv-1.1.0 folder you just downloaded contains a wealth of docs and samples that will help you understand and explore OpenCV. Be sure to look around once you've finished this chapter!

Setting Up XCode

You've built OpenCV, which is arguably most of the hard work out of the way. Now let's use it!

1. Open up Xcode.

2. Create a new iPhone project using the "View-based application" template and name it "FaceDetect" (see Figure 5–3).

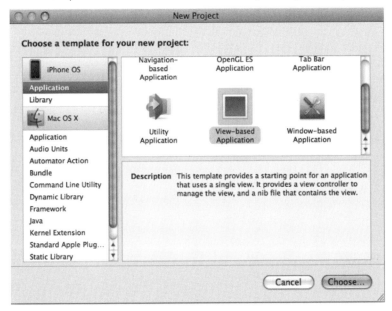

Figure 5–3. *Creating a view-based application*

3. Drag the opencvlib folder you just created into the root of the project (see Figure 5–4). Check the "Copy items into destination group's folder" box and click "Add," as shown in Figure 5–5.

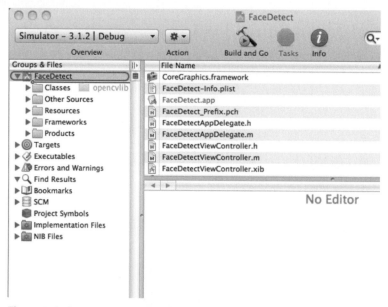

Figure 5–4. *Drag the "opencvlib" folder to your project's root*

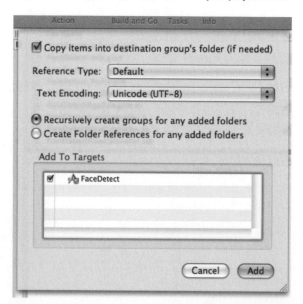

Figure 5–5. *Ensure you check the "Copy items into destination group's folder" box*

4. On the top menu bar, go to **Project ➤ Edit Project Settings**. This will bring up the settings window. Select the "Build" tab. Ensure that the "Configuration" dropdown is set to "All Configurations", so the changes apply to both debug and release builds. Now search for the "Other Linker Flags" setting (the search box is there for a reason!) and add a new entry to it with the string "-lstdc++". This allows GCC to link standard C++ libraries statically, preventing a stream of nasty linker errors (Figure 5–6). You can close the settings window.

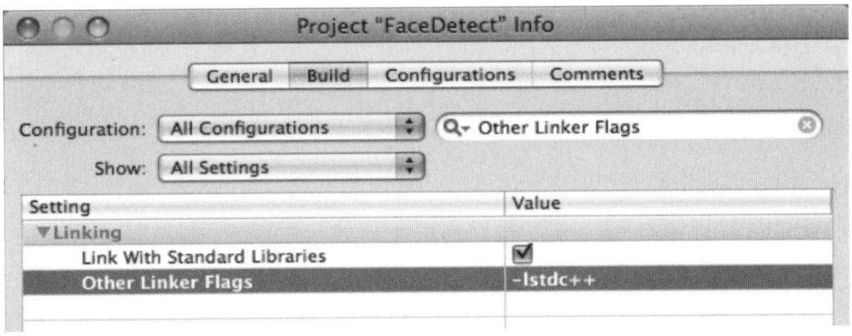

Figure 5–6. *Setting the appropriate linker flags*

Adding Image Conversion Functions

Besides getting OpenCV to compile, this is the most important step in getting it to run on the iPhone. OpenCV uses IplImage, its own data structure to store images and without a way to convert them to and from CGImage, nothing interesting can be done. It's time to implement those functions. Thankfully, IplImages have very similar structures to CGImages—an array of pixels with a header, making your job easy!

1. Open up FaceDetectViewController.h (under the "Classes" group) and import cv.h. This provides access to OpenCV functions:

```
#import <UIKit/UIKit.h>

#import "cv.h"

@interface FaceDetectViewController : UIViewController {
```

2. You will be using Apple's Image Picker to select images later on. This requires your view controller to implement two interfaces: UIImagePickerControllerDelegate and UINavigationControllerDelegate. Add them in the class declaration:

```
@interface FaceDetectViewController : UIViewController
    <UIImagePickerControllerDelegate, UINavigationControllerDelegate> {
}
```

3. Now add the following two method declarations to FaceDetectViewController.h:

```
- (IplImage *)iplImageFromUIImage:(UIImage *)image;
- (UIImage *)uiImageFromIplImage:(IplImage *)image;
```

4.   And their corresponding definitions in FaceDetectViewController.m:

```
// You should always release the image returned by this method.
- (IplImage *)iplImageFromUIImage:(UIImage *)image {
```

Firstly, you must create the return value and data structures to hold the metadata for your image. cvCreateImage() initializes an image header and allocates a contiguous array of pixels. The size and structure of this array depend on how many color channels and bits per channel are used. Here you will use a general 4-channel (RGBA) image with 8 bits per channel. It is the least space efficient but most flexible way to store an image.

```
CGImageRef imageRef = image.CGImage;
CGColorSpaceRef colorSpace = CGColorSpaceCreateDeviceRGB();
IplImage *iplImage =
    cvCreateImage(cvSize(image.size.width,image.size.height), IPL_DEPTH_8U, 4);
```

With the image space allocated, you need to set its pixels. One way to do this is to create a bitmap context to be drawn on by passing CGBitmapContextCreate(), the pointer, to the IplImage's pixel array (imageData).

```
CGContextRef contextRef =
    CGBitmapContextCreate(iplImage->imageData, iplImage->width, iplImage->height,
                          iplImage->depth, iplImage->widthStep, colorSpace,
                          kCGImageAlphaPremultipliedLast|kCGBitmapByteOrderDefault);
```

The context has the same dimension, properties, and color encoding as the IplImage. To transfer the image data, you can simply draw the UIImage onto the context, whose pixel array is in fact the IplImage's imageData.

```
CGRect imageRect = CGRectMake(0, 0, iplImage->width, iplImage->height);
CGContextDrawImage(contextRef, imageRect, imageRef);
```

Finally, you clean up the bitmap context and the color space object, returning the converted image. You can now manipulate your image in all sorts of ways using OpenCV.

```
CGContextRelease(contextRef);
CGColorSpaceRelease(colorSpace);
return iplImage;
}
```

You'll also need a function to convert IplImages back to UIImages.

```
- (UIImage *)uiImageFromIplImage:(IplImage *)image {
```

To start out, you create an NSData structure and copy the IplImage's whole pixel array into it.

```
NSData *data = [NSData dataWithBytes:image->imageData length:image->imageSize];
```

In order to construct the UIImage, you'll need a colorSpace reference and a data provider for the NSData just created.

```
CGDataProviderRef provider = CGDataProviderCreateWithCFData((CFDataRef)data);
CGColorSpaceRef colorSpace = CGColorSpaceCreateDeviceRGB();
```

In this case, converting the image is a little easier. You create a CGImage of the appropriate size and type, using data, then wrap it with a UIImage. That's it.

```
CGImageRef imageRef =
    CGImageCreate(image->width, image->height, image->depth,
                  image->depth * image->nChannels, image->widthStep,
                  colorSpace, kCGImageAlphaLast|kCGBitmapByteOrderDefault,
                  provider, NULL, false, kCGRenderingIntentDefault);
UIImage *uiImage = [UIImage imageWithCGImage:imageRef];
```

Once again, you clean up and return the brand new UIImage.

```
CGColorSpaceRelease(colorSpace);
CGDataProviderRelease(provider);
CGImageRelease(imageRef);

    return uiImage;
}
```

Creating a Simple GUI

Like most iPhone apps, ours will be interacted with through a GUI. It will be simple and built in Interface Builder (IB) rather than programmatically, keeping this section quicker and shorter than a rocket-powered midget.

1. Open up FaceDetectViewController.h and add a variable declaration inside the @interface block.

```
IBOutlet UIImageView *imageView;
```

This imageview will be used to display the output of your app.

2. Also add the following method declaration below the @interface declaration in FaceDetectViewController.h. You'll implement it soon, I promise!

```
- (IBAction)detectFaces;
```

3. Save your file (⌘S). This will allow IB to see the changes you've just made.

4. Double-click FaceDetectViewController.xib under the "Resources" group. This will open Interface Builder.

5. Bring up the window for this .xib's View and the IB object library (⌘⇧L).

6. From the objects library, add an Image View that takes up most of the screen, so you can see what you're doing!

7. Bring up the ImageView's Attributes window (⌘1). Under the "view" bar, set the "mode" to "Aspect Fit". This prevents large images from rendering past the ImageView's boundaries.

8. Now add a Round Rect Button under the Image View and set its title to "Detect Faces". It should look somewhat like Figure 5–7.

Figure 5–7. *What the GUI should look like*

9. Right-click the translucent orange cube (File's Owner) to bring up the connections dialog. Now drag the "imageView" outlet onto the UIImageView in your GUI (Figure 5–8).

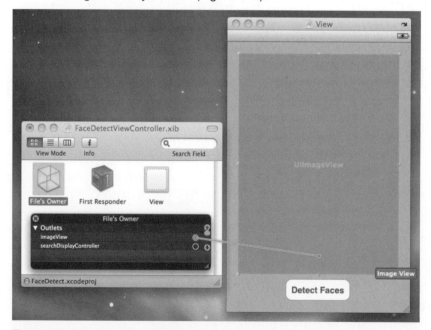

Figure 5–8. *Connecting the "imageView" outlet to the main Image View in the GUI*

10. The button also needs connecting. Right-click File's Owner and drag the "detectFaces" outlet onto the button. Select "Touch Up Inside" from the pop-up list that appears (see Figure 5–9).

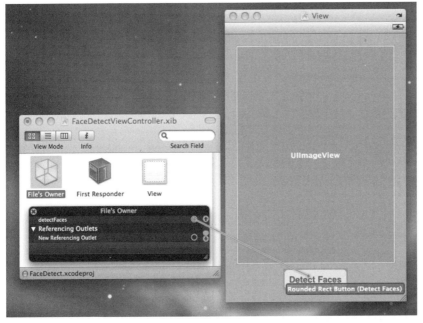

Figure 5–9. *Connecting the "detectFaces" method to the "Detect Faces" button*

11. Save your work in IB (⌘S) and go back to Xcode.

Loading Images from the Photo Library

To use images from the photo library, you will bring up the built-in image picker screen and implement the method that handles the chosen image. This is the picker that comes up when selecting an image to e-mail, for example. The delegate business is so the picker knows to which view will be shown to the user once an image has been chosen.

1. Open up FaceDetectViewController.m and implement a detectFaces method that brings up the picker:

```
- (IBAction)detectFaces {
  UIImagePickerController* controller = [[UIImagePickerController alloc] init];
  controller.delegate = self;
  [self presentModalViewController:controller animated:YES];
  [controller release];
}
```

2. Now define the following method to allow you to do something when an image is chosen from the picker. Remember to add a corresponding declaration for it in FaceDetectViewController.h.

```
- (void)imagePickerController:(UIImagePickerController *) picker
    didFinishPickingMediaWithInfo:(NSDictionary *) info {
  // Load up the image selected in the picker.
  UIImage *originalImage = [info objectForKey:UIImagePickerControllerOriginalImage];
  IplImage *iplImage = [self iplImageFromUIImage:originalImage];

  // We will do some CV magic here later.
  // ...

  UIImage* newImage = [self uiImageFromIplImage:iplImage];
  // IplImages must be deallocated manually.
  cvReleaseImage(&iplImage);

  [imageView setImage:newImage];
  [[picker parentViewController] dismissModalViewControllerAnimated:YES];
}
```

For now, this method will simply convert the UIImage into OpenCV's IplImage format and then back so it can be displayed. Later, you will add some processing on the IplImage.

3. Cross your fingers and push the "Build and Run" button. If you get errors/warnings, take a step back (or ten!), so as to see where things went wrong.

4. Pat yourself on the back. Not only do you have a working app that you can re-use for your next projects, but most of the code transcription is now finished. Well done, little scribe!

Doesn't seem very exciting, but your program is already capable of converting images in the library to the OpenCV's IplImage format, back to UIImage, then displaying the UIImage. This is the starting point for any iPhone application using OpenCV. However, this doesn't quite tick the "Cool" box, so up next I'll show you how easy it is to add some real Computer Vision once a good foundation has been laid.

Loading the Haar Cascades

One way to perform face detection with OpenCV is by using Haar object detection. It works by summing and subtracting the pixel values of rectangular shapes or "features." These shapes are scanned across the image, and the pixel intensities in the black regions are subtracted from the intensities in the white regions (see Figure 5–10). The result is a sum that encodes the edge properties (edge intensity, angle, and polarity) from all pixels at each location into a single number, greatly simplifying processing. Unsurprisingly, the nerve cells in your eyes work in a similar way. This compression partly explains why we have 120 million photoreceptors in each retina but only 1 million axons running down each optic nerve.

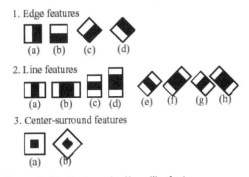

1. Edge features

(a) (b) (c) (d)

2. Line features

(a) (b) (c) (d) (e) (f) (g) (h)

3. Center-surround features

(a) (b)

Figure 5–10. *Rectangular Haar-like features.*

Haar object detection is essentially a template matching approach, trying to match facial features at every position in the image at a variety of scales. In order to use it, a trained Haar cascade needs to be loaded. Thankfully OpenCV already comes with some examples.

1. For this project, you will use a frontal face detector, so it will not detect tilted or turned faces! **"haarcascade_frontalface _alt_tree.xml"** works well, so let's use it. This file is located under **opencv-1.1.0/data/haarcascades.** Copy it to the Resources group in your project (see Figure 5–11).

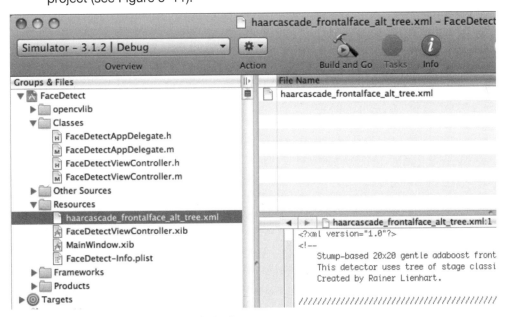

Figure 5–11. *The Haar cascade file goes in the Resources group.*

2. Create the necessary static variables by adding the following code at the top of FaceDetectViewController.m, right below the import declarations:

```
#import "FaceDetectViewController.h"

// Filename where the Haar Cascade is stored.
static const char *CASCADE_NAME = "haarcascade_frontalface_alt_tree.xml";

// Temporary storage for the cascade. Due to its size, it is best to make it static.
static CvMemStorage *cvStorage = NULL;

// Pointer to the cascade, we also only need one.
static CvHaarClassifierCascade *haarCascade = NULL;

@implementation FaceDetectViewController
```

3. Loading a cascade is a time-intensive procedure that uses a lot of memory. XML is a very inefficient way to store numbers and on top of that, OpenCV's XML parsing is very wasteful. Therefore, you only want to do it once if possible. For this simple app, it suffices to place the cascade initialization in the viewDidLoad: method in FaceDetectViewController.m.

```
- (void)viewDidLoad {
    [super viewDidLoad];
    cvStorage = cvCreateMemStorage(0);
    NSString *resourcePath =
        [[[NSBundle mainBundle] resourcePath] stringByAppendingPathComponent:
            [NSString stringWithUTF8String:CASCADE_NAME]];
    haarCascade = (CvHaarClassifierCascade *)cvLoad([resourcePath UTF8String], 0, 0, 0);
}
```

Keep in mind that you cannot use cvLoadImage in the same way! You have to load it as a CGImage using the built-in methods and convert it into an IplImage later.

Performing Face Detection

You now have the means to obtain an image from the photo library and have a cascade loaded on startup. It is time to expand the imagePickerController:didFinishPickingImage:editingInfo method to detect faces in an image and draw a box around them.

1. Implement the drawOnFaceAt:InImage method by adding the following code to FaceDetectViewController.m. This method will be called for each face found in the image in the next step. Again, *be sure to add a corresponding declaration in the header file.*

```
- (void)drawOnFaceAt:(CvRect *)rect inImage:(IplImage *)image {
    // To draw a rectangle you must input points instead of a rectangle. I know, I know...
    cvRectangle(image, cvPoint(rect->x, rect->y),
            cvPoint(rect->x + rect->width, rect->y + rect->height),
```

```
                    cvScalar(255, 0, 0, 255) /* RGBA */, 4, 8, 0);
}
```

2. Now add some real functionality to the method below by modifying it as shown in the following code:

```
- (void)imagePickerController:(UIImagePickerController *) picker
    didFinishPickingMediaWithInfo:(NSDictionary *) info {
  UIImage *originalImage = [info objectForKey:UIImagePickerControllerOriginalImage];
  IplImage * iplImage = [self iplImageFromUIImage:originalImage];

  // Clear the memory storage from any previously detected faces.
  cvClearMemStorage(cvStorage);

  // Detect the faces and store their rectangles in the sequence.
  CvSeq* faces = cvHaarDetectObjects(iplImage, // Input image
                              haarCascade, // Cascade to be used
                              cvStorage, // Temporary storage
                              1.1, // Size increase for features at each scan
                              2, // Min number of neighboring rectangle matches
                              CV_HAAR_DO_CANNY_PRUNING, // Optimization flags
                              cvSize(30, 30)); // Starting feature size

  // CvSeq is essentially a linked list with tree features. "faces" is a list of
  // bounding rectangles for each face found in iplImage.
  for (int i = 0; i < faces->total; i++) {
    // cvGetSeqElem is used for random access to CvSeqs.
    CvRect* rect = (CvRect*)cvGetSeqElem(faces, i);
    [self drawOnFaceAt:rect inImage:iplImage];
  }

  UIImage* newImage = [self uiImageFromIplImage: iplImage];
  cvReleaseImage(&iplImage);

  [imageView setImage:newImage];

  // Optional: save image.
  UIImageWriteToSavedPhotosAlbum(newImage, self, nil, nil);

  [[picker parentViewController] dismissModalViewControllerAnimated:YES];
}
```

NOTE: For more information on each of the cv* functions and their parameters, take a look at the OpenCV documentation. It is very useful!

3. Now run your application on the simulator and try detecting some faces (see Figure 5–12).

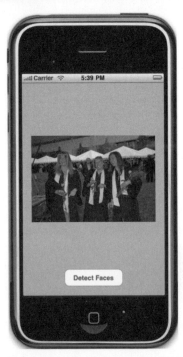

Figure 5–12. *The finished app in the Simulator*

If you try running this app on the device, you'll see that it will either run really slow or crash outright, depending on the size of the input image. I'll get to this in the Performance section shortly.

This is a very simple example, but it provides all that you need to unleash the full power of OpenCV on your iPhone! There are plenty of guides and documentation online to help you choose your next exciting project!

Bonus

It is very easy to do some seemingly complex tasks thanks to OpenCV. For example, to turn this app into an automatic face blurrer like the one used in Google Street View, you just have to tweak the drawOnFaceAt:InImage method (see Figure 5–13).

```
- (void)drawOnFaceAt:(CvRect *)rect inImage:(IplImage *)image {
    IplImage* faceImage = cvCreateImage(cvSize(rect->width, rect->height), 8, 4);

    // The Region Of Interest acts as a temporary crop of the image.
    cvSetImageROI(image, *rect);

    // Create a copy of the face and apply gaussian blur to it.
    cvCopy(image, faceImage, NULL);
    cvSmooth(faceImage, faceImage, CV_GAUSSIAN, 51, 51, 0, 0);

    // Let's build a (elliptical) mask to apply blur only around the facial area.
    IplImage *copyMask = cvCreateImage(cvGetSize(faceImage), 8, 1);
```

```
    // Center of the ellipse.
    CvPoint center = cvPoint(faceImage->width / 2, faceImage->height / 2);
    cvZero(copyMask);
    // Draw the ellipse.
    cvEllipse(copyMask, center, cvSize(faceImage->width * 0.5, faceImage->height * 0.6),
              0, 0, 360, cvScalarAll(255), CV_FILLED, 8, 0);

    // Pixels in faceImage will only be copied if they are non-zero in copyMask.
    cvCopy(faceImage, image, copyMask);

    // Clean up.
    cvReleaseImage(&faceImage);
    cvReleaseImage(&copyMask);
    cvResetImageROI(image);
}
```

Figure 5–13. *Your app, improved with face blurring*

Voilà! Google ain't got nuthin' on ya now! Use this app to take photos of your in-law or ugly cousins at social events, keeping your photo library untarnished!

Performance Tweaking

If you tried running this program on the device, you'll have noticed that it is slow! The effect is usually not noticeable in the simulator. This is because the simulator doesn't try to emulate the iPhone's CPU speed and a multi-core Intel CPU is typically faster than a tiny ARM chip.

Don't fret though! Computer Vision, like AI, is all about trimming down on the amount of computation at the right places. Tweaking parameters so they are optimized to your exact use cases is also immensely helpful. Done carefully, your program will be orders of magnitude faster with a small loss or even a gain in reliability.

You can easily get more than 10x performance improvement with the following tweaks:

- Reduce the resolution of the input image. You won't need a 1600×1200 image to find faces, and most photos are blurry anyway, wasting pixels. 400×300 will do the trick just fine and give your app 16x less data to process. Just use a smaller IplImage in the iplImageFromUIImage:image method:

```
...
CGColorSpaceRef colorSpace = CGColorSpaceCreateDeviceRGB();
IplImage *iplImage =
    cvCreateImage(cvSize(image.size.width/4,image.size.height/4), IPL_DEPTH_8U, 4);

// Use the IplImage as a bitmap context.
...
```

- Read the OpenCV documentation to learn how to tweak parameters in cvHarrDetectObjects(). As an example, the following settings are much faster and still work reasonably well when people are up close:

```
cvHaarDetectObjects(iplImage, haarCascade, cvStorage,
                    1.2, // scale_factor
                    2, CV_HAAR_DO_CANNY_PRUNING,
                    cvSize(50, 50));  // min_neighbors
```

The fourth parameter (scale_factor) controls how much the features are enlarged each time they are scanned over the whole image. Setting this number higher greatly decreases the number of runs required for them to reach the image's size. However, your detector won't find faces unless they happen to have a very similar size to the features. Setting scale_factor too high will lower reliability.

The last parameter (min_neighbors) controls the starting size of the features. The ratio of this size to the image size greatly affects speed, especially if scale_factor is small. Larger is faster but no faces smaller than that can be found.

- If you're feeling adventurous, edit OpenCV itself. The iPhone is much faster at integer calculations than floating-point (FP) ones. Unfortunately, cvHarrDetectObjects() uses FP calculations in a lot of places where it doesn't really need to. Replacing some frequent calculations with fixed point math will boost speed further. The code looks really hairy but is manageable if you spend some time on it. Searching the web might save you the work!

- You could also convert the XML Haar Cascades into a more compact format that doesn't require parsing (e.g., as binary data), which will greatly boost loading times as well as cutting down on the size and RAM usage of your app.

Another thing that you'll soon notice, if you haven't already, is that the app is not very good at picking up tilted faces. That's because Haar object detection is essentially a template matching algorithm. It is already attempting to match faces of many different sizes in thousands of positions across the image. Duplicating those searches for face rotation in three axes would make it prohibitively slower due to a combinatorial explosion. Newer and better algorithms do exist, but they usually have a higher complexity and memory cost.

Going Further

This was just a very simple example to illustrate what a few lines of code are capable of with OpenCV. In the following, you'll find some other interesting projects to explore, progressing in difficulty from trivial to clinically insane:

- *Group photo fun*: Modify the program you've just built to add moustaches, hats, and ties to people in pictures. Randomly deform their heads or replace them with celebrities' faces!

- *Mobile photo editing tools*: Use OpenCV's image in-painting algorithm to repair damaged images or remove pimples from one's face. Then, apply visual effects using morphological operators, blurring and segmentation.

- *Real-time, real-life pong*: Play pong with a friend by holding rulers or broomsticks, or bounce a virtual ball around virtually any environment. Canny Edge detection followed by a Hough Transform can be used to find major lines in an image, the paddles. To run this at several frames per second even on a 2G iPhone, use frame-grabbing on the iPhone's virtual viewfinder. Since you'll be looking for large image features, it is fine to use very-low resolution images for internal processing. 320×200 would be plenty for this.

- *Play board games using the camera*: Sudoku Magic, my first app, captures, grades, and solves Sudoku puzzles visually by applying 20 distinct image processing steps in sequence. A Checkers solver would be a great starting point due to its simple, regular visual structure. Use the Hough Transform to find the board edges, apply a perspective transform to rectify it, then perform segmentation and color matching at the now fixed tile centers to extract piece arrangement.

- Emotion detector: Great for sizing up new people you meet. Use feature extraction functions and Delaunay Triangulation to measure relative distances between facial features. This can be used to represent facial expressions as a small set of numbers. Then use a learning algorithm from OpenCV's Machine Learning library to recognize a person's emotional state based on their portrait. Easy peasy lemon squeezy…or not, but the sky is the limit with OpenCV!

Whatever it is that you choose to do, there is a vast amount of material available online to help you achieve it with OpenCV. Be sure to browse around!

Summary

In this chapter, you learned a little bit about Computer Vision. You then got OpenCV running on the iPhone by building a simple app that detects and blurs faces, converting the results back into a UIImage. I hope you enjoyed reading this as much as I enjoyed writing it. I would love to hear about your ideas and projects in mobile Computer Vision! If you have any questions/comments or want to get in touch, drop me an e-mail at iphonecompvis@gmail.com.

Scott Penberthy

Company: *North Highland Partners*

Location: *New York City*

Former Life as a Developer: *Scott began coding shortly after the Apple II was launched in the '70s. His addiction to coding bloomed into a scholarship to MIT, earned by writing a multiplayer online game that brought his school's antique computer to its knees. After graduating, Scott took a job at IBM Research, the birthplace of IBM's web products and services. After running up the corporate ladder in the 1990's building massive web sites, Scott jettisoned himself in 2005 to return to his true love of coding. Now a successful entrepreneur, Scott runs an app studio in New York City.*

Life as an iPhone Developer: *Scott cracked open the iPhone SDK in 2007 while running engineering for Photobucket. It wasn't until Apple announced in-app purchases in 2009 that his entrepreneurial itch became unbearable. Scott jumped into apps full-time in 2009, writing a messaging app for push services, an app for a major movie studio, and an app for sharing photos on FourSquare. As of early 2010, Scott's studio has several apps under development.*

Apps on the App Store:

- *Flame It!*
- *iSlide Camera*
- *Pushtones*

What's in This Chapter:

- *A study of Gutenberg's printing press and how it applies to OpenGL*
- *Objective-C classes for representing the steps of Gutenberg's printing process*
- *A simple production application that uses the Gutenberg process*
- *Tools for preparing to use any TrueType font in the Gutenberg process*

Key Technologies:

- *A study of Gutenberg's printing press and how it applies to OpenGL*

- *TrueType fonts*

- *Texture atlases*

- *Objective-C classes for the above*

Chapter 6

How to Use OpenGL Fonts without Losing Your Mind

Here I sit in my office, building an app for a major movie studio. It's a dream job. The alpha code drop is due shortly before Christmas. I'm trying to use Core Animation and Cocoa touch, keeping my costs down. The brand designers want something special, with custom menus, buttons, animated graphics, sounds, the works. "Ah," I say to myself, "It's time to dive into OpenGL. This should be straightforward, just like the old days."

The graphics are screaming right along. The sound engine is coming together, as long as you ignore the occasional simulator crash and inability to pause. I haven't seen my wife or kids in days. More on that later. Then it hits me. Marketing calls.

"We need some text describing each dragon, each with their own font."

As I scurry through the iPhone documentation, I realize Apple is not too fond of mixing UIView and UIFonts with OpenGL. The documentation, blogs, and forums warn against mixing Cocoa Touch and OpenGL. Blasphemy! They seem to fight each other for the frame buffer. Timing can be an issue.

I take a peek at the available open source libraries for True Type fonts, as well as numerous gaming engines. They appear to work well, but the interfaces are a bit onerous, and I tremble at the idea of having to recreate all of Apple's handiwork for a single app. Do I really need all that complexity? I don't want physics, a game engine, levels, and all that rot. With the deadline looming, it's too late now to switch. I need a pragmatic approach, something fast, lightweight; something that just works.

This chapter describes pragmatic font techniques in OpenGL. As it turns out, these techniques are nearly identical to those employed by the inventor of the printing press. They're not too different from what I learned in kindergarten. As fast as technology changes, human nature really does stay the same. I call these techniques "fontery."

History

n the medieval days of fontery, there were monks and monasteries. Monks were fond of wearing heavy, woolen garments in the heat of the day. Some would spend years with painstaking calligraphy, creating massive books that were four to five times the size of their head. Once produced, they'd blame it on the devil. Literally. One of the most famous of all such books is the Codex Gigas, the "devil's bible" that took a single monk more than 20 years of toiling, largely in solitary confinement. Legend has it that he created the work in one massive night of furious calligraphy, driven by the devil after selling his soul.

Most monks would craft elaborate fonts with interesting artistic tastes, such as the letter "I" used to introduce the preceding paragraph. These dropped capitals were quite elaborate. In this illustration, a monk has depicted a dog biting a bone while being attacked by jellyfish, a lizard, and perhaps some holly in the background. Others would adorn their letters with fruit, wild animals, trees, and just about anything that was on their mind.

These elaborate works inspired a German goldsmith born in 1398. Johannes Gutenberg was working as an apprentice to a card maker, who was stamping the back of the playing cards with a copper engraving, dipped in ink. Gutenberg wondered if he could produce copies of the monk artwork, jellyfish and all, in a similar fashion. Instead of engraving an entire page, as was done for the playing cards, Gutenberg decided to engrave individual letters, then position them along tracks held together by a vise grip.

In Figure 6–1, you see a replica of Gutenberg's engravings, where bins are used to sort the engravings for faster retrieval. The vise grip is seen on top of these bins in the figure.

Figure 6–1. *Parts from Gutenberg's movable type*

Gutenberg would dip his vice grip full of letters into card ink, pressing it to paper, producing the written word. Later, he would attach and align several vise grips on the back of an Olive Oil press, pressing down onto sheets the size of monk bibles. Voilà. Gutenberg's printing press was born, enabled by his invention of "movable type."

Gutenberg's movable type is credited with starting the European Renaissance, and perhaps is the most important invention of the 15th century. His technique of engraving individual letters and aligning them by hand is at the core of many font engines today.

Terminology

We've all played with ink and stamps, starting with our first years in preschool and kindergarten. It's fun! You pick up a stamp, press it into a mat of colored ink, and then stamp it on paper to create letters, words, and pictures. Suppose you wanted to create an entire book or pamphlet by just stamping letters and placing them on the page. It's a laborious process. You'll need help. Next, you'll have to describe how you want your helpers to do their job. For the book to look professional, you'll need to make sure everything is spaced well, lines up, and is easy to read.

Suddenly, the little stamps from kindergarten get a lot more complex. Centuries of playing with words made from stamps and ink have produced a common nomenclature. You'll see a lot of this nomenclature in the modern documentation for Cocoa Touch, Quartz 2D, and other libraries that display text. Sadly, OpenGL provides none of it. Zip. Nada. Not a word.

You'll be creating an OpenGL font system from scratch in this chapter, as part of a real (though embarrassingly trivial) fortune cookie app. I provide the complete source code to the app, as well as tools I've used to create fonts in other apps.

Your font system will rely on the techniques and nomenclature honed over centuries. If you're like me, you like to cut to the chase and start coding, so enough with the pretense and background story.

Bear with me. It's really important that you understand some basics about fonts before writing a font system. This is one of those instances where history does indeed teach us a valuable lesson.

Figure 6–2 shows several of these ancient terms, annotating the imaginary word "Fontery."

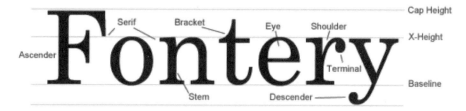

Figure 6–2. *The different components of a font*

Imagine for a moment that the word "Fontery" was stamped from engravings in the era of Gutenberg. A single engraving of a character is called a *glyph*. I guess "engraving" had too many syllables or didn't sound erudite. "Stamp" would have been too demeaning. So, we have glyph. *C'est la vie*.

Gutenberg found that some glyphs don't look good when stamped side by side—they leave too much space. For example, the letters "f" and "i" in the word "fish" actually touch each other. Being the pragmatist, Gutenberg would simply create a single engraving for the "f" and "i" together. To distinguish these from his "glyphs," they were called ligatures, as shown in Figure 6–3. Common ligatures are "fi," "ly," and "ae."

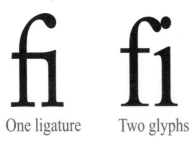

One ligature   Two glyphs

Figure 6–3. The letters "f i" as a single ligature or two glyphs.

A *typeface* is a set of glyphs and ligatures for an entire alphabet and number system. Typefaces have common treatment for the strokes and shapes, providing an aesthetic look and feel. In Figure 6–2, you see many names for the different glyph elements. You need to remember two of them. The ascender is the part of a character that sits "above" most other glyphs. The descender is the part that lies below.

Gutenberg would line up his engravings using a common baseline. Every glyph would appear to "sit" on the baseline, dangling descenders below. To ensure a consistent size for the typeface, Gutenberg would draw two imaginary lines above the baseline. The x-height line aligns the top of lower case letters. The cap height aligns upper case. Ascenders for characters such as "h" would rise above the x-height line. Finally, the maximum descender and the maximum ascender would define the line size for a single line of text.

Gutenberg's process for printing was straightforward. First, he chose a typeface, and set the line size by changing movable tracks within his Olive Oil-inspired printing press. Every word was assembled by hand, choosing appropriate glyphs and ligatures from bins of engravings for his chosen typeface. The engraving sat on a base block of metal that was carefully designed to have the appropriate level of spacing. This made layout very efficient. Individual engravings were placed side by side, clamped down, forming words that were a close approximation to the handwritten calligraphy.

Pragmatic Fontery

You're going to use Gutenberg's 15th century techniques to create a font system in OpenGL, demonstrating its use in an iPhone app. The system contains some basic data structures for representing Gutenberg's glyphs, typefaces, vise grips, and olive oil presses. The system captures Gutenberg's techniques in three algorithms, one for laying out glyphs into words, a second for laying words out on a vise grip, and a third for applying the vice grip full of glyphs to your digital display.

I like to call this replica of Gutenberg's process "Pragmatic Fontery." This system is quite useful for head-up displays, game status, simple help screens, display titles, tickertape, and more.

fCookie

I'll review the algorithms, data structures, and code for pragmatic fontery by describing a simple app called "fCookie." Think of this as the "Hello World" version of fontery, with a twist. This app is available on iTunes for free. I've included the entire source code at the Source Code area of the Apress web site at www.apress.com, so that you can get started immediately on fontery in your projects. Two screenshots of fCookie are seen in Figure 6–4.

Figure 6–4. *The fCookie iPhone App*

fCookie selects a random fortune from an array of character strings, then selects one of six different typefaces for displaying the fortune. Figure 6–5 shows a typeface for a "Bonzai" font, as well as a peek at the property list describing all the glyphs it contains.

Key	Type	Value
▼ Root	Array	(93 items)
▶ Item 0	Dictionary	(7 items)
▼ Item 1	Dictionary	(7 items)
name	String	A
width	Number	17
height	Number	32
x	Number	19
y	Number	1
ascent	Number	23
descent	Number	-11
▶ Item 2	Dictionary	(7 items)
▶ Item 3	Dictionary	(7 items)
▶ Item 4	Dictionary	(7 items)

Figure 6–5. *The Bonzai typeface and a property list describing its glyphs*

fCookie uses the algorithm's I'll show you, stitching together the letters and words into a fortune. OpenGL routines display the fortune, creating a ticker tape animation by shifting the letters to the left on each frame. A random color is chosen for each display and the transparency is slowly shifted in and out. These crude effects illustrate how OpenGL can manipulate the various characteristics of a font, including color, size, rotation, transparency, and more.

Creating a Font's Texture Atlas

There are thousands of professionally designed fonts available on the Internet, many for free. Pragmatic Fontery will be using TrueType fonts, the fonts originally invented for the Mac in the early 90's. The fonts on your Mac are stored in /Library/Fonts in OS/X and have "ttf" extensions, which stands for "True Type Font." My 10.6 version of OS/X has 230 such fonts at the time I wrote this chapter in early 2010.

The first challenge you face is to convert these font files into something usable and fast on the iPhone. It's time to break out the terminal app, which is located in the Utilities folder of your Applications directory (see Figure 6–6).

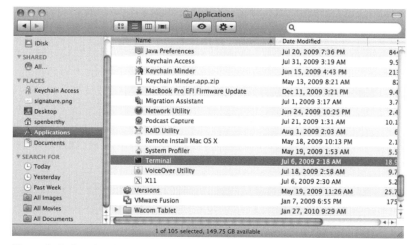

Figure 6–6. *Opening the Terminal Application*

Go ahead and launch a terminal window. You'll be greeted by a command prompt in a new window, much like the one in Figure 6–7.

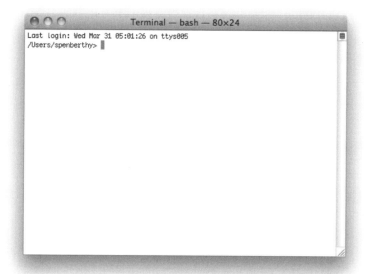

Figure 6–7. *The Terminal window for entering commands*

You're going to use an open source tool for image manipulation, in combination with scripts I've written for this chapter, transforming TrueType files into a PNG image and a property list (.plist) file.

If you're new to open source on the Mac, you'll want to download a tool called MacPorts. This provides a "port" command that lets you search and install software packages that have been pre-compiled for your version of Mac OS/X. MacPorts is available at http://www.macports.org/install.php#pkg.

Follow directions and install the appropriate software. MacPorts can be finicky. It requires that you install the "Unix Support" that comes with Xcode, found on the Xcode DVD that shipped with your Macintosh. The instructions in this chapter assume that Macports has been installed and working correctly. If you get stuck, check out more tips on this issue at https://trac.macports.org/ticket/21062.

Make sure your MacPorts packages are up-to-date by issuing the following command in your terminal window:

```
% sudo port -v selfupdate
```

The "sudo" (pronounced "soo-doo") command attempts to grab administrative privileges on your machine, as the installation will have to touch many system directories. You'll need your administrator password, or run this from an administrator account on your Mac.

With MacPorts in hand, you can download and install ImageMagick with the following command:

```
% sudo port install ImageMagick
```

ImageMagick has been around for years, starting in academia as students and faculty exchanged code for manipulating computer images. It's the secret sauce behind many online services for creating avatars, advertising banners, image overlays, Twitter badges, and so on. We used it at Photobucket for processing billions of images every day. The initial installation is quite large but well worth the wait. A friend of mine installed this on a slow connection, and had more than enough time for a cup of coffee and a slice of pie.

Let's grab a few handy utilities that will make your job easier. You'll use MacPorts again:

```
% sudo port install wget
% sudo port install php5
```

The wget tool was used to create the original search database for Google. It retrieves any web page or item from the Internet and stores it locally. php5 is the language I use for scripting in this chapter, ensuring you have the latest version as of this writing.

After all the software has been installed, close and restart your terminal window. The new window should now have access to all this software.

Now let's create a directory for storing the source code with this project. I call it fontery. You'll then download source code from my company's site, so as to create texture atlases from any true type font (*.ttf):

```
% mkdir fontery
% cd fontery
% wget http://bit.ly/fontery1
% tar xfvz code.tar.gz
% rm code.tar.gz
```

The mkdir line creates a directory "fontery" in your home directory. You change to this directory with the cd command. The wget command downloads a compressed "tarball" that contains the sample code for this chapter. A tarball is a common technique for bundling files together for transmission on the Internet. You'll see a bunch of text printed out as your computer reaches out to the Internet, downloading content. Finally, the tar command extracts (x) the content from a file(f) "code.tar.gz", being quite verbose (v), decompressing (z) as it goes along. This will print dozens of lines, showing all the individual files that are being placed on your machine. Since you now have the files, you no longer need the tarball, so delete it with the remove (rm) command.

The code bundles a sample True Type font, "bonzai.ttf," a font that evokes Chinese writing for the fCookie app. While this example is shown to use bonzai.ttf, you can use any of the files in /Library/Font, as well as other TrueType fonts you download or purchase. Assuming you've installed everything correctly, generating a texture atlas is straightforward. Let's try it.

```
% ./genfont bonzai.ttf
Working...........
We created a fontmap font0.png and property list font1.png
using font size 32.
%
```

The genfont script produces two files:

- font0.png: A PNG graphic that contains all readable Latin characters of your font into a single 256x256 image. The script tries multiple point sizes until it finds one that just fits. The glyphs are painted in white on a transparent background. This will allow you to change the colors by applying filters in OpenGL, and map the fonts to any underlying image (e.g., a signpost, a car, a heads up display). Inspired by Gutenberg, the script also includes extra spacing for each character so that they flow properly when laid out on the screen. This spacing will vary as specified in the original TrueType font.

- font0.plist: A property list (plist) file that will be read by your Objective-C classes. This property list stores font information including the location of each glyph on the PNG graphic, plus its width, height, descender, ascender, and baseline.

Texture Mapping

These PNG and PLIST files form the core of your Gutenberg font system. You use a graphics technique known as *texture mapping*. Texture mapping is the process of painting pieces of an image onto a display. There's a small bit of math involved, which you'll need to understand. The math helps you position characters exactly on the screen. It also lets you rotate and scale the characters to handle different font sizes. Let's take a quick diversion to learn more about the underlying math now, so that the rest of the chapter makes sense.

The "mapping" is formally defined with two coordinates:

- ■ (x, y) is a point on the display

- ■ (u,v) is a point on the image

Let's assume for this discussion that (x,y) starts at (0,0) in the upper left of the screen, increasing x to the right, and y to the bottom. In this example, you will use the full dimensions of the iPhone in portrait mode, where the upper left is (0,0) and the lower right is (320,480). See Figure 6–8.

The (u,v) coordinate of an image has a similar coordinate system, starting at (0,0) in the upper left of the image, and continuing to the right until you reach the width w of an image, continuing to the bottom until you reach the height h the image. But, the values of (u,v) are *normalized*.

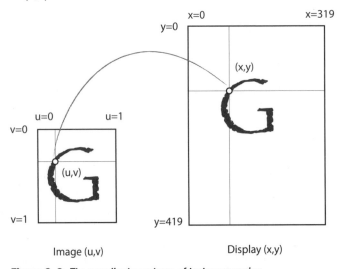

Figure 6–8. *The coordinate systems of texture mapping*

You may recall that normalization maps an interval of numbers to the range [0,1]. The value u, which represents a point along the horizontal axis, starts at 0.0 and progresses to 1.0 for the entire width w. For example, 0.5 represents halfway across the image, 0.25 is one quarter from the left, 0.75 is one quarter from the right. The value v, which represents a point along the vertical axis, starts at 0.0 at top and progresses to 1.0 at the bottom height h.

Texture mapping takes a piece of an image as defined in (u,v) coordinates, then maps the bits in the image to (x,y) coordinates on the screen. In Figure 6–8, you see the letter G in (u,v) space being mapped to a different location on the iPhone screen (x,y). This operation is quite fast and accelerated by the graphics processing unit or GPU. OpenGL will automatically scale and transform the image bits in hardware to maintain a fast frame rate.

So to recap, (x,y) is a point on the display screen, and (u,v) is a point on your image. I'll be referring to these throughout the rest of the chapter. Feel free to come back and review this section if you get lost. Now, on to the app.

Opening Your App

Return to your terminal window. You want to use the texture maps and the uv values created by the genfont utility in your app. The texture map is captured in the file font0.png. The uv values and size of each glyph are kept in font0.plist.

Let's rename these to something you'll remember:

```
% mv font0.png bonzai.png
% mv font0.plist bonzai.plist
```

Let's get these fonts into your app. Open the Xcode project included with the download (see Figure 6–9).

```
% cd FortuneCookie
% open FortuneCookie.xcodeproj
```

Figure 6–9. *A snapshot of the Fontery classes in fCookie*

The Fontery Classes

After you open the FortuneCookie Xcode project, you should see the familiar workspace for building iPhone apps. Take a look at the classes included with the file, available in the main pane (as in Figure 6–9). If you don't see all the names here, click on the Fontery folder to expose them.

The bulk of the code lies within APFontMap. This class does the heavy lifting of reading texture atlases from an external PNG file, then chopping the texture into little bits for each glyph as specified in the font's PLIST file. Since texture atlases consume resources in mass quantity, APFontMap maintains a singleton Dictionary that maps font names (e.g. "bonzai") to the texture.

```
@interface APFontMap : NSObject {
        NSMutableDictionary *glyphLibrary;
        NSMutableDictionary *mapLibrary;
}
```

The mapLibrary variable is a Dictionary of texture atlases. In this demo app, I use a single dictionary for all of the glyphs as well. You map from a character like "z" to an instance of an APGlyph. In a production app, you'll want to have a set of glyphs for each map to avoid duplicates.

APGlyph

Individual glyphs within a font map are represented by instances of APGlyph. This class has the instance variables discussed earlier:

```
@interface APGlyph : NSObject {
        CGFloat *uv;
        CGFloat width;
        CGFloat height;
        CGFloat ascent;
        CGFloat descent;
        NSString *mapKey;
        NSString *glyphName;
}
```

Recall that (u,v) represents a coordinate on the texture atlas. The APGlyph points to this location, and captures the glyph's width and height in (u,v) pixels. See Figure 6–10 for an example of an APGlyph for the capital letter "H," as seen on a fragment of a texture atlas.

The ascent and descent variables are used for lining up glyphs on a line. These, too, are measured in pixels. The mapkey variable represents the name of the font map from which this glyph was pulled. This is useful during game loops, to ensure that the font map is first loaded into OpenGL before texture mapping is done. The glyphName will be helpful in mapping from characters in a string to this glyph. In Figure 6–10, glyphName would have the value @""H".

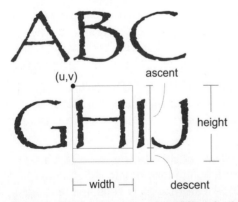

Figure 6–10. *The dimensions of an APGlyph for the letter "H"*

APChar

Glyphs represent the individual engravings from Gutenberg's printing press. Recall that Gutenberg would place these glyphs in a vise grip, forming words and sentences. You need to capture the placement of glyphs in two dimensions, ensuring that everything lines up on a baseline. This is the purpose of the APChar class:

```
@interface APChar : NSObject {
        CGFloat x;
        CGFloat y;
        CGFloat width;
        CGFloat height;
        CGFloat baseline;
        CGFloat r;
        CGFloat g;
        CGFloat b;
        CGFloat a;

        // The following are taken from the glyph map,
        // then cached here.
        CGFloat minU;
        CGFloat maxU;
        CGFloat minV;
        CGFloat maxV;
}
```

As you see, there are a few more values you capture than the (x,y) position. You cache the color and size of your glyph for speed in *rendering*, the process of stamping your glyph in digital ink, then pressing it to the digital display.

Figure 6–11 shows all the values for an APChar for the letter "H" as it is mapped to the iPhone screen, where H" begins the green text string "Hello world." You'll recognize (x,y), the location of a character on the iPhone screen. You add r, g, b, and a to represent the amount of red, green, blue color, as well as the alpha transparency. A value of 0.0 means no color and 1.0 means full color. Similarly, an alpha value of 0.0 means completely transparent or invisible while 1.0 means completely opaque. You also cache the width, height, baseline values for speed, to avoid chasing pointers at render time. Finally, you compute the *bounding box* of the glyph. The bounding box is the smallest rectangle in (u,v) coordinates that completely surrounds the glyph. The upper left is (minU, minV) and the lower right is (maxU, maxV). Bounding boxes are helpful for quickly positioning and layout out text on a screen, abstracting a line of characters into a rectangle.

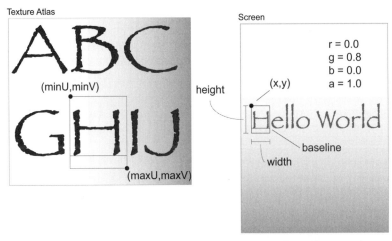

Figure 6–11. *An APChar maps an APGlyph from the texture atlas to the screen.*

APChar captures the placement of an individual glyph on a vise grip. You want to take these placements and have OpenGL do the bidding, cutting glyphs from the larger texture map, dipping them in ink, and pressing them to your display.

Recall that OpenGL has no notion of a font. Don't worry in Gutenberg's day, the olive oil press had no idea it was being used to print bibles. Gutenberg hacked it. He used screws to attach vise grips into the underside of the large, wooden press. He replaced the grate that extracted olive oil with a solid block of wood. He substituted paper for olives. Finally, Gutenberg painted ink on the vice grips moments before he screwed the press down, pressing the vise grips into his paper.

You need to replicate this elegant hack in the world of OpenGL. OpenGL speaks in triangles, polygons, and colors. You'll split your glyphs diagonally, creating two triangles for each glyph, as shown in Figure 6–12. OpenGL likes to have all of its triangles at once, much like the olive oil press likes to have an entire page at a time. You'll accommodate OpenGL by figuring out all the triangles for your string of font characters, keeping them in a single array. Since this is memory intensive, keep a pool of these triangles handy, pulling from them whenever your string grows, returning triangles to the pool when your string shrinks.

Figure 6–12. *Splitting a glyph into two triangles for OpenGL rendering*

APText

You abstract this complexity away with an APText class. APText houses most of the fontery complexity, mapping from a set of APChar placements to triangle arrays in OpenGL.

```
@interface APText : NSObject {
        NSMutableArray * chars;
        NSMutableArray * unusedChars;

        GLfloat * uv;
        GLfloat * vertices;
        GLfloat r, g, b;
        CGFloat alpha;

        NSInteger vertexIndex;
        NSInteger vertexCount;
        NSInteger alignment;
        NSInteger charCount;
        NSString *string;

        CGFloat lineWidth;
        CGFloat lineHeight;

        NSString *fontName;
        BOOL needsLayout;
        BOOL okToRender;
}
```

An APText instance represents a character string that you want to display on the screen. Interesting character strings will change. Examples are the hit count in a front-person shooter, trash talkin' text from another user, elapsed time, status messages, and more.

APText is optimized for speed. It pre-allocates all the memory it will need for the largest string it could display. I typically set this limit to the number of characters that will fit on a single line, say, 64. APText keeps track of memory with two mutable arrays. Assume for now that 64 is the limit you've chosen.

The unusedChars array is first filled with all 64 instances of APChar, one for each character in the string. The chars array is initially empty. Class methods will pull characters from unusedChars and place them in chars when needed, or returning them from chars to unusedChars if they're no longer needed (for shorter strings).

The uv array specifies the (u,v) locations of all characters you'll display, in order from the first to the last. Since you'll be displaying this with OpenGL and a GPU, you cut each glyph into two triangles, as shown for the letter "F." Six coordinates are used, specifying the triangle formed by (1,2,3), then the triangle formed by (3,2,4). Figure 6–12 shows the vertices (1,2,3,4) and the two triangles that are formed for the letter F. You pre-allocate enough memory to store 64*6 or 384 of these.

The vertices array specifies the (x,y) locations on the iPhone screen that correspond to each (u,v) coordinate in or text string. These are matched one for one with the (u,v) coordinates in the uv array, splitting characters into the two triangles (1,2,3) and (3,2,4) as show in the letter "F". You pre-allocate enough memory to store 384 xy pairs.

So far, APText has enough memory allocated for 64 characters, storing the (u,v) and (x,y) pairs in tight arrays. You add a few more instance variables to keep track of your current string, whose size could vary. See Figure 6–13 for an example using the string "Hello World," pulling triangles from a texture atlas in the font Papyrus.

- `string` is your current string of characters, up to 64 characters in length.

- `vertexCount` tracks the total number of vertices you need from (u,v) and (x,y). It will be the same for both.

- `charCount` tracks the total number of characters in your string.

- `lineHeight` tracks the line height of our font. This is useful for positioning multiple APText instances in a paragraph, for example.

- `lineWidth` tracks the total width of your character string, in pixels.

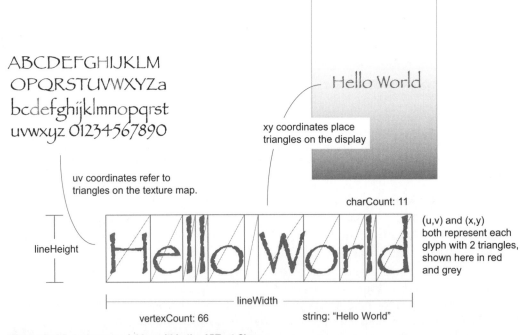

Figure 6–13. *Instance variables within the APText Class*

So far you've sent the basic elements of Gutenberg's press. APGlyphs are placed on your virtual vise grip with APChars. A set of APChars are mapped to your OpenGL printing press with an APText instance, which represents a vise grip being screwed into the back of an olive oil press.

Now you need to capture the physical act of screwing the press down onto paper. This is the role of APRenderController.

This class organizes OpenGL calls to set up, display, and animate your APText instance. This class was derived from the ESRenderer* classes in the standard OpenGL template available in the iPhone SDK. You have a few instance variables:

```
@interface APRenderController : NSObject
{
@private
        EAGLContext *context;

        // The pixel dimensions of the CAEAGLLayer
        GLint backingWidth;
        GLint backingHeight;

        // The OpenGL names for the framebuffer and renderbuffer
        // used to render to this view
        GLuint defaultFramebuffer;
        GLuint colorRenderbuffer;

        APText *ourText;
        CGFloat offset;
}
```

The context is an OpenGL drawing context. Think of this as housing the state of graphics processing unit (GPU), keeping track of all the OpenGL switches for color, transparency, shading, scaling, rotation, and more. You refer to the context every time you want to draw to the screen.

The dimensions of your screen are kept in (backingWidth x backingHeight). The names were taken from the ESRenderer class.

When drawing in OpenGL, one "frame" is usually being shown while a second "frame buffer" is being filled with the contents of the next frame. Once the frame buffer is complete, a single call to OpenGL will copy the contents of the frame buffer to the live frame. The process repeats ad infinitum, producing animation. You'll create these two frame buffers in memory, ask OpenGL for their "handle," and store the handle in defaultFrameBuffer and colorRenderBuffer. Therefore, point all your drawing and texture mapping operations to defaultFrameBufferefaultFrameBuffer.

Putting It All Together

You've used open source tools to convert True Type fonts into texture maps and property lists. You've seen Objective C classes that ingest these into font maps, creating modern versions of Gutenberg's tools. To recap, review the following:

- A PNG file and a property list capture the essence of any True Type font.

- APGlyph's are Gutenberg's individual engravings, cut from a master design kept in an APFontMap.

- APChar's represent the placement of glyph's on a single Gutenberg track.

- APText represents Gutenberg's vise grip, holding the glyphs in place and attaching them to the back of the OpenGL oil press.

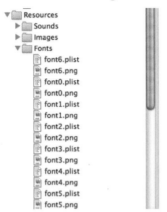

Figure 6-14. *The six fonts and their property lists within fCookie*

Let's do some oil pressing, Gutenberg style!

First, load up the resources. Make sure the PNG image and PLIST property list are part of the Resources folder within XCode. You'll notice in Figure 6–14 that I've loaded 6 different fonts, each starting with "font" and ending in a number from zero (0) to (6). I also organized these into a "Fonts" group for clarity.

Your app begins as a modification of the OpenGL template in the iPhone SDK. You have a single view, EAGLView, that contains an OpenGL layer. This view contains an instance of your APRenderController in the renderer instance variable. When your controller is created, you do three things:

1. Create your OpenGL context, essentially Gutenberg's workspace.

2. Create your frame buffers.

3. Create your APText object, picking a random fortune and font.

Most machines need some "setup" time. Even an oil press needs to oiled, placed on a solid footing, and cleared of debris. A clean bucket needs to be placed beneath the press for capturing olive oil. OpenGL is no different. Let's take a moment to review how you get OpenGL ready for displaying text.

Setting Up the Display

You'll use the simplest and oldest of the OpenGL interfaces, version 1.1, using the initWithAPI call:

```
- (void) createContext
{
        context = [[EAGLContext alloc initWithAPI:kEAGLRenderingAPIOpenGLES1];
        if (!context || ![EAGLContext setCurrentContext:context])
        {
                [self release];
                context = nil;
        }
}
```

Your framebuffers are the digital equivalent of Gutenberg's paper, of the olive oil bucket. You create them with a handful of OpenGL calls:

```
- (void) createFrameBuffers
{
        glGenFramebuffersOES(1, &defaultFramebuffer);
        glGenRenderbuffersOES(1, &colorRenderbuffer);
        glBindFramebufferOES(GL_FRAMEBUFFER_OES, defaultFramebuffer);
        glBindRenderbufferOES(GL_RENDERBUFFER_OES, colorRenderbuffer);
        glFramebufferRenderbufferOES(GL_FRAMEBUFFER_OES, GL_COLOR_ATTACHMENT0_OES, ⏎
 GL_RENDERBUFFER_OES, colorRenderbuffer);
}
```

"OES" in the function names refers to "OpenGL Embedded System." The first call tells OpenGL to create a frame buffer internally, and return to you a handle for referring to it in the future. OpenGL handles are all unsigned integers, perhaps a pointer in memory. The frame buffer is used to draw items before they're rendered. You'll keep this handle in defaultFrameBuffer.

The next call tells OpenGL to create a render buffer for display to the screen. I know this seems a bit redundant. On the iPhone, you never draw directly to the screen. Other versions of OpenGL allow this, an "immediate" mode. You'll still keep this handle around to tell OpenGL to do the drawing for you, copying from the framebuffer.

The next two calls "bind" the framebuffers to the live, graphics pipeline. Binding tells the graphics hardware which memory to use for certain operations. This could allow you, for example, to create multiple framebuffers, and only bind the one you want to use at a given time. You bind your single frame buffer to the live frame buffer, and your render buffer to the live render buffer.

The final call tells OpenGL to hook up a feed from the live frame buffer to the live render buffer. This way the hardware will know the ultimate target, so it can figure out which color schemes to use, how many bits to use per each color, and so forth. These hardware attributes are determined whenever you associate the render buffer with a Layer. This critical connection is done in the resizeFromLayer method of APRenderController, which is called from the main view at startup:

```
glBindRenderbufferOES(GL_RENDERBUFFER_OES, colorRenderbuffer);
```

```
[context renderbufferStorage:GL_RENDERBUFFER_OES fromDrawable:layer];
```

You capture the dimensions of the hardware in your two instance variables, using the following calls into OpenGL:

```
        glGetRenderbufferParameterivOES(GL_RENDERBUFFER_OES,
GL_RENDERBUFFER_WIDTH_OES, &backingWidth);
                    glGetRenderbufferParameterivOES(GL_RENDERBUFFER_OES,
GL_RENDERBUFFER_HEIGHT_OES, &backingHeight);
```

So far you've created an OpenGL graphics context, created your frame buffers, hooked them together, connected the render buffer to your layer, and retrieved the raw hardware dimensions. Your next and final step is to specify how you'll map from your math coordinates to physical screen coordinates. This is done once, in setupPortraitMode of APRenderController, in APRenderController.m:

```
- (void) setupPortraitMode
{
    glBindFramebufferOES(GL_FRAMEBUFFER_OES, defaultFramebuffer);
    glViewport(0, 0, backingWidth, backingHeight);
    glMatrixMode(GL_PROJECTION);
    glLoadIdentity();
    glOrthof(-backingWidth/2.0, backingWidth/2.0,
             -backingHeight/2.0, backingHeight/2.0,
             -1.0f, 1.0f);
}
```

The call the glOrthof specifies the x-range, y-range, and z-range that you'll use to represent the physical screen. Here I've chosen to make the center of the screen (0,0), and have the X axis go from –w/2 to +w/2 from left to right. Similarly, I've chosen to make the Y axis start at –h/2 on the bottom, to +h/2 on the top. I won't be using the Z range, so I left it at –1.0 to 1.0.

Your digital olive oil press—the OpenGL context—is now ready for drawing!

Creating Your Fortune

You want to display a fortune, and have it scroll across the screen. For this example, I've hardwired the character strings in C. Open the file Fortunes.h. You'll see the following near the top of the file:

```
#define kFortuneCount 441
#define kFontCount 6

static char* kFortunes[] = {
    "He who climbs a ladder must begin at the first step.",
    "The one who snores will always fall asleep first.",
    …
}
```

kFortunes is an array of ASCII character strings, 441 to be exact. I've also defined a total number of fonts, kFontCount as 6.

Now switch to the file APRenderController.m, where you create an instance of APText, initializing it with a random quote from the kFortunes array. This all occurs in the createObjects method which follows:

```
- (void) createObjects
{
        int fortune = round(randomPercent * (kFortuneCount-1));
        int fontid = round(randomPercent * kFontCount);
        NSString *quote = [NSString stringWithUTF8String: kFortunes[fortune]];
        NSString *font = [NSString stringWithFormat: @"font%d", fontid];
        NSLog(@"Showing fortune:\n%@\nin font %@",quote,font);

        ourText = [[APText alloc] init];
        [ourText useFont: font];
        [ourText setString: quote];
        ourText.r = 0.7*randomPercent;
        ourText.g = 0.7*randomPercent;
        ourText.b = 0.7*randomPercent;
        offset = 0;
}
```

You'll notice the use of randomPercent, C shorthand defined as

```
#define randomPercent (((CGFloat)(arc4random() % 40001))/40000.0)
```

This uses an improved random function generator, arc4random, to determine a value from 0.0 to 1.0. I find it much more "random" than the stock rand() function, as it initializes itself based on current time and the content of CPU registers. But I digress.

Next, you choose a random number, then pick one of the C strings out of your Fortunes array and convert it to an NSString, as follows:

```
NSString *quote = [NSString stringWithUTF8String: kFortunes[fortune]];
```

You also pick a font from font0 to font6, which as you recall are stored with your resources:

```
NSString *font = [NSString stringWithFormat: @"font%d", fontid];
```

Creating the actual APText is straightforward. You allocate an instance then tell APText the name of the font, and the value of your string:

```
ourText = [[APText alloc] init];
[ourText useFont: font];
[ourText setString: quote];
```

You also choose random values for the red, green, blue colors, representing the relative intensity of each color from 0 to 70%:

```
ourText.r = 0.7*randomPercent;
ourText.g = 0.7*randomPercent;
ourText.b = 0.7*randomPercent;
```

I've kept the range from to nothing higher than 70% saturation, producing a darker range of colors that will be placed on a white background. If you let value range all the way to 100% saturation, you could get bright, white colors that are impossible to see.

Finally, record the "offset" for shifting the text on the display as 0. Increase the offset on every frame, shifting your text to the left. Once the text is completely off the screen, reset the offset to zero and repeat.

Displaying the Fortune

You now have an OpenGL layer ready for display, and an APText object containing your lucky fortune. Now let's look at how you use fontery to display the string on the display.

The render method of APRenderController is called for every frame. You break this down into three steps, as seen in APRenderController.m:

```
- (void) render
{
        [self beforeRender];
        [self renderObjects];
        [self afterRender];
}
```

The beforeRender step chooses your graphics context, clears the OpenGL display, and gives a fresh perspective, with no translations, rotations, color changes, etc. It resets the math and engine state so you don't get confused.

```
- (void) beforeRender
{
        [EAGLContext setCurrentContext:context];
        glMatrixMode(GL_MODELVIEW);
        glLoadIdentity();
        glShadeModel (GL_SMOOTH);
        glBlendFunc(GL_ONE, GL_ONE_MINUS_SRC_ALPHA);
        glEnable(GL_BLEND);
        glClearColor(0.9f,0.9f,0.9f,0.6);
        glClear(GL_COLOR_BUFFER_BIT | GL_DEPTH_BUFFER_BIT);
}
```

The renderObjects step iterates through all objects in your display, asking them to render themselves. For this app, you only have one – ourText.

```
- (void) renderObjects
{
        offset += 2;
        if (offset > ourText.lineWidth + 160) {
                offset = 0;
                ourText.r = 0.7*randomPercent;
                ourText.g = 0.7*randomPercent;
                ourText.b = 0.7*randomPercent;
        }
        glTranslatef(-offset,0,0);
        ourText.alpha = 0.6+0.2*(cos(offset*3.1415926/180)+1.0);
        [ourText render];
}
```

To spice things up a bit, change the offset of each iteration, then use glTranslatef to shift the display to the left (negative x values). Also, play with the transparency of the text, using math to make it oscillate between 40% and 80% opaque. Once the offset moves the text completely off the screen, reset the offset and change the color for the next scrolling display.

You then call the render method of APText:

```
-(void)render
{
        // Choose font atlas and uv mapping
        if (fontName != nil) {
                [[APFontMap sharedFontMap] bindMaterial: fontName];
                glEnableClientState(GL_TEXTURE_COORD_ARRAY);
                glTexCoordPointer(2, GL_FLOAT, 0, uv);
                if (glGetError()) printf("Error setting texture uv\n");
        }

        // Load (x,y) mapping
        glEnableClientState( GL_VERTEX_ARRAY);
        glVertexPointer(2, GL_FLOAT, 0, vertices);
        if (glGetError()) printf("Error setting vertices xy \n");

        // Set paint color
        GLfloat red = (r < 0) ? 0 : ((r > 1) ? 1 : r);
        GLfloat green = (g < 0) ? 0 : ((g > 1) ? 1 : g);
        GLfloat blue = (b < 0) ? 0 : ((b > 1) ? 1 : b);
        glColor4f(red, green, blue, alpha); //, alpha, alpha);

        // Apply triangles to the screen
        glDrawArrays(GL_TRIANGLES, 0, vertexCount);
        if (glGetError()) printf("Error drawing vertices\n");

        // Clean up our work area
        glColor4ub( 255, 255, 255, 255);
        glDisable( GL_TEXTURE_2D);
        glDisableClientState(GL_VERTEX_ARRAY );
        glDisableClientState( GL_TEXTURE_COORD_ARRAY );
}
```

Let's now step through this algorithm and how it executes at runtime.

1. Bind your texture map in OpenGL.

```
        // Choose font atlas and uv mapping
        if (fontName != nil) {
                [[APFontMap sharedFontMap] bindMaterial: fontName];
                glEnableClientState(GL_TEXTURE_COORD_ARRAY);
                glTexCoordPointer(2, GL_FLOAT, 0, uv);
                if (glGetError()) printf("Error setting texture uv\n");
        }
```

You have to choose your font. Use the fontName string as a key, mapping from the fontName to an OpenGL texture stored in a shared dictionary. This is done in the file APFontmap.m, as follows:

```
-(void)bindMaterial:(NSString*)mapKey
{
        NSNumber * numberObj = [mapLibrary objectForKey:mapKey];
        GLuint textureID = [numberObj unsignedIntValue];
        glEnable(GL_TEXTURE_2D);
                glBindTexture(GL_TEXTURE_2D, textureID);
}
```

2. Specify (u,v) locations for each glyph triangle.

You next tell OpenGL to use the UV coordinates that correspond to the particular glyphs in your string. This is the purpose of the two lines of code:

```
glEnableClientState(GL_TEXTURE_COORD_ARRAY);
glTexCoordPointer(2, GL_FLOAT, 0, uv);
```

The first, glEnableClientState, tells our OpenGL olive press that you'll be using texture mapping as a technique for painting on the screen. You're "turning on" the ability to pass in a set of UV coordinates in a single array. The next call, glTexCoordPointer, actually passes your array of UV coordinates for all the characters you need from your font.

> **NOTE:** Production applications will want to behave a little better than what you've shown here, keeping track of the state of the OpenGL graphics pipeline. Calls to glEnableClientState and glDisableClientState can get expensive. You'll want to make these calls only when absolutely necessary. For example, you might set up a texture mapping mode, then map all your textures, before switching to other modes. Your sample code turns these on and off for each APText display.

3. Specify (x,y) screen locations for each glyph triangle

You have to map these textures to locations on the screen. Recall that you position the glyphs in your string with APChar instances. Each of these has an x,y value, and you collect all the XY values into an array named vertices. You tell OpenGL to use this array with two API calls:

```
glEnableClientState( GL_VERTEX_ARRAY);
glVertexPointer(2, GL_FLOAT, 0, vertices);
```

The first call enables the use of such a "vertex array," and the second call says you're only specifying 2 dimensions, (x,y), using floating point values.

4. Choose your ink color.

You then set up the color of your font. Your font texture atlases are created with white characters on a transparent background. You can use a single call into OpenGL to shade this white to whatever color you want, at a transparency set by your alpha value. Neat. First, you turn the r,g,b values into a valid range from 0.0 to 1.0:

```
GLfloat red = (r < 0) ? 0 : ((r > 1) ? 1 : r);
GLfloat green = (g < 0) ? 0 : ((g > 1) ? 1 : g);
GLfloat blue = (b < 0) ? 0 : ((b > 1) ? 1 : b);
```

Then, you tell OpenGL to turn on its color shader:

```
glColor4f(red, green, blue, alpha);
```

5. Paint the triangles on the framebuffer

Finally, draw the entire character string in a single OpenGL call:

```
glDrawArrays(GL_TRIANGLES, 0, vertexCount);
```

OpenGL will use the (u,v) positions and (x,y) positions you gave it earlier, iterating through the array, mapping each (u,v) triangle to an (x,y) triangle on the screen. OpenGL "presses" the triangle into an off-screen framebuffer. Think of this as the raw sheet of paper on the olive oil press. With the glDrawArrays call, you've now imprinted one copy of your APText string onto the virtual display.

These five steps are repeated for all the text strings on your display. This completes the renderObjects step of your APRenderController. You have one step left, done once for the entire set of images rendered to the frame buffer.

The afterRender step asks OpenGL to dump the frame buffer into the render buffer, displaying your text on the screen. This is the equivalent of lifting the head of the olive oil press, allowing you to reach inside and see the final work product.

```
- (void) afterRender
{
        glBindRenderbufferOES(GL_RENDERBUFFER_OES, colorRenderbuffer);
    [context presentRenderbuffer:GL_RENDERBUFFER_OES];
}
```

You're done. You repeat this every frame to create an animated, scrolling fortune.

Summary

This chapter has demonstrated "pragmatic fontery," a technique first devised by Gutenberg in the 15th century. Gutenberg created individual carvings for each letter, casting them into individual blocks that also included spacing. He would space these blocks together on a track, holding them in place with a vise grip. The vise grips were attached to the back of an Olive Oil press, which was then pressed down on monk-sized paper.

Your digital version mirrors his invention. An APGlyph class instance represents an individual character block, cut from a larger APFontMap image with (u,v) coordinates. An APChar class places this glyph on a track using (x,y) screen locations. An APText class gathers all characters together to represent a single track, with its own lineWidth and lineHeight. Your APRenderController class acts as the Olive Oil press, essentially "pressing" an APText into your iPhone screen, by first casting it in a framebuffer with a chosen (r,g,b) color, then swapping the framebuffer for the live display.

I demonstrated the use of pragmatic fontery in a simple fortune cookie app, fCookie. Source code for the app and its supporting scripts are available on the Apress web site at www.apress.com . I hope you enjoy using these classes, extending them for use in heads up displays, counters, menus, status messages, and more!

Ben Britten Smith

Company: EscapeFactory
(http://escfactory.com)

Location: Melbourne, Australia

Former Life as a Developer: I have been writing software in one form or another since grade school. Back then, I wrote in BASIC and Logo. Over the intervening quarter century or so, I have ranged all over the map, from writing low-level assembly for embedded systems through all the major (and not so major) languages settling now and again on the big ones, like C, C++, Perl, Smalltalk, Obj C, and PHP.

Somewhere along the way, I got involved with a visual effects company called Spydercam and wrote their industrial motion control system. This system is still in heavy use and is used on many feature films. In 2005, Spydercam's lead hardware designer, lead mechanical engineer, and I were awarded an Academy Award for Technical Achievement for our efforts in 3D motion control. Some interesting trivia: the system we designed is the only one that I am aware of that runs on a Mac, written entirely in native Cocoa/Obj-C.

I am also active in the Multitouch surface open source community. I wrote an open source tracker called xTouch and an open source OSC implementation called BBOSC. I also collaborated on a Unity-based Multitouch framework called uniTUIO.

Life as an iPhone Developer: Recently, I have relocated from New York City to live in Melbourne with my wife Leonie. Here I have started offering my services as a freelance cocoa developer, and once the SDK became public, the market for iPhone work exploded. I have worked on a half dozen apps that are on the store now for various clients, like Anti-Stress, Blackout, and aSleep. Just after the SDK was released, I was approached by a few clients interested in game development. My first iPhone game was SnowDude and it was entirely in Cocoa/OpenGL. On the heels of the SnowDude release late in 2008, Unity3D announced their Unity for iPhone tools, so I started making games using Unity3D. By the time of this printing, I will have over a half dozen games in the app store, both Unity and OpenGL/Cocoa.

Apps on the App Store:

- *Mole: The Quest for the Terracore Gem*
- *Gamebook Adventures Volume 1: An Assassin in Orlandes*
- *Gamebook Adventures Volume 2: The Siege of the Necromancer*
- *Snowferno*
- *SnowDude*

What's in This Chapter: *In this chapter Ben explores the power of the Unity3D game engine. During this gentle introduction to the Unity API, Ben shows you how to get around in the Unity editor, takes you through the process of importing 3D models, building a 3D scene, and attaching custom scripts to your game objects, explores touch interaction and a simple GUI interface, and even shows you how to control a fully animated 3D character.*

Key Technologies:

- *Unity3D*
- *3D Modeling/Texturing*
- *Asset Management*

Chapter 7

Game Development with Unity

Most of us have built our own game engine in one form or another. If you are a programmer and you build games, then it is like a rite of passage. I have done it. In fact, I have done it a few times. 2D-game engines based on Core Animation, both 2D and 3D engines based on OpenGL and OpenGL ES, the list goes on. I love making my own engines. They do exactly what I need them to do, no more and no less. The downsides: it takes a long time to write your own engine and unless you make the exact same kinds of games over and over again, you will be spending a long time adding features to your engines to match your new game designs. It is often hard to see this happening to yourself because writing game engines is fun!

At some point along the way, I realized that if I was really going to be serious about game development, I needed to stop writing game engines and start writing games. After I had built a handful of games for clients using my own custom 2D/3D OpenGL ES–based engine, I decided that I really wanted to branch out and build my own games.

Once I started thinking about my own games, I wanted to add things like physics and complex object interactions, cool lighting effects, and particles—all in 3D, of course. Now, there was nothing stopping me from adding all these features to my own little engine and using that, except time.

I first started looking around at the various physics libraries available, and began mapping out what it would take to properly integrate a physics library with my little 3D engine. I took a look at a few various options, made some notes, and decided that no matter which way I went I would need at least a few days to get myself even a bit familiar with the physics API, a few more days of testing and fiddling with the bits and pieces to figure out how it would best integrate with my existing code, and then a few more days to actually add it in. On top of that, there would be at least a few more days worth of bug fixing and issues down the line. Therefore, to add one feature to my engine, it would take me a couple of weeks of work.

I am a freelance programmer, so my hours have dollar values attached to them. Any time I am not spending on client projects is money that I am not earning. With this in mind, it was easy for me to put a fairly large monetary value on my two weeks of time and come to the conclusion that simply buying some pre-built engine would make so much more sense.

What Is Unity?

This brings us to Unity3D (`http://unity3d.com`), the main Unity application, which is usually just called Unity. It comes in two flavors: a Pro version, which costs money, and a free version, which does not. There is also another standalone app which is Unity iPhone, and it also comes in two types: Unity iPhone Basic, which is a few hundred dollars and Unity iPhone Advanced, which is a bit more expensive. As of this writing, Unity 3.0 was just announced. It will bring the iPhone and "desktop" versions into the same package. This will make cross platform development even easier.

But, really, what is Unity? I used some terms like "game engine" earlier, but Unity is not really a game engine. It is a game creation tool that happens to have a game engine built into it. What does that mean? It means that if you want to build a game (or any 3D application) and you want to focus on the game play aspects of the game yet not worry about the esoteric 3D rendering issues, then Unity is a good place to start.

This is not all though. The folks at Unity are very keen to provide as many platforms for easy deployment as possible. This means that if you use Unity to build a game for the iPhone, or iPad, you will be able to easily port it for the browser or the desktop (even the Windows desktop). The recently announced Unity 3 will also support Android deployment as well as a handful of consoles.

As an indie game developer, the cross platform support is one of the reasons I consistently choose Unity for my projects. I can prototype game designs and build them for the browser so that our team members can easily game test from any computer. After we have settled on a working game design, I can build the game and quickly produce an iPhone version; then tweak the interface and display to build an iPad version, and then maybe add gamepad or keyboard support so as to produce a desktop version. Finally, I could add Facebook integration to deploy on Facebook or another social network. This flexibility is simply not possible with any other engine out there.

So, let's get into Unity.

The Unity application is also known as the Unity Editor, and at first it can be a bit overwhelming (see Figure 7–1).

The Unity Editor is where you will do most of your game building work. This is also where you store your assets and make object connections. The Unity Editor is where you will be able to quickly build your game objects and place them in your scenes. The inspector allows you to easily change the variables for all the various game objects and scripts you will be using and writing. It holds all the images and materials you will use for your textures and user interface elements. It is all very simple to use and you will spend a great deal of time in the Unity Editor.

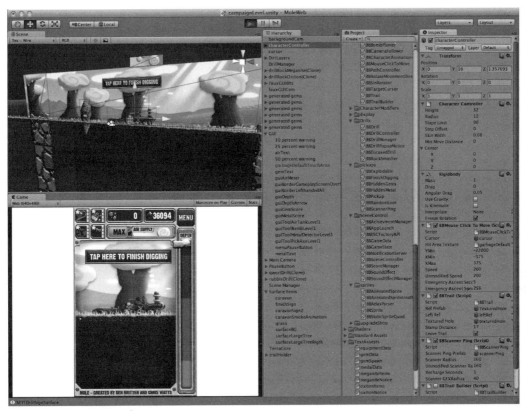

Figure 7–1. *The Unity Editor window. Unity Pro working on my game, Mole.*

The other thing you will need is a good text editor. Unity comes with one, called Unitron, and it is really quite good if you are just starting out. It gives you easy auto-completion of the API calls and quick access to the documentation.

For this chapter, I would suggest you go to http://www.unity3d.com and download the free Unity editor. As of this writing, you can get a 30 day free trial of the iPhone Basic version. You can also use the desktop version if you are just starting out with iPhone development and have yet not gotten your Apple development account. The desktop version will not allow you to build for the iPhone, and some of the specific iPhone API calls are not available (like the touch processing). However, you will be able to implement the code in this chapter and I will point out anything iPhone specific. This way you can get a feel for the Unity API and building a game, the Unity way.

Why Use Unity?

I already talked a bit about why I initially started using Unity: the price/performance ratio was far higher than what I could accomplish on my own. I also talked a bit about cross platform deployment.

Additionally, with Unity I also get a nice asset management interface and a nice 3D scene modeler for my game scenes. Building all that on my own would have taken me years.

Let's pretend you already have an OpenGL|ES code base that does most everything you want. I still think that you could find some value in Unity. First, the Editor provides a handful of primitive shapes and game objects that allow you to very quickly put together game prototypes. This is so much more helpful than I ever thought it would be. Do you have a crazy idea for a game, but you don't know if it is going to be fun or not? You can probably knock out a rough game play prototype with boxes and spheres in a few hours.

Add to that built-in physics, collisions, particles, texture handling, audio handling, and anything you need to build a game is there.

If you have been building games on the iPhone, you also know of the dreaded iPhone Simulator issues. There is no accelerometer, which means you can't do more than very basic double-touch gestures. This doesn't feel like an iPhone, which means that when you are building your game and testing it, to get a real feel, you have to always build for the device. This can take a long time and really slows down your process. Unity provides you with an iPhone app called Unity Remote that allows you to use a device like a gamepad and test games right in the editor. Therefore, if you are doing a rolling-ball game, like you did with Snowferno, then you just hit the play button in the editor, and the game shows up on your device instantly, so you can test it without having to compile or install every time. You'll see this in the "Using the iPhone As a Game Pad" section later in this chapter.

You can change your scenes and your game objects while you are play testing. If that bit of the scene is in the wrong place, you can just grab it, move it, and play on.

There are many more pros to using Unity, and you will see many of them during the rest of the chapter, but to summarize all of them: Unity makes it easy to build games. It is made specifically to build games and it does it very well.

However, Unity is not a panacea and is not without its downsides. The biggest issue for me when I first began using Unity was that I could not use Objective-C and Cocoa. If you are familiar with Objective-C and the Cocoa APIs you will need to learn some new stuff. (Others who do not like Objective-C might find this to be a big upside.) I am a big fan of Objective-C. I love the Cocoa APIs and generally dislike writing in the other C languages. That said, it took me only a few days to really get comfortable with the scripting for Unity. Unity uses the Mono scripting project, which means you can pick a few different languages. The most popular are Javascript and C#.

There is some debate as to the best scripting language to use within Unity. Truth be told, there is no better language for scripting in Unity. At the time of writing this chapter, there was some internal discussions of whether we should be using Javascript or C# for the sample code.

Javascript has an advantage in that is very simple to use and building scripts in Javascript can be very quickly done. Much of the Unity documentation is also provided with Javascript samples. I built my first Unity-iPhone game, Snowferno, entirely with Javascript and it works great.

That said, I think that C# is a bit more of a programmer's language. By that, I mean C# is more strongly typed, and I find it a bit easier to do more complex things in C#. Sometimes I want to be specific with my variable types, and I often want to take advantage of Object Oriented design patterns. These types of things are easier in C# in my opinion.

Ultimately, I decided to do the sample code in C#. I think that most programmers reading this will be familiar with the C languages and Objective C in particular. I tend to design my C# code in a very cocoa-like fashion, so it should be easy to transition.

How do you build a game in Unity? Read on!

Exploring the Unity Interface

I only have one chapter here, so I am not going to make a comprehensive guide to all things Unity. What I plan to do is introduce you to some common features of Unity while making a simple game. At the end of the chapter, I hope you will have an appreciation for how simple Unity can be and yet how you can leverage Unity's pre-existing architecture to build your own games quickly and easily.

If you haven't gotten a version of Unity, download the iPhone version from the Unity3d.com web site, then run the installer and sign up for the 30 day trial.

With that in mind, the first thing you will need to do is get familiar with Unity's interface. Over the course of the chapter, you will be using lots of different art assets, from 3D models to textures to scripts. In all of the cases, you can substitute your own 3D models or images, but to make things a bit easier I have built a sample project. You should be able to find the source here: http://apress.com/book/sourcecode. Once you have it, open up the sample code in Unity by going to the **File ➤ Open Project** and selecting the CoolerUnity folder.

In Figure 7–2, you see the five major sub window types in unity. These five are the ones you will be looking at most of the time, so you will start with these.

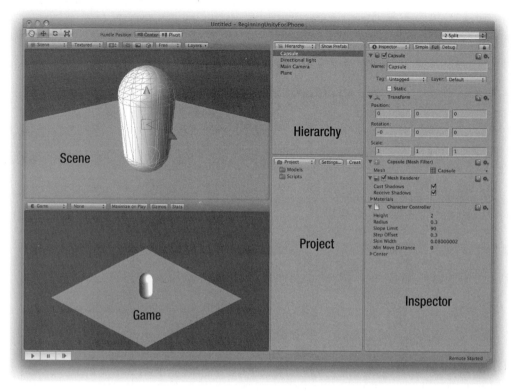

Figure 7–2. *The five main chunks of the Unity editor. This is what you are staring at for the majority of your time in Unity.*

If you opened up Unity and it doesn't look quite like this that is OK. As of this writing, the desktop version is slightly different from the iPhone version pictured here. However, don't let the slight differences in UI worry you, the functionality is almost identical. Everything you do in this chapter, with the exception of the iPhone specific things will work just fine in the desktop version, and I will point out how to replicate touches in the desktop version as well, so if all you have is the free Unity download, you will be just fine.

Let's have a look at each one of these sub windows.

The Scene View

The scene is similar to a 3D editor. It allows you to move objects around in your scene and view your scene from anywhere. You can grab your scene objects and rotate, scale, and move them.

The scene provides you with some basic manipulation tools in the upper-left corner as shown in Figure 7–3.

Figure 7–3. *The scene manipulators: the pan/zoom/tumble tool, move tool, rotate tool, and the scale tool.*

The leftmost tool is the pan/zoom/tumble tool. If you just click and drag in the scene window, then that tool will have a hand icon and you will pan the camera around the scene. If you hold the option key while dragging, the icon will change to a little eye and you can tumble the scene. If you hold the command key while dragging, the scene will zoom. If your mouse has a scroll wheel, then the scroll will zoom as well.

The next three tools are for manipulating a single object. If you select an object in the scene then these tools will allow you to move it around, spin its orientation, and scale it. You can also do this from the Inspector view by typing in the exact values you want and you will talk about that in a second.

The Game View

The game view is what the player will see when they play your game. When you hit the play button to test out your game, you will be playing the game in this view, and this is what will show up on your device if you are using it as a remote (more on that later). You can set this view to show various different resolutions and aspect ratios, but generally when developing for the iPhone you want to stick to the iPhone screen size.

If you have a look at Figure 7–4, you are going to be making a game that is in the landscape format, so you want to lock the game view into the iPhone wide resolution. This way you know exactly what the player is seeing and you can tweak your camera angles and scene design to that screen size.

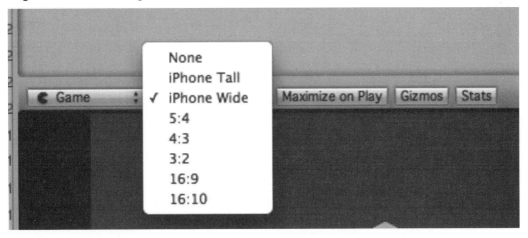

Figure 7–4. *Setting the game view to only show the iPhone landscape aspect.*

The Project View

The project view is a shortcut to all the assets in your project. There is a folder in your Unity project called Assets. Everything in that folder (including other folders) will show up in the project view. One of Unity's unique and awesome features is the way that assets are imported. Any time you make a change to anything in the assets folder, Unity automatically imports it into your project or updates the existing assets. For example, if you have a texture you are tweaking in Photoshop, you can open it up right out of the assets folder and every time you save, your changes will appear in Unity automatically. This even works while you are playing the game in the Game View.

The Hierarchy View

The hierarchy view shows only those objects that you have in the scene currently. Most games have multiple scenes.

The Inspector View

The Inspector is where you can change the values of your object's attributes. In the scene view, you could rotate, scale, and move the objects. Similarly, in the inspector, you can simply type in new values for the various transform properties. The inspector also exposes various attributes of all the components of the objects, from the material that you are using to render the object to the customized script variables that you choose to expose to the editor. More on all of this later, but suffice it to say, you will be using the inspector quite a bit.

Now that you have seen the interface, you are going to have a quick look at how you put objects into your games and how you interact with them in the editor.

How the Pipeline Flows

Each object in your game is built up of various bits and pieces. Things like the material you are using, the mesh of vertexes that define the shape of your objects and the transform that defines where in space the object is. In Unity, these are called Components. The container that holds a bunch of components is known as a GameObject.

Most every object in your scene will be either a game object or a component of a game object. The asset pipeline is about getting various art assets into components and attaching those components to a game object, which becomes part of your scene.

This sounds a bit convoluted and complicated, but it is actually very simple. I am going to go through the process of making a game object from scratch, so that you can get familiar with each of the major components. Then, I will show you how to do it the easy way.

Any given game object can have a dozen or so different types of components attached to it. You are going to look at the most common of these: the renderer, the transform, the collider, and the script. You will look at each one individually and look at how you import assets into these components.

Before you can look at components, you need a game object container. If you haven't already, make a new scene in your project. This can be found under File ➤ New Scene.

The Transform: Everybody Has One

In this new scene, you should see a blank scene view and your hierarchy has a Main Camera object in it. You want to add a new empty game object. Go to the menu GameObject ➤ Create Empty.

Now your scene should look something like Figure 7–5. Your object shows up in the scene as an empty box because it has no renderer attached to it. We will get to that in a moment.

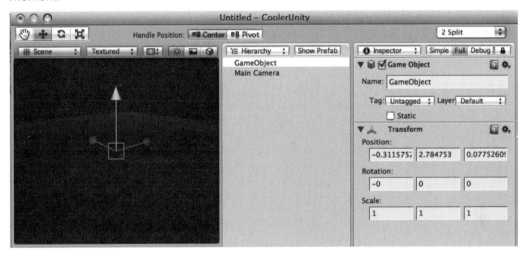

Figure 7–5. *A new empty game object*

For now, have a look in the inspector. You can see two components there: the Game Object and the Transform.

The Game Object isn't actually a component; it is the instance variables of the game object itself. For now, let's just change the name to something besides "GameObject", I will call it: "Rotating Barrel".

The next thing to look at is the transform. Every object has a transform, even empty ones like this one. The transform lets you adjust the general transformations like position, scale, and rotation.

In the case of new empty objects, Unity has a tendency to put the object at the last place you were looking at, or at some other inexplicable place. When you are dealing with objects that have meshes, then it is obvious that they are out of place, but with the empty ones, it is sometimes hard to tell. I tend to automatically set the transform position for any new object to 0,0,0 just so I can tell where it is easier.

> **TIP:** Keeping the empty objects at 0,0,0 is a good practice to get into, because later on when you are using empty objects to group other objects together, or make pivot points, then the position becomes more important.

Meshes, Renderers, and Materials

Empty objects are very handy for lots of things, but if you want to be able to see them, then you need a renderer.

With your new Rotating Barrel selected, go to the **Component ➤ Mesh ➤ Mesh Filter** menu item. This will add a mesh filter to your Rotating Barrel object, as shown in Figure 7–6.

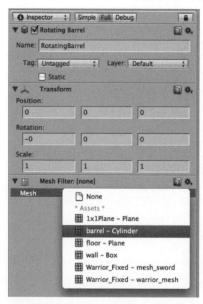

Figure 7–6. *Selecting the Barrel mesh for the Rotating Barrel Object.*

What is a mesh filter? A mesh filter is the object that handles all of the actual vertex data for your models. In this case, you want to use a barrel mesh, and there is one already conveniently located in the project. If you open the tiny popup menu in the mesh filter component, you will get a list of all the meshes in the project, something similar to Figure 7–6. Select the barrel - Cylinder mesh. The drop-down triangle that indicates that the meshes is a list is small and off to the right. It is not immediately obvious that it is a drop down, but it is, and those are very handy.

Ok, now you have a mesh, but you still can't see your object!

You need a Mesh Renderer component. Go to the **Component ➤ Mesh ➤ Mesh Renderer** menu item. Now you should be able to see your barrel object. If you can't see your object, there are a few things that may have gone wrong.

First off, check to make sure that your barrel is at position 0,0,0. Second, check to see if your Scene View is pointing at your barrel. You can do this by just tumbling around in the scene view a bit to try and find it, or select your barrel in the hierarchy view, then roll the mouse pointer into the scene view and hit 'f'. This will automatically frame your selected object in the Scene View (see Figure 7–7).

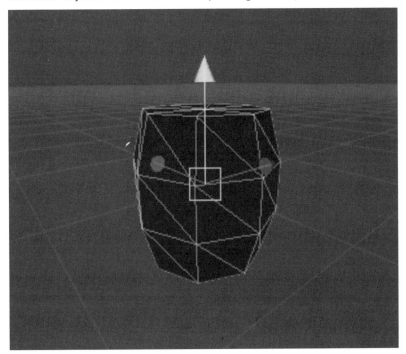

Figure 7–7. *The barrel mesh, rendered*

This is a pretty boring barrel, you need one more thing: a material. Currently, the mesh renderer is using a default none material, so you are getting a black colored object.

A material is basically a texture and a shader. Like everything else in Unity, you can tweak all of the various settings for your materials to get just the right thing, but for now you will just grab the one that was prepared earlier.

Just like with the mesh filter, if you pop open the menu under the materials in the inspector, you get a list of all the available materials. Choose the barrel-cylindermat material, like in Figure 7–8.

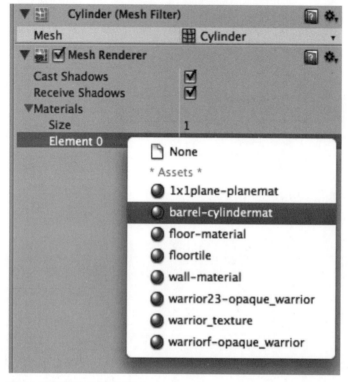

Figure 7–8. *Material Selection*

Now you should be able to see the barrel in all of its glory.

Since you don't yet have any lighting, the barrel might be very dark. In this case, you need to shut off the scene lighting. In the scene view at the top-center, there is a little button that looks like a sun. That is the scene lighting. When it is on, it lights the scene view using whatever lights you have in your scene. You don't have any lights in your scene, so when it is on, your scene is awfully dark. Turn it off, and you will get some nice ambient lighting, as shown in Figure 7–9.

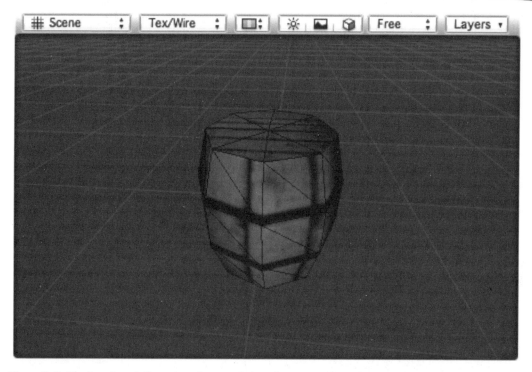

Figure 7–9. *Finally, a barrel. If your barrel seems dark, make sure you have the scene lighting turned off in the Scene View.*

Let's step back and have a look at what you have done. First, you have an empty container object then you added a mesh to it. The mesh is just a list of vertexes, UVs, and normals. Then, you added a mesh renderer that took that mesh and drew it to the screen. Finally, you added a material for the renderer to use and you can now see your final object.

This is roughly the same thing you would need to do if you were writing your own OpenGL engine. Also, it is good to know that the process you just went through is the hardest way to build an object, but it shows you the various bits that go into how each object is drawn on screen.

Now if you wanted to make an object with the same mesh, but a different texture, then you can just assign a different material. I encourage you to play around with the materials, colors, and other options in the mesh renderer component to see how it affects the barrel.

If you would like to know the easy way to do what you just did, select your rotating barrel and use either the transform component in the inspector, or the drag tool, and move the rotating barrel off to the left or right of center. In the project view, find the directory Models. Inside that is a model called: barrel. Drag that from the project view into the hierarchy view. Now you have two barrels.

Importing Assets

In the sample project, I have already imported a bunch of assets, like the barrel model and material. At some point, you will want to use your own models and images, which is where importing comes in.

For the most part, the importing of objects into your scene is as simple as dragging and dropping them. Generally, you simply grab your asset from the desktop and drag it into the Project View in Unity. In this case, the barrel was created and textured in a 3D modeling program (specifically, Cheetah3D) and just saved into the Models folder. Either way Unity automatically imports the model into a mesh and the texture into a material. All you have to do is drag the model into your scene.

If you want to apply a new texture, you could go back into 3D modeler and remap the texture, or you could just drag the new texture image into Unity and create a new material then assign that image to the material. Then, assign the new material to my object like you just did. It is very easy.

Let's try it now. In the project view, select the folder Materials. Then go to the **Assets ➤ Create =➤ Material** menu item. This should put a new material asset into the materials folder. Rename it something useful, like "Gray Barrel". Now open the Images folder in the project view and find the image: barrelTextureHigh. Select your new Gray Barrel material and then drag the barrelTextureHigh into the image well for that material. This can be seen in Figure 7–10.

You now have a new material. You can assign that material to one of your barrels in the same fashion you did previously by selecting that object, and then selecting the material from the mesh renderer material drop down, or you can simply drag the material from the project view onto the object, either in the hierarchy view or the scene view.

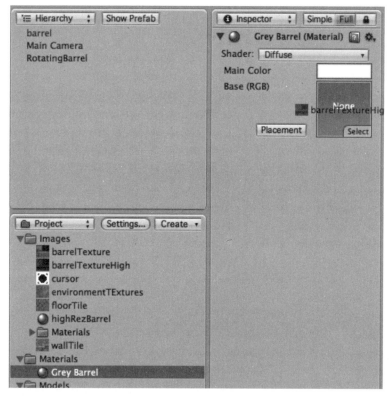

Figure 7–10. *Creating a new material and assigning a texture*

Custom Scripting

Now that you have a few objects in your scene, you need them to do something besides just sit there. If you have been following along, then you should have two barrels, one grayish and one brownish. One of them will be called "Rotating Barrel" while the other will be called 'Grey Barrel'. Let's focus on the rotating one for now.

As the name might imply, you would like to have this barrel rotate. Not because barrels are generally found to be rotating, but because rotating is a nice easy place to start talking about scripting.

What you will do is go ahead and make the script to rotate this barrel, make it work, and then we will come back and have a look at the bigger picture of how all these things work together.

Go to the project view, find the scripts folder, and select it. From here, you can either right-click the folder and select **Create ➤ C Sharp Script**, or you can go to **Assets ➤ Create ➤ C Sharp Script** in the menu bar.

In either case, you will get a new script called "NewBehaviourScript". Rename this "RotateBarrel" and then double-click the script to edit it (or click on the edit button in the inspector).

Unity will nicely preload your new script with a few empty methods.

```
using UnityEngine;
using System.Collections;

public class NewBehaviourScript : MonoBehaviour {

        // Use this for initialization
        void Start () {

        }

        // Update is called once per frame
        void Update () {

        }
}
```

If you are not familiar with C Sharp, don't worry it is pretty easy, and you won't be doing anything particularly esoteric with it. It is a derivative of C, just like Obj-C so it should come fairly easy if you know any of the other C based languages.

The first thing you need to do for your script is rename the object to match the file name. You named your file "RotateBarrel", so the class name needs to be RotateBarrel. Change the NewBehaviorScript to be RotateBarrel. This is not a C# thing, but a Unity thing. Unity is going to precompile all of your scripts, and it needs to have the file names match the class names or it will not be able to make to proper links.

You can see from the class declaration that this object inherits from some object called MonoBehaviour. MonoBehaviour is required for any script you want to be able to attach to a game object. Not only that, but MonoBehaviour has lots of useful methods that you can override to implement custom functionality. Two of these are Start() and Update().

Start() is called before the first time the object is ever rendered. It is only ever called once for any object. It is a good place to put any initialization you may want. You don't really need to do anything in the Start() method, but you can add some code there just to show that it is doing something.

```
        void Start () {
                gameObject.transform.rotation = Quaternion.identity;
        }
```

Ultimately, this script will be attached as a component to a game object. If you want to get a handle to the gameObject you are attached to, you can call it via the gameObject instance variable. From there, you are calling the transform, and finally the rotation part of the transform. You are setting it to the quaternion identity.

A quaternion is a way of expressing an arbitrary orientation in space. The identity basically means that the object is at rotation 0,0,0. In the case of the barrel, that is upright if you haven't rotated your barrels, so they are probably still in the identity rotation orientation.

Overall, you are making sure that the barrel is upright before you start to rotate it.

```
// Update is called once per frame
void Update () {
        transform.Rotate(Vector3.right, 1.0f);
}
```

As the comment would imply, update is called every frame. Here you are grabbing a handle to the transform, and rotating it around the X axis (which is also known as Vector3.right) at one degree per frame.

Before you had to use: gameObject.transform to get a handle to the transform, but here you do not? Well, actually, you never really need to call gameObject to access the standard components like transform, collider, renderer etc. It is implied that you are referencing your gameObject when you call one of those components so you can reference it like I do in the Update() method.

Now you have finished your script, save it and go back into Unity.

If your scripts have any errors, then you will get compile errors right away once you go back to Unity (as long as you saved your script).

As you can see in Figure 7–11, the status bar will pop up a red X if you have compile errors. If you click the status bar once, then you will get the console window and it will have more detailed information. If you double-click, the error in the console window, or in the status bar, it will open your editor and send you to the offending line.

Assets/Scripts/RotateBarrel.cs(14,9): error CS1002: Expecting `;'

Figure 7–11. *The status bar at the bottom of the editor tells you if you have any errors.*

Once you have a working script with no errors, then you can attach the script to your barrel object. This is just like assigning a material, because you can simply drag the script from the project view onto the object in the hierarchy or in the scene view. Once attached, it will appear as a component of that object in the inspector, as shown in Figure 7–12.

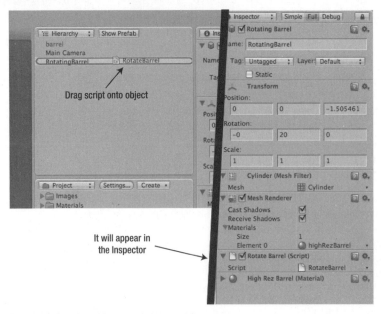

Figure 7–12. *Attaching a script to an object*

Playing Your Game

Now you should have some movement in your scene, but nothing is happening. This is because you are not playing the game.

In the lower-left corner of the editor is a play button, press that now. If all goes well, you should see your barrel in the scene view spinning, like in Figure 7–13. If all you see is a blue background, then you are probably looking at the Game View. You haven't set up the game view yet, so you may or may not see much happening in there.

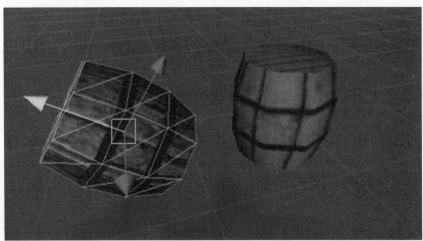

Figure 7–13. *You can see the effects of our RotateBarrel script in the rotating barrel.*

Let's make one more adjustment to your barrel spinning script.

```
public class RotateBarrel : MonoBehaviour {
        public float speed = 1.0f;
        .
        .
        // Update is called once per frame
        void Update () {
                transform.Rotate(Vector3.right, speed);
        }
        .
        .
        .
```

You are adding a public instance variable called speed to the top portion of the script, and then you are using speed in your rotate method instead of just hardcoding a value in there. Functionally, this is no different then what you just had, except now you can access the speed variable from within the editor.

If you go back into Unity and select your rotating barrel, then you will see your new variable exposed in the editor, like in Figure 7–14.

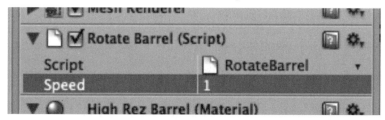

Figure 7–14. *Now you can change the speed of your barrel right from the editor.*

Next, hit play. Your barrel should be spinning just as before, but now you can go into the editor and change the speed value to 5 or 10 so the barrel will spin much faster. Find a nice rotating speed that is appealing to your sense of spinning barrels. I have chosen 3.2. Now click on the play button again to stop the game preview.

Wait! Your speed changed back to 1! This is because you changed it during a game preview. Since your game can be altered during play by any number of internal and external forces, any changes made to an object's state during game preview are not saved. If you find a value for the speed that you like using the live preview, then you have to stop the preview, set the speed, and save your scene. Otherwise, you will lose your changes.

In any case, the important thing to take away from this is that you can expose values from your scripts in the editor, so that you can change them easily and in real time during a game preview. This will speed up your game balancing and tweaking process hugely.

Coroutines Not Updates

I am going to take a minor tangent and talk about a very important topic in the world of Unity scripting: Coroutines. A coroutine is a scheduled method call that runs outside of the main game loop.

What does that mean? Every frame of the game, any object with an `Update()` method gets called to update itself. I hope you are running your game at a nice high frame rate, so you want to keep these updates to a minimum. Very often there are things in the scene that may be constantly updating, but are not so important that they need to update every frame.

For example, your rotating barrel is pretty fantastic, but it would probably be just fine rotating at about 10 fps, thus costing you one-sixth of the resources, if you are trying to run your game at 60fps.

How do you use these mystical coroutines?

Let's have a look at how the barrel script might look if you used coroutines:

```
void Start () {
        gameObject.transform.rotation = Quaternion.identity;
        StartCoroutine(this.periodicRotate());
}
 IEnumerator periodicRotate () {
        while (true) {
                transform.Rotate(Vector3.right, speed);
                yield return new WaitForSeconds (0.1f);
        }
}
```

This looks very similar to your current code. The few big things: in your `Start()` method, you call `StartCoroutine()` and pass it another method: `periodicRotate()`.

In the `periodicRotate()` method, you want to spin forever, and you have the exact same transform function call as before, but now you have this strange line:

```
        yield return new WaitForSeconds (0.1f);
```

This command may look a bit odd, but the upshot is that it will wait for however long you tell it to, and then come back to this method, right where it left off.

Practically speaking, it makes this a loop that runs about ten times a second. Of course, this will affect your rotation speed, but you can tweak that in the editor with your exposed variable to get it to look right again.

Coroutines are hugely important in iPhone development with Unity. On the desktop, where you generally have extra CPU to burn, you can get away with moving things every frame, even if they don't need it, but on the iPhone every CPU cycle is precious, so don't waste any. Use coroutines (and really you should be using them on the desktop as well, no need to waste cycles if you don't need to).

The Game View

The game is pretty lame so far. Even on the app store I don't think people will pay a dollar for this new app: "Two barrels, one spinning". But it does bring us to that other view down in the lower left that you haven't really used yet: the game view.

The game view is where you get to actually play your game. Once you hit the play button, unity loads up your scene as if you are the user and you can play the game right there in the editor. This is immensely useful, and makes for a nice quick testing turnaround when you are building your scenes.

You add an object, or tweak a script, and you can just hit play and see right away whether it looks right or behaves the way you think it should. You can even change inspector values, add objects, and generally do whatever you want while the game is playing and see your changes taking place in real time.

This brings us to the camera object. Up to this point, you have been interacting with the objects in the scene view. In the game view, you see the scene as the user would, and that means you are seeing it through the in-scene cameras.

In this case, youhave one camera called Main Camera. You can actually have as many cameras as you want in your scene, and they all will display at the same time to the game view. I will talk about this setup in the "Multiple Cameras" section later. For now, you can focus on just the one.

Depending on whether you have moved your camera from the default starting position or not, you will probably be looking at a mostly blue screen with some small barrels near the center. This is not exactly what you want to see in your barrel spinning app, so let's move the camera to a better spot.

Go to the scene view, and tumble, pan, and zoom your scene view until it looks something like the scene view in the top of Figure 7–15. (if you don't remember how to do this, see the section called The Scene View.) Then, select your Main Camera object in the hierarchy view and go to **GameObject ➤ Align With View** in the menubar. This should align your main camera with the scene view orientation, and your game view should resemble something like the lower portion of Figure 7–15.

This is a nice quick way to get the game camera lined up on something or get it close to what you want. You can also adjust the camera position and orientation right in the scene view, like any other object, or just type the values into the inspector if you know what they are. Most often, you will be scripting your cameras to follow the main character or similar behavior. You will be doing that in a few pages.

First, you need to fix the darkness issue in your game view and that requires lights.

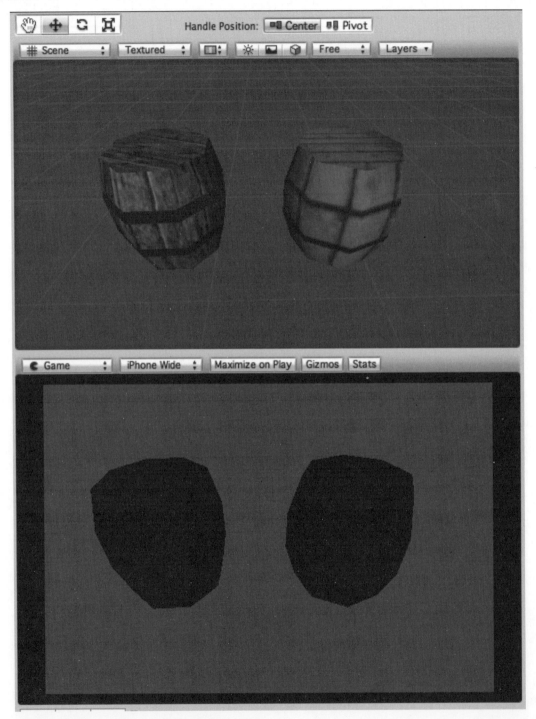

Figure 7–15. *Aligning the camera with the Scene view*

Adding Lights

Currently, in the lower portion of Figure 7–15, you are looking at your two barrels and they are being illuminated with the default ambient lighting. In terms of performance, ambient is the cheapest lighting and if your game can get away with it, I would suggest using the ambient as your major source of light.

If you go to **Edit ➤ Render Settings** in the menu bar, then the render settings will appear in the inspector (see Figure 7–15). You want to change the ambient light to something nice and bright, like white. This will mean that your objects will be fully lit all the time from any angle. This looks great, but for now let's pick a nice 50% gray. This way you can add some light to the scene and actually see it.

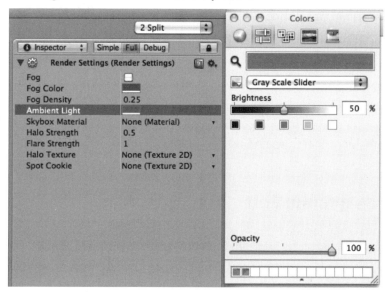

Figure 7–16. *Changing the ambient light setting*

The three types of lights are described in the following, but you can see them in Figure 7–17.

- *Point light*: This is the equivalent of a bare lightbulb. It radiates light in all directions for a certain range.

- *Spot light*: This is the equivalent of a flashlight or searchlight. It radiates light out in a cone from the source.

- *Directional light*: This is roughly equivalent to sunlight. Whatever direction the light is coming from, it will hit all faces from that same direction. The position of the directional light does not matter, only the orientation.

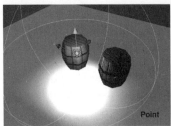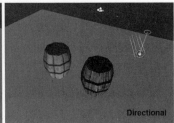

Figure 7–17. *Three types of lights: Point, Spot, and Directional*

It is important to remember that for every light you add, Unity has to do an extra draw call for any objects that are hit by that light. By adding a single directional light, you effectively double your draw time. Be sparing with your light sources on the iPhone.

Let's add a point light. **GameObject ➤ Create Other ➤ Point Light.** This will add a new light to your barrel scene. Grab the light in the scene editor and move it around so as to get a feel for how the light affects the rendering. Again, it may need to be moved to 0,0,0 to get it close to your barrels. Once you have it near your barrels, adjust the range and attenuation settings in the inspector to play around with it.

You have nearly seen enough of the Unity interface to start looking at a more realistic game situation. There is one more thing you should have a look at briefly: the Unity Remote.

Using the iPhone as a Game Pad

One of the best things about Unity for the iPhone is the ability to preview your game on the device instantly. This is done using an application called the Unity Remote. If you have Unity for the iPhone, one of the things that comes with it is an Xcode project called Unity Remote. You build this project with your own certificates and install it on your device. Then, whenever you have Unity running and a WiFi network going, you can run Unity Remote and use your iPhone as a gamepad to control the Unity editor.

Unity Remote streams a low-quality compressed version of the game video to your device as well as catching all the touch inputs and accelerometer data. This sends that all back to the editor so you can get a feel for how your game will play on the actual device. This also allows you to build and test your game very quickly because you don't have to constantly build and deploy to your device to check to see if the touch points are working or if that one model looks too big.

Installing Unity Remote is more about doing an Xcode build than anything else, and I am presuming that if you are reading this book, then you already know how to do that, so I won't waste lots of page space going into that. If you are feeling particularly lazy, you can also download Unity Remote off of the App Store, because it is a free app. Overall, you should have Unity Remote up and running for the next parts of the chapter dealing with the more iPhone specific inputs.

Your Game

You have seen a brief glimpse of the Unity pipeline, built a few objects, and wrote a script. Now you are going to combine all of those things into an actual game scene as well as explore a few new topics, like animations.

Before you can get started in Unity, you need a game design. This is usually the most important step of any game development project. I realize that you are not really making a game, but a game-like environment. I also realize that this game is designed less to be a fun game and more to be able to highlight the various things I want to show you about Unity. That said, the game design is the foundation that you build your game from, so without a good foundation, you cannot have a good game.

I have always been partial to dungeon crawlers, so I think you should have a dungeon-crawler sort of game. You are going to be on the iPhone, so your control interface should be as simple as possible. You don't want to have giant faux-joysticks in either corner forcing you to cover 50% of the screen with your thumbs the entire time, so you should implement some tap-to-move sort of interface.

A third person isometric sort of setup would work well for this. You can have the simple tap interface to move the character and tap on an object to interact with it, whether to open a chest or to attack a foe. This keeps your interface nice and simple.

This also means you need a main character, some environment elements that you can interact with, and maybe some enemies.

You are doing an isometric view game where you tap the scene and the character moves to that position, so you need some touch input controlling mechanism to handle those taps. You will also want objects that you can attack, some that you can interact with, and some that you can pick up.

Admittedly, this is a pretty lame game design, but it should give you plenty of topics for the rest of the chapter. Your final game won't really be a game so much as a collection of game-like interactions, but it will give you a good idea how to handle the more complicated object interactions needed for good gameplay.

So, open up a new scene in your sample project and you can get started.

Adding a Base to Work From

The first thing you are going to need is some terrain on which your game will take place. In this case, it will be a simple dungeon floor.

A floor gives you the opportunity to use one of Unity's primitives. In your new scene, go to **GameObject ➤ Create Other ➤ Plane** in the menu. This will put a nice plane down somewhere in your scene. Make sure that it is at position 0,0,0, and name it something nice. I called it "Floor".

It might look a bit dark in your game view. This is because the ambient light settings are per-scene. Therefore, you will need to go back in and set the ambient light to a 50% gray.

It is also a bit small. A primitive plane is 10 units square at a scale of one. It is usually helpful to keep the units in your game to match something simple, like one unit is one foot. With this in mind, your character model will be about 6 feet tall, so you will make this starting area 50 square feet. Change the plane scale to 5,5,5 (the y scale doesn't really do anything, it's beneficial to keep these things consistent).

Next, you must set the camera angle. You want an isometric feel to your game, but I don't think that you want a real isometric rendering, so you will keep the default camera perspective, but lock the angle.

Select your camera and set the position to: –12,15, –12, and then set the rotation to be 30,45,0. This gives you an isometric viewpoint.

To finish off the floor, you should add a texture to it. Gray is pretty boring. In the Images folder, in the project view, there is an image called "floorTile". If you just drag that image onto the plane, a material will be automatically created and applied to the plane.

Now your scene should look something like Figure 7–18.

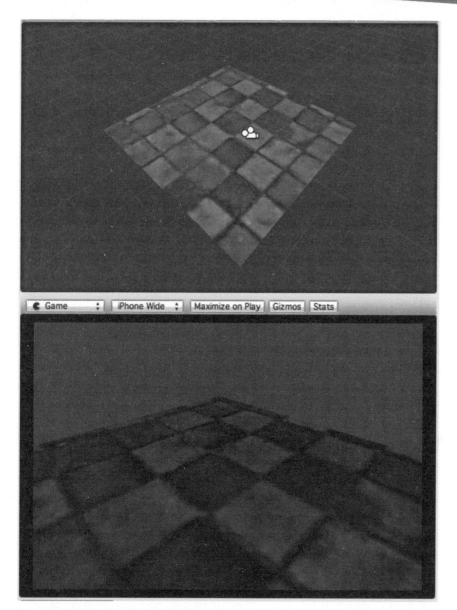

Figure 7–18. *The floor of your dungeon*

Currently, your floor is meant to be 50 feet square, in which case those tiles are nearly 8 feet across. It would be better if you could repeat the tile texture across the floor.

If you select the floor object, in the inspector you will see the material component. There is a small button there labeled "placement". If you click that then you will get the texture placement options. Set the tiling to 5 for both x and y, like in the bottom of Figure 7–19.

Figure 7–19. *Setting your X and Y tiling multipliers so that you can have many more tiles on your floor*

Now your floor is beginning to look more like a floor.

The Main Character

You now have a floor, so you need a character to wander around on your floor. The creation of the main character in your game needs to have some control mechanism, whether a warrior maiden who wields a mean broadsword or a snowball that rolls around.

Enter the CharacterController component. The CharacterController component is a specially made kind of collider that has some special methods that allow for easy control. There is nothing stopping you from taking your barrel, modifying the rotate script to look for touch inputs or acceleration, and making that the main character. By using a CharacterController component, you have much finer control over the object's movements.

Let's go ahead and add a CharacterController to your scene. First, you need an empty GameObject, so: **GameObject ➤ Create Empty.** Make sure that your new game object is at 0,0,0 position and name it something clever like "Character".

Next, make sure that your new Character object is selected, so go to **Component ➤ Physics ➤ Character Controller.**

You are going to use the character controller in its most basic capacity to motivate your character model around the scene and to provide simple collision detection. If this were a high-paced action-shooter, then you might also use the character controller to handle more complicated collision dynamics like platforming and keeping the player from walking up too steep of a slope. For today, you will keep it simple.

Because of this, you need to adjust your CharacterController collider capsule to be slightly above the ground you just made. Select the character and in the CharacterController component, set the height to 5, the radius to 1.1, and the center Y value to 3. It should look something like Figure 7–20.

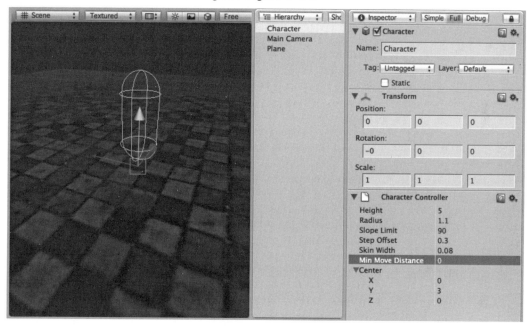

Figure 7–20. *Your new character controller looks like a big pill. This is the collider that will contain your character model.*

What have you really done here? Well, by moving the capsule center up by 3 and making the capsule height 5, your capsule is actually hovering just off the ground.

This will be handy later when you start to add colliders to the scene. For now, what you really need is a character model. You actually have a great animated warrior model that you are going to add into the scene, but that involves a complex discussion of character animation. I just want to talk about moving around the floor for now, so you will just add a placeholder model.

Go to **GameObject ➤ Create Other ➤ Cube.** Name it something like "Faux Character" and set the position to 0,3,0 and the scale to 2,6,2. This new cube primitive also has a box collider attached to it. You are going to be using this as your character stand in model. Your CharacterController already has a collider so you don't need the box collider. Select the new faux character. To the right of the collider component in the inspector is a small gear-menu, click that and select Remove Component (you can also just right-click the component name to get the same menu). This will remove the box collider from your cube.

Now, you should have a 6 foot square pillar sitting on your floor. Next, make the character controller object the parent of your new character model. This is done simply by dragging the faux character onto the character controller object in the hierarchy view. Much like adding a document to a folder in the Finder, your scene should now look like Figure 7–21.

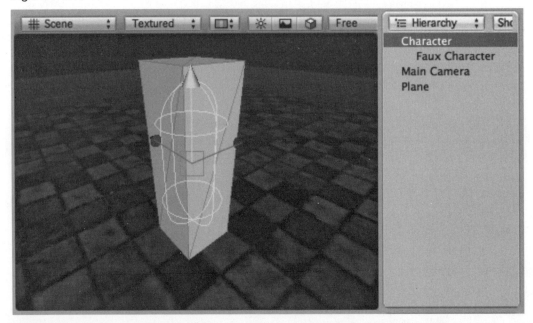

Figure 7–21. *Your CharacterController object is now the proud parent of a Faux Character model.*

What does it mean to be the child of another object? Wherever the parent moves, the child moves, if the parent is rotated then the child is rotated and so on. In mathematical terms, the child transforms are multiplied by the parent transforms. In practical terms, it means that if you attach a script to move the character controller around then you character model will follow.

Before you get into the code, you should attach the script to your character. Remember way back in the early part of the chapter when you attached a rotation script to your barrel? You are going to do the same thing here. Grab the BBCharacterController script and drag it from the Scripts folder up onto the Character object (the parent, not the faux character). That is it, now you should see the BBCharacterController script in the inspector right under the CharacterController component.

Now double-click the BBCharacterController script in the Scripts folder. Let's look at the code.

```
public class BBCharacterController : MonoBehaviour {
        public float moveSpeed = 7.0f;
        public float attackRange = 3.0f;
```

```
public int attackDamage = 5;

public GameObject cursor;
public GameObject characterModel;

private Vector3 movementDestination;
private CharacterController controller;
```

First, you have a whole handful of public and private instance variables. At the top, you have some `floats` and an `int`. You have seen this kind of thing before in the rotating barrel example, and it allows you to change your character's attributes from the editor (or from other scripts). Next, you see some interesting public `GameObject` declarations.

You can expose pretty much any kind of variable. In this case, you are saying that you want to be able to attach another game object to this script. Don't worry too much about that, I will discuss it in detail within the "Animations" section.

Next, you have some private variables. These are things that you don't want to expose to the interface either because changing them during play would cause badness to happen, or because I just don't need them to be cluttering up the editor interface.

Next up is your final instance variable and your first method.

```
private static BBCharacterController sharedInstance = null;

public static BBCharacterController instance {
    get {
        if (sharedInstance == null) {
            sharedInstance = FindObjectOfType(typeof (BBCharacterController)) as
BBCharacterController;
            if (sharedInstance == null)
                Debug.Log ("Can't find a BBCharacterController. You must have an
object with a BBCharacterController attached to it.");
        }
        return sharedInstance;
    }
}
```

You are doing some mildly esoteric C# magic here, but it is not too bad. This is a static accessor method, which implements the Singleton design pattern. This will allow other objects to easily get a handle to the character controller script. This works when another object calls this method, like so:

`BBCharacterController theController = BBCharacterController.instance;`

If it does not already have a static reference to the controller, it will use the `FindObjectOfType()` method to look through all the objects in the scene until it finds an object that is of type `BBCharacterController`. Then, it returns it.

The next time this method is called, the static reference will not be null, and it will return immediately a reference to the controller object. This ensures that anyone who calls this method will get the same controller back. This will come in very handy later on when your touch manager object needs to tell the character to go somewhere.

Now you begin the Start() method. Recall that this gets called once, right before the object is rendered for the first time.

```
void Start ()
{
        movementDestination = transform.position;
        controller =
(CharacterController)gameObject.GetComponent(typeof(CharacterController));
        if (characterModel != null) {
                characterModel.animation.wrapMode = WrapMode.Loop;
                characterModel.animation["Attack"].wrapMode = WrapMode.Once;
                characterModel.animation["Attack"].layer = 1;
        }
}
```

Here you are initializing two of your private variables. The movementDestination is where you want your character to move to, so you want it to be initially set to your current position. Next, you are caching a reference to the CharacterController component. You are going to be using the CharacterController component quite a bit, even in your tight loops like Update() which gets called every frame. GetComponent() is not a particularly slow method, but it is not very fast either. If you are going to be calling something every frame, you want it to be as fast as possible, so that is why you are making a local reference to the CharacterController component. This way you can have much faster access to the character controller.

That last bit about the characterModel is basically initializing your animations, which you don't have yet. You just have a big gray block, so I will cover those later in the "Animations" section.

```
void Update () {
        Vector3 moveDirection = movementDestination - gameObject.transform.position;
        moveDirection.y = 0.0f;

        if (moveDirection.sqrMagnitude > 0.5) {
                controller.Move(moveDirection.normalized * Time.deltaTime * moveSpeed);
                if (characterModel != null) characterModel.animation.CrossFade ("Walk");
        } else {
                if (characterModel != null) characterModel.animation.CrossFade ("Idle");
        }
}
```

Now, you have your main method, the Update(). I will say this a few more times probably, but remember that the update is called every frame, so anything you put in an update method should be fast, fast, fast.

Here you are making a new vector that points to where you want to be moving. You are going to keep all of your movements in the y=0 plane, so you will just set your movementDirection.y = 0 just in case. You don't want your character flying off the floor or burrowing into the ground accidentally.

Next, you are checking the square magnitude of the movement vector. This will tell you whether you are actually moving or not. You use the square magnitude instead of the actual magnitude because it is a much faster operation. If you are moving, then you call the Move() method on the character controller.

The Move() method is one of those special methods that is only available on a character controller component. It is actually doing some complex stuff, but the upshot for is that it will handle collisions automatically. It is not like you are just setting the position to the next incremental move value, by using Move() on a CharacterController component you are telling Unity to be clever and check way ahead to see if you are going to collide with anything, or if the terrain goes up or down, and a whole slew of other things. This is one of the main reasons to use a CharacterController component instead of rolling your own control scripts.

Note that in the Move() call you are doing some data wrangling:

```
moveDirection.normalized * Time.deltaTime * moveSpeed
```

Move takes a Vector3 as the parameter, and you are using your moveDirection vector as the basis for that parameter. This makes sense because you want to get to your destination point. But you don't want to teleport there instantly; you want to move at some regulated speed. Therefore, you are normalizing the vector first, which reduces it to a new vector that points in the same direction, but has length of 1. This way you can now multiply it by a few scalers and make a new, probably much shorter movement vector. Time.deltaTime is the amount of time that has passed since the last frame. You don't know how many fps your game will be running at, so this allows you to move at a constant rate no matter how fast or slow the actual device is working. Finally, you multiply by your moveSpeed. This is how many units your character will cover in one second.

So, to sum up: You are reducing the movement vector to a unit vector so you can use it just for its directional attribute. Next, you are scaling that vector so that it is the length of a single frame's worth of movement at your move speed. Finally, you call Move(). Practically speaking, when some other script tells the character to move to some other point, the character will smoothly move there.

After your move, you are calling some animation methods. I will go into this in the "Animations" section later, but you probably managed to figure out that when you are moving, you want to be playing the walking animation. When you are not moving, you want to be playing the idle animation. That is what those lines do for you.

You have this variable movementDestination, which is where you want to move to. In order for you to move anywhere, you need to let other scripts be able to set this for you. You could just make it public, but you want it to have a few side effects, so you will instead make a public method.

```
public void moveTowards(Vector3 position)
{
        position.y = 0.0f;
        movementDestination = position;
        transform.LookAt(position);
        position.y = 0.1f;
        if (cursor != null) cursor.transform.position = position;
}
```

This is a pretty simple method because you are limiting your movement to the y=0 plane. Therefore, first filter the input to make sure no other scripts are trying to make the character leave the floor. Next, set your `movementDestination` to this new position. You could stop right there and your character would diligently move toward this new position during the next `Update()` loop. However, you want to have a few other things happen as well.

```
transform.LookAt(position);
```

This will take your orientation and spin it so that it is facing your destination. This doesn't matter so much when you just have a block, but when you get your actual character model attached, it will be fairly important.

Next, take your position and move it up very slightly and move your cursor object so that it is just off the floor at your destination.

You haven't made a cursor object yet, but you will do that after you figure out the touch handling. What you want to happen is that there is some indication of where you are moving to, so you will have some object that indicates your target position.

```
void OnControllerColliderHit (ControllerColliderHit hit)
{
        movementDestination = gameObject.transform.position;
        movementDestination.y = 0.0f;
        if (cursor != null) {
                Vector3 cursorPosition = movementDestination;
                cursorPosition.y = 0.1f;
                cursor.transform.position = cursorPosition;
        }
}
```

`OnControllerColliderHit()` is another one of the handy things that you get by being attached to an object that has a `CharacterController` component. Basically, when you are calling the `Move()` method in your update loop, if your capsule collider bumps into any other collider, then this method will be called.

What you are doing here is pretty simple. If you bump into anything, you stop trying to move, and you set your cursor so that it is right under you. This way if you try to walk though a wall, then when you bump into the wall, your destination will change to right where you are and your cursor will also jump there as well, showing the user that you are not going to be trying to walk through the wall.

This would be the point where you could add in some kind of path-finding algorithm, so that your character would walk around the wall, but for your game you will make the user be your pathfinder.

You have a character that should move when you tell it to, but now you need some way to tell it to move. This brings you to input handling.

Inputs and Colliders

So far you have a floor and you have a character. You need to implement a touch system so that you can tell your character where to move to on this floor. In order for your touch system to work, you will need some colliders in the scene that you can touch. Now you can just put invisible colliders into the scene. However, that is not very good, so you want to make the floor so that you can attach a collider to it and build a touch system to interact with it. Overall, your floor needs a collider, which is an excellent segue into a discussion about colliders.

What is a collider? When working with objects in a 3D space, figuring out if one object is hitting another object becomes a very complicated problem. Luckily, you don't have to care very much about that because Unity handles all the tedious math and complicated space segmenting issues for you. All you need to know are the relative costs of each kind of collider and when to use them.

There are four basic collider types: Sphere, Capsule, Box, and Mesh. Figure 7–22 shows the first three.

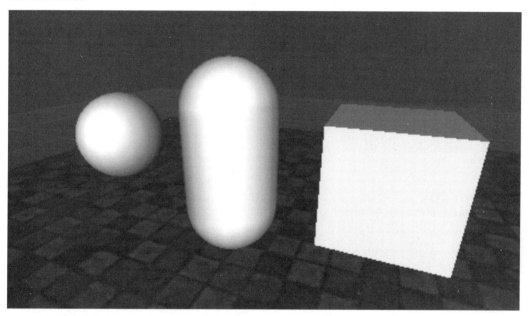

Figure 7–22. *The three primitive collider shapes and also three primitive solid objects that you can make in Unity.*

A sphere collider is just what it sounds like. It is a sphere that extends a certain radius around a central point. Sphere colliders are the least expensive type of collider in terms of processing. If you can get away with just using a sphere collider, it will always help performance.

The next best thing is a capsule collider. This looks like a cylinder with round ends. A capsule collider has a length and a radius. It extends by the radius amount out from a line segment.

After that, a box collider has simply six sides. it doesn't have to be square.

Finally, there is mesh collider. This is a collider that will be the exact shape of whatever mesh you assign it to. These kinds of colliders are very useful if you have some complex geometry and you must have proper collisions where a simpler collider just won't do.

However, beware of the mesh collider: your performance will suffer if you use too many of these.

Generally, it is best to pick a primitive collider that closely matches your object in shape. If you have complicated geometry, it is almost always better to use a few different collider primitives than to use a mesh collider.

You want to add a box collider to the floor. However, astute readers will have noticed that the plane already has a mesh collider. As discussed, mesh colliders are expensive, and you don't really need a mesh collider when a box collider would do fine, so you are going to replace the mesh collider with a box collider. Select the floor object in the hierarchy, then go to **Component ➤ Physics ➤ Box Collider**, and say OK to replace the existing collider.

Now you have a floor and it has a collider, so what now? Let's write some code.

Go to your Scripts folder in the project view and find a script called BBTouchInputController. This will be the script that handles all the touch inputs and distributes them to any objects that might be looking for touches.

```
void Update () {
    if (Input.GetMouseButton(0)) {
        // show the crosshairs
        Vector2 touch = new Vector2(Input.mousePosition.x, Input.mousePosition.y);
        this.handleTouchAtPoint(touch);
    }
}
```

This is your Update() method. It is pretty simple really. Essentially, once every frame you check to see if there has been a mouse button pressed, and if so, you deal with it. Wait a minute; this is a touch input device, so there is no mouse. This makes no sense!

Unity does provide you with a whole slew of iPhone based input mechanisms. If you need to access more than one touch at a time, then you will want to use the iPhoneInput class to access the touches.

However, Unity remaps some of the iPhone specific inputs to the Unity desktop inputs. For example, GetMouseButton(0) usually refers to a mouse left click. On the iPhone, it refers to the first touch to hit the screen. This is handy for many reasons; when testing in the editor, you don't always have a device handy or attached. By using the mouse button mapping, both mouse clicks and screen taps work fine. Also, if you plan to port your game to a web preview or reuse your code for another game on a different platform, this increases the portability. I always use the remapped inputs unless it is absolutely necessary to use the iPhoneInput class.

You have your update method and it is checking for inputs. Therefore, it grabs the input point and converts it to a Vector2, which is just x,y with no z. Then, you send it off to the next method: handleTouchAtPoint().

```
public void handleTouchAtPoint(Vector2 touchPoint) {
        RaycastHit hit = new RaycastHit();
        if (Physics.Raycast(Camera.main.ScreenPointToRay(touchPoint),out hit,
Mathf.Infinity)) {
```

```
          BBTouchable touchableObject =
(BBTouchable)hit.transform.gameObject.GetComponent(typeof(BBTouchable));
          if (touchableObject != null) touchableObject.handleTouch(hit.point);
     }
}
```

Here you are doing some physics magic, but again Unity does all the heavy lifting for you. Therefore, you are taking the point on the screen that was touched and converting it into a ray. A ray is basically just a line going from the point on the screen straight out into the scene. The `Physics.Raycast()` method returns true if any colliders are hit by the ray, and the first one to be hit is put into the hit object.

It is important to note that you are calling `ScreenPointToRay()` on `Camera.main`. What is this? `Camera.main` is a convenience reference to whatever camera is tagged as the main camera. In this case, it will be the only camera in the scene. Later on when you have more cameras, you will have to change this code slightly.

When the `Physics.Raycast()` hits something, you get a hit object back. Therefore, you need to figure out if it is something that can respond to a touch command. To do this, you need to access the base game object that the hit is referring to, and then ask that base game object if it has a specific class of component attached to it. Calling `hit.transform.gameObject` gives you a handle to the gameObject that your raycast hit. You then call the `GetComponent()` method which returns the first component of the specified type that is attached to that object.

Remember when you attached the `RotateBarrel` script to your barrel in the first half of the chapter? What you were doing was actually attaching a component of type `RotateBarrel` to that object.

In this case, you are looking for objects that have a script attached to them of type `BBTouchable`. You will look at that script next. Using `GetComponent()` is how you go back in and programmatically get a handle to that script.

In the next line, you check to make sure that the script handle you got back is not null. If it is null, then the object you hit had a collider, but did not have a BBTouchable component attached, so you will ignore it.

Now you have this script, and it needs a place to live in your scene. Go to **GameObject ➤ Create Empty** in the menu. Rename this new object: InputManager and attach your BBTouchInputController script to it.

Your scene now has an input manager. You have nothing that is touchable, but you have an input manager.

At the start of this section, I mentioned attaching a collider to your floor, and then I got off on a tangent about the Input Manager. Now your floor has a collider, and you have an object that is monitoring the inputs, ready to send them to any object that has a BBTouchable script attached. You will want to find the BBTouchable script and attach it to your floor. Now your floor is touchable.

Let's open up the BBTouchable script and see what is happening here.

```
public class BBTouchable : MonoBehaviour {
```

```
        public virtual void handleTouch(Vector3 worldPoint) {
                BBCharacterController.instance.moveTowards(worldPoint);
        }
}
```

Wow, really not a whole lot going on. You get called by the touch manager with the world point of where you were touched, and you basically just pass it right on to the character controller. Why didn't you just have the input manager call the character controller directly?

Have a close look at the function declaration, especially the word: virtual. This is a bit of C# jargon that you don't have to worry about in ObjC, but it does mean that you can have objects inherit from this object and be able to override this method. You are going to have a few different objects that behave in slightly different ways when touched, so this is the basis for those classes.

By decoupling the actual processing of the touches from the touch input manager, you have created a very flexible touch input system.

Now for the exciting moment! Hit the play button and tap or click somewhere on the floor. Be sure you are clicking in the game view and not the scene view. Your big gray block should slide back and forth across the floor to wherever you clicked.

If it is not working, have a look at the console and see if you can figure out what the problem is. Make sure that you have a BBTouchInputController script attached to a Game Object in your scene. Also, be sure the floor has a collider and a BBTouchable script attached to it. Finally, make sure that your character controller has a BBCharacterController script attached (note: the parent object, not the faux character model).

Your First Design Iteration

So far, so good. You have a character model (a big block) and it is wandering around the floor (well, sliding around the floor). However, you may have noticed a few problems.

First, try to move to a space that is directly behind the character model. In other words, tap right on the model itself. You should be moving to a position behind, but it does not move. Why is that?

The CharacterController is a collider, so when your touch input manager does its raycast, it is hitting that collider before it is hitting the floor collider behind. Since the character collider is not a touchable collider, it is ignored, so you don't move.

You want the character collider to collide with stuff in your scene, but not your raycasts. This is actually a very common problem; so common, in fact, there is a very quick and easy fix.

Select your Character Controller (the parent, not the model) and have a look at the inspector. At the top, under the object name are a few drop-down menus, one called Tag and one called Layer. Tags and Layers are convenience attributes that allow you to find objects quicker and filter objects easily. You are concerned mostly with the Layer for now. All the objects you have made so far are in the Default layer. This means they are visible to just about anything that is looking for objects, and this includes the Raycast method. You can add your own layers and use them to hide objects from cameras or exclude them from various operations.

As mentioned, the raycast issue is so common that Unity already has a built-in layer called Ignore Raycasts just for this. Set your Character controller into the "Ignore Raycasts" layer. You will get a popup asking if you want to change the children too. Since the faux character does not have a collider, it doesn't really matter either way, but I like to keep things consistent so I changed all the children as well.

Now try to play the game again, you should be able to tap just behind the model and have it move directly away from the camera.

Speaking of the camera, right now you can move all over the floor that you can see, but you can't go any further. This may be great for some games, but this is a dungeon explorer game, so you want to be able to explore. This means that you want the camera to move with your player.

For this, you need a new script. Have a look at the BBSimpleFollower script.

```
public class BBSimpleFollower : MonoBehaviour {
        public GameObject target;
        private Vector3 offset;

        void Start() {
                offset = transform.position - target.transform.position;
        }

        // Update is called once per frame
        void Update () {
                transform.position = Vector3.Lerp(transform.position,
target.transform.position + offset,0.1f);
        }
}
```

True to its name, it is a very simple script. You have a few instance variables. One is a GameObject that is your target, the object you want to follow. The other is a private variable which will be the offset vector that you will use to determine your position in relation to the target.

Your Start() method defines your offset by measuring the current relationship between your object and the target. In the update, all you do is set yourself so that you are at that constant distance from the target.

You are doing something a bit funky here, though. What is a Lerp?

Lerp is a shorthand way of saying Linear Interpolation. Linear interpolation is the process by which you find a point that is some percentage of the way between two known points. In this case, your points are where you are now and where you want to be. You are finding the point that is 10% of the way between those two points and using that point to set your position.

What is this doing? This is a simple and easy way to make your camera movement a bit smoother. When the character is moving, your camera will be lagging behind by a bit, and then when the character stops, you will smoothly catch up.

In fact, this is a perfect opportunity to try to add your own public variable to this script. Change that 0 to a public variable so you can change it in the editor to see the effects. Remember that the lerp value should generally be between 0 and 1. Zero being never moving and 1 being never lagging.

If you attach this script to your main camera and look in the inspector, you see that your Target variable value is "None". You need to attach a target. This will be your Character Controller. Drag the character controller object from the hierarchy menu then down into the target slot in the editor for your simple follower script. Alternatively, you can use the drop-down menu to the right of the target field and select the Character out of the scene portion of the drop down.

Now press play and move around the scene. The camera will follow you at a slight lag, but you can now explore the entire floor.

Adding More Touchable Objects

As much fun as moving a block around a floor is, you would most likely love to have a few more interesting things in your scene. Remember your barrel from the first part of the chapter? Let's add one of those.

Find the barrel model in the Models folder and drag it into the hierarchy view. You will get a tiny barrel in your scene. It may be right under your character, so go ahead and move it out where you can see it.

It is very small. Currently, the barrel is only 1 foot high. Let's change the scale so that the barrel is 3,3,3. This will make it proportional to your 6 foot tall character block. You will also have to move it up, so that it looks like it is sitting on the floor (see Figure 7–23).

Now if you hit play and walk around, you will see that you can walk right through the barrel. Not exactly what you want. Your barrel needs a collider. As you saw earlier, there are lots of options for colliders, but you always want to use the cheapest one. Your barrel is pill shaped, so you should go for the capsule collider. Select the barrel and go to **Component ➤ Physics ➤ Capsule Collider** to add your collider. This will possibly cause a popup notice warning you that you are losing your prefab. This is fine for now, but I will talk more about prefabs in the next section.

The default collider size is a bit small, so let's make it a bit taller set the collider height to 1.5. That will work well. Now if you hit play, you will bump into the barrel and stop.

One barrel is pretty great, but more barrels would be even greater.

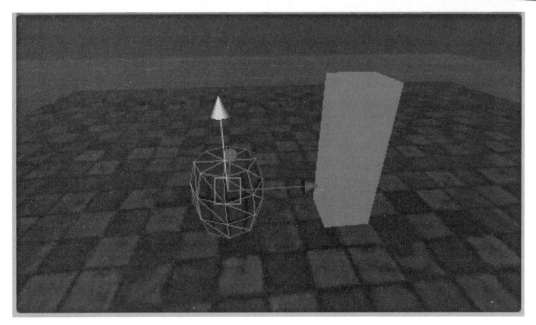

Figure 7–23. *Your barrel is back again.*

Prefabs

This brings us to the wonderful topic of prefabs. Prefabs are, as you might suspect, pre-fabricated objects. This is a wonderful feature that Unity provides to make your scene building go very quickly. I am going to show you just how easy prefabs can be.

There is a folder called Prefabs in the project view. It has some prefabs already, but you want to make a new one. Just like making a new material, you can right-click or go to the **Assets ➤ Create** menu and select **Prefab**. This will make a new prefab, and it will be colored gray. This means that it is empty. You need to put something in it, why not your new barrel with attached collider? Drag the barrel from the hierarchy view down on top of the new prefab. It will change to blue, meaning that it now has something in it. Rename this something like "barrelWithCollider".

That is it, you have made a prefab. Yes, it is that easy. Now you can drag that barrel prefab from the prefabs folder into your scene, and you will get a new copy of that object. You can drag it in a few times if you want to make more than one barrel. You can close this scene, open another new scene, and drag your barrel prefab into that scene. Prefabs are easy to make and easy to use because they multiply your productivity. You should be using prefabs for any object in your game that appears more than once. You will see a bit more about the power of the prefab when you want to change your barrel.

Animations

Animations are not particularly difficult to deal with in Unity, but the subject of animations covers a very broad spectrum of functionality. You are going to just dip your toes into the lake of possibilities that are animations.

What is an animation exactly? Technically speaking, your rotating barrel could be considered an animation. However, in the context of Unity, and game development in general, usually animations refer to prebuilt sequences of movements and transformations, usually made in some external 3D editor like Maya or Cheetah3d.

If you are not familiar with making animations in a 3D editor, then some of this won't make much sense to you, but that is OK. As a programmer, you will hopefully have artists who make your animations for you. As long as you understand the parts where you have to play the animations back, you will be fine.

Making animations for a game engine is a bit different than making them for a video sequence, or for whatever other reason you may want to make an animation. For an animation to be useful in Unity, it generally needs to have multiple stages. For example, if you want to make an animation of a treasure chest opening then you would need some number of frames that would be the "closed" animation. Probably a closed chest is not doing too much, so it could be a very short animation. Then, you would need some more frames that animate the chest opening, and some more to animate it closing, if needed.

These animations are generally built into the same file in your 3D modeling program. In your treasure chest example, you might have frames 1–10 be the "idle" animation where the chest just sits there. Then, you might make frames 11–45 be the frames where the chest opens up, and then frames 46–60 might be the frames where the lid closes.

This is the simplest kind of animation. You can also have rigged characters, but the premise is the same. Frames 1–100 might be an idle animation, where the character taps her feet or something. Frames 101–200 might be a walk cycle that you can loop over and over again to simulate walking, and frames 201–300 might be an attack with a sword, frames 301–350 might be an attack with a bow, and so on.

How you go about making these animations depends on your choice of 3D modeler and what it is you are animating. I am not going to go into the specifics of how you would go about making an animation in a 3D modeler; instead, you will work with one that I had made for this chapter.

Adam Taylor is an animator and character rigger here in Melbourne where I am based, and he very generously donated some of his time to rig and animate a warrior maiden character for you to use in our sample game. Here she is in Figure 7–24.

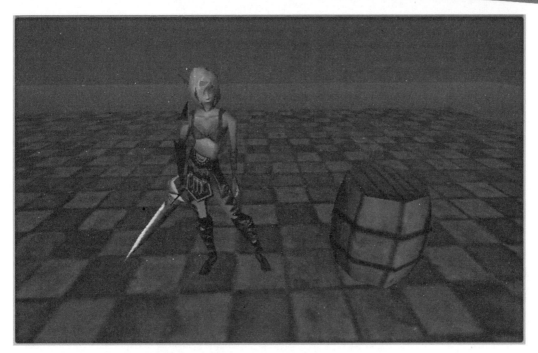

Figure 7–24. *Your leading lady, thanks to Melbourne, AU animator Adam Taylor* (http://www.adamtaylorfolio.com).

Animation Import Settings

The leading lady can be found in the Warrior folder, in a file called "warrior fbx animations". Before you drag her out to be part of your scene, you need to have a look at the import settings. Select the "warrior fbx animations" file and at the top of the project view is a button labeled: 'Settings', hit that and you will get a new window that will look like Figure 7–25. (This is one place where the newer desktop version of Unity looks quite a bit different. If you are following along with the desktop version, then you will see most of the same options, but in the inspector.)

If you were importing a new animation, then it would look the same, only there would be no clips at the bottom, you would need to add those.

Remember how I talked about each set of frames being a different animation state? This is how your warrior model is set up. Frames 1 to 141 is the "Idle" animation. This is a looping animation that shows your character shrugging a bit and looking around. Next is the Walk cycle between frames 142 and 173. This is a single step, meant to be looped when walking. Finally, you have an Attack animation that is of the warrior swinging her gigantic sword.

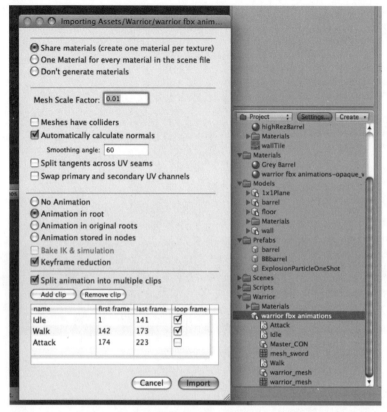

Figure 7–25. *The animation import settings for your warrior model*

You are very close to having a working, walking model. Close the settings window. Find the Faux Character model and delete it from the scene using z-Delete. Be sure to delete just the Faux Character and not the parent Character controller. Now drag the "warrior fbx animations" file out into the scene.

Yikes, she is tiny! When you first bring her in, she is about ten times too small (see Figure 7–26).

This is a common issue and is easily fixed. Delete the warrior from your scene, and go back to the import settings. There is a setting called Mesh Scale Factor. Change that to 0.1 (instead of 0.01) and re-import. Now drag a new warrior into the scene, and she should be the right size.

Now double-check that your warrior model is at position 0,0,0 and that the CharacterController is also at 0,0,0. Then, in the Hierarchy view, drag the warrior model onto the character controller, so the warrior is a child to the Character Controller, just like your Faux Character block. You should have a hierarchy like Figure 7–27. Notice how the capsule collider lines up with the character model. If your collider and character do not line up properly, move the warrior model back out of the Character parent, and make sure everything is at 0,0,0 and try again.

Figure 7-26. *It is like Alice in Wonderland. Your model scales are off. Back to the settings window!*

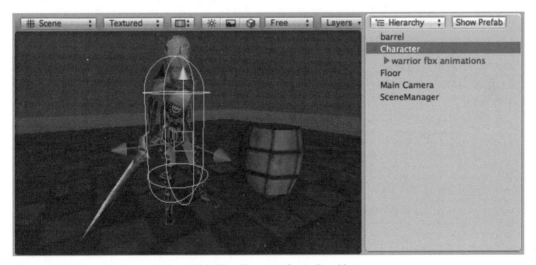

Figure 7-27. *Your warrior model is a child of the Character Controller object.*

Recall your Character Controller script had some exposed GameObject variables and one of those was the character model. Therefore, select the Character Controller object and in the inspector, find the BBCharacterController component. Now drag the warrior model from the hierarchy view down into the character model slot. It should look something like Figure 7-28.

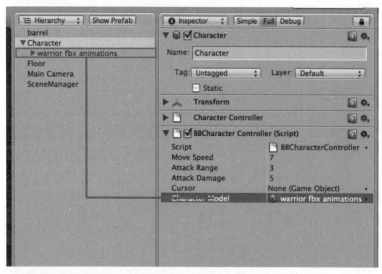

Figure 7–28. *Connecting your Character Model to the warrior animation.*

If you don't like to drag and drop things, you can also select the warrior fbx animations object from the drop-down menu to the right of the Character Model variable in the inspector. However, be aware that you now have two things that are called "warrior fbx animations". One is in the assets section and one is in the scene section. In this case, you want to link to the instantiated object in the scene, so be sure to pick the correct version.

At this point, you should be able to hit play and have the character walk around the scene. Let's go back and have a look at that BBCharacterController script that is doing this work for us.

```
void Update () {
        Vector3 moveDirection = movementDestination - gameObject.transform.position;
        moveDirection.y = 0.0f;

        if (moveDirection.sqrMagnitude > 0.5) {
                controller.Move(moveDirection.normalized * Time.deltaTime * moveSpeed);
                if (characterModel != null) characterModel.animation.CrossFade ("Walk");
        } else {
                if (characterModel != null) characterModel.animation.CrossFade ("Idle");
        }
}
```

You saw this previously, but now you can focus on the animation related lines. When you imported your model with animations, you had to set up each animation as a separate clip and gave each clip a name. That name is how you reference those clips, it is important to be sure you use the exact name, capitals and all, or it won't work. So what is happening here?

When you are walking, you call characterModel.animation.CrossFade ("Walk") and when you are not moving you call characterModel.animation.CrossFade ("Idle"). How do you crossfade from a character animation?

Unity uses a fairly common technique in game development known as animation blending. When your character comes to a stop, you just stop the walk animation and start the idle animation. But, the motion would jump, especially if you stop in midstride.

Animation blending fixes that problem. It takes the actual keyframes for the animation currently being played and averages them with the new animation that you want to play. This has the effect of a nice smooth transition from walking to idle. Walk around the scene a bit and pay close attention to the split second when the animation changes from walking to idle and back again. Animation blending is crucial to keep your character movements nice and smooth.

You can actually play multiple animations at one time, giving each one a certain weight in terms of how much that set of keyframes effects the actual movement of the model. You will do this with the attack animation, and it makes handling complex animations very easy.

However, before you can attack anything, you need to add some object interactivity.

Interacting with Something Besides the Floor

You have already seen quite a broad range of functionality that Unity can provide, and hopefully you have gotten a bit familiar with the Unity interface. I am going to move a bit quicker in these last few pages because there are still a handful of things I want to cover. However, what you will be doing in the rest of the chapter is the same thing you have been doing all along: make objects, attach scripts to them, and test them. That is the basic iteration.

At this point, you want to be able to interact with your environment a bit more than just walking around and bumping into things. You want to be able to use your cool attack animation, and for that you need some objects that are attackable.

Have a look at the BBAttackable script.

```
public class BBAttackable : BBTouchable {

        public float armor = 0.0f; // higher armor is harder to hit
        public float health = 1.0f; // at health = 0 i am dead

        public override void handleTouch(Vector3 worldPoint)
        {
                // this will cause the player to attack me
                BBCharacterController.instance.attack(this);
        }

        public virtual void applyDamage(int damage)
        {
                health -= damage;
                if (health <= 0) this.die();
        }

        public virtual void die()
        {
                // need to play a death animation or something
```

```
                    // for now, we will just destroy
                    Destroy(gameObject);
            }
    }
```

First, you can see that this is inheriting functionality from the BBTouchable class, so it will get touch events. You have added a few public instance variables to control how much health and armor the object has.

In your touch handler, you are calling a new method on the Character Controller called attack(). You also have a public method that applies any damage you might have sustained. If you go below 0, you call your die() method which removes your object from the scene.

If you jump to the BBCharacterController script and have a look at the attack method, you can see how this is working.

```
public void attack(BBAttackable target)
{
        // first off, am I close enough to hit it?
        // if not, then move towards it
        if (Vector3.Distance(transform.position, target.transform.position) >
attackRange) {
                this.moveTowards(target.transform.position);
                return;
        }
        Vector3 lookAt = target.gameObject.transform.position;
        lookAt.y = 0.0f;
        transform.LookAt(lookAt);
        if (characterModel != null) characterModel.animation.CrossFade ("Attack");
        StartCoroutine(this.doDamage(target));
}
```

The first thing to do is check to see if you are within your attack range to actually attack the other object. You shouldn't be able to hit an object with your sword unless you are right in front of it, so if you are not close enough to hit it, you move towards it.

Next, you turn to face the object you are hitting. Generally, you will already be facing it because you will have moved toward it to get close enough to hit it. If you happen to already be close enough to hit an object that is behind you, then you need to turn to face it.

Now you cross fade to your attack animation.

Astute readers will be thinking, the next time the update loop runs, it will just override this crossfade with a walk or idle animation. This can't work.

That would be true, unless you make the attack animation worth more than the other animations. You can play multiple animations at once, each one having a weight which is used to determine how much the different animations effect the overall movement of the model. In the case of the Attack animation, you actually want it to have 100% of the weight while it is playing, so you will just assign it a higher layer. Each animation has a layer, and the highest layer basically gets the most weight.

Have a look at the Start() method in the BBCharacterController script.

```
        if (characterModel != null) {
                characterModel.animation.wrapMode = WrapMode.Loop;
                characterModel.animation["Attack"].wrapMode = WrapMode.Once;
                characterModel.animation["Attack"].layer = 1;
        }
```

Here you are initializing your animations. First, set all of the animations to loop. Next, single out the attack animation and set it so it only plays once then stops. The last line is the important line. You set the attack animation to be layer 1. Animations are by default layer 0.

So, if you play the attack animation, it will play out to its completion no matter what other animations are playing.

Back to the `attack()` method, the last line:

```
StartCoroutine(this.doDamage(target));
```

Recall way back in the beginning of the chapter I talked about coroutines as a way to schedule periodic events outside the update loop? This is a perfect place to use them.

```
IEnumerator doDamage(BBAttackable target)
{
        yield return new WaitForSeconds (1.0f);
        if (target != null) target.applyDamage(attackDamage);
}
```

Instead of a loop like you had in the spinning barrel example, you are just waiting a certain amount of time, then calling applyDamage to the target. This is timed so that it is about where the sword moves through the center of its swing.

Let's have a look back at how this all works. Let's say that you have some object, like a barrel, and you attach the Attackable script. When it is touched, it tells the player to come and attack it. If the player is close enough, it plays the attack animation and applies some damage to the barrel. If the player is not close enough, then the attack command basically turns into a `moveTowards()` command.

Now, you want to actually add this BBAttackable script to all of your barrels. You could add it to them one by one, but wait! They are all prefab copies. That must mean something! It means that you can add the script to the prefab, and if you haven't broken the prefab connection, all the prefab copies in the entire game will gain that new script. Attaching a script to a prefab is just like attaching a script to a normal scene object.

Find the barrel prefab that you made earlier, make sure it is the prefab, and not the barrel model. When you select it, you will see its attributes in the inspector. Now find the BBAttackable script and drag it into the barrel prefab inspector, or right onto the prefab itself. You should see the BBAttackable script show up in the inspector, and now all of your prefab barrel copies will be attackable.

If you play the game now, you should be able to walk up to a barrel and attack it, causing it to vanish, like in Figure 7–29.

Figure 7–29. Your warrior attacking a defenseless barrel

User Interface

Unity provides for a few different kinds of UI methods. It has a whole set of GUI objects that provide things like buttons, scroll areas, and things of that nature. It also has an intermediate set of GUI classes that are used to make your own GUIs. These are the GUITexture and the GUIText. I would encourage you to play with both the GUITexture and the GUIText classes, but I would avoid the GUI objects like GUI.Button and GUI.Box or anything that requires an onGUI() method call.

The GUI class of objects are fairly heavy in terms of performance, and on the iPhone even the simplest of GUI style interfaces can bring the phone to its knees. The simpler GUITexture and GUIText objects are much more lightweight so I would recommend using those if you need to do any GUI type displays.

What is a GUI object? The GUI objects are a special breed of objects that live in the screen space and always appear flat to the camera. Add a GUIText object to your scene, then walk around a bit, you will see what I mean.

However, I tend to build my GUIs out of plain old quads and have them live in the world space. This method is slightly more complicated to set up, but it allows me to reuse all of the interaction scripts that I have already made for 3D objects, saving lots of time and keeping code clean and consistent.

Let's have a look at a very simple example.

Multiple Cameras

You want to add a button to your interface that makes more barrels. To do this, you are going to need a new camera. **GameObject ➤ Create Other ➤ Camera.** This will add a second camera to your scene, and this camera will make it look like everything has vanished. Dont worry, that is just because you are now looking through the new camera, and it is not set up right yet.

First, rename it something like GUICamera. Then remove the Audio Listener component from the new camera. You can only have one listener, and your Main Camera already has one.

Now you are going to do some new stuff. You need to make a new layer. At the top of the inspector, under the camera's name is the Layer menu. You saw this earlier with the Ignore Raycasts layer. Now you want to make a new custom layer. At the bottom of the Layer popup is: Add New Layer.... Select that and you will see all the layers in the inspector. Pick any one of the user layers and name it something like, "faux gui". This will be the layer that your fake GUI objects live in and this will allow you to filter their visibility from your main camera.

 Now, select the GUICamera. In the inspector you will see a bunch of options, one of which is the Culling Mask. The culling mask tells the camera which objects it should be rendering. By default, a camera will show everything. You just want it to show your new faux gui layer. First thing is to select "Nothing" in the CUlling mask drop down. By selecting Nothing, you can quickly clear the list of visible objects. Now in the same Culling Mask drop down, select your new layer, faux gui. This camera will only show objects that are in the faux gui layer. Before you leave this camera, change the Clear Flags to Depth Only. This effectively makes this camera have a clear background color, and now you should be able to see your scene again. Your GUICamera attributes should look like Figure 7–30.

The last thing that you need to do is set the Culling Mask to filter out any faux gui layer objects on your Main Camera. Select the main camera and uncheck the faux gui layer in its Culling Mask drop down (it should already be unchecked as new layers do not get added to the culling mask by default, but it is good to check these things).

What have you done here? You have made a new camera, and set it so that it only shows objects in a certain layer. You have also made sure that your other camera does not show these objects. This means you can effectively use this new camera to build an overlay scene. In this case, you will use it to add a button.

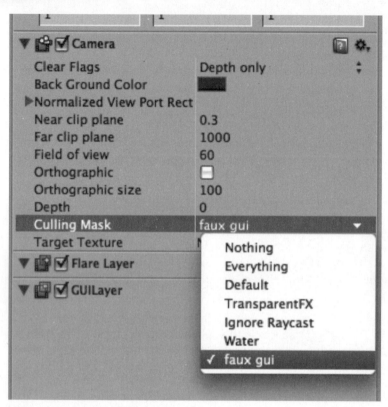

Figure 7–30. *The GUICamera attributes*

3D Objects As GUI Items

Set your new GUICamera position to 0,0,–5. Now find the prefab in the Prefabs folder, in the project view, called barrelButton. Drag this out into your scene, so it should now look something like Figure 7–31.

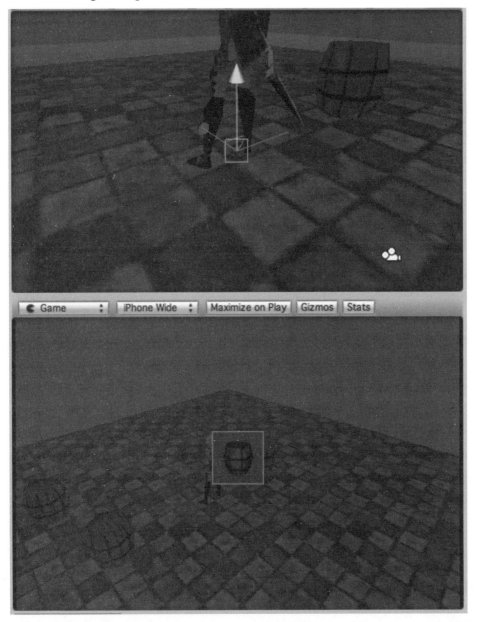

Figure 7–31. Your new barrel button. In the game view, it is in the center of the screen, even though in the scene view it seems to be half-poking out of the floor.

Here you can see what is going on. In your scene view, you can see all of your objects. Your new button is just poking out of the floor at 0,0,0. In the game view, your Main Camera, the one that can see the barrels and the warrior does not show the button poking out of the floor, but the second GUICamera which can only see the button shows it as center screen.

Keep in mind you only have the one little button, but your GUI interfaces can get quite complicated, and having them all cluttering the scene view can be a bit annoying. There are lots of ways to fix this. The simplest I find is to make a new empty Game Object, and put all the faux gui layer objects into that parent object, then you can deactivate the whole lot of them by deactivating the parent object (just uncheck the checkbox that is at the top of the inspector, next to the object name). This allows you to turn off your entire gui so you can focus on your scene or vice versa. Your scene is simple enough so you don't need to worry too much about it.

Everything is working properly, but your button is in a bad spot. In the scene view, or by using the inspector, move your button to one of the corners. I put mine at 3.5,-2.1,0, but you should be able to drag it all over the screen and see how it looks in other positions.

Now you need to make it do something. You have a touchable interface going on, so you should take advantage of that. Have a look at the BBTouchableButton script.

```
public class BBTouchableButton : BBTouchable {

        public GameObject buttonDelegate;
        public string message = "doButtonAction";

        public override void handleTouch(Vector3 worldPoint)
        {
                if (buttonDelegate == null) buttonDelegate = gameObject;
        buttonDelegate.SendMessage(message,SendMessageOptions.DontRequireReceiver);
        }
}
```

Very simple. I like to keep my scripts as simple as possible, because there is less chance for bugs that way.

You can see that your touchable button is a subclass of BBTouchable, so it will work within your current touch handling scheme. Your script is basically just calling this one method:

```
buttonDelegate.SendMessage()
```

What is this doing? SendMessage() is a generic way to try to call a method on another object. SendMessage() is a bit slower than finding the script component and calling the method like you have done previously, but it allows for a bit more flexibility. SendMessage() attempts to call the specified method call on any components of the object that it is being called on. By adding the SendMessageOptions.DontRequireReceiver constant, you are basically saying: try to send this message out, but if there is nobody to hear it, then that is OK.

At the top of your file, you define a public GameObject to attach any delegate object you want in the editor, but the default (when the delegate is null) is to just send the message to whatever object your script is attached to.

You also make the message a public variable, so if you want to call some other method when the button is tapped then you can easily change it.

Next, you need a script to actually perform the action. Open up the BBSpawnBarrelsAction script.

```
public class BBSpawnBarrelsAction : MonoBehaviour {

        public GameObject barrelPrefab;

        public void doButtonAction()
        {
                // are there any spawned barrels left?
                if (GameObject.Find("Spawned Barrel") != null) return;

                // We want to spawn some barrels
                this.spawnBarrelAtPoint(new Vector3(10.0f,1.5f,10.0f));
                this.spawnBarrelAtPoint(new Vector3(-10.0f,1.5f,-10.0f));
        }

        void spawnBarrelAtPoint(Vector3 spawnPoint)
        {
                        GameObject newBarrel =↵
(GameObject)Instantiate(barrelPrefab,spawnPoint,Quaternion.identity);
                        newBarrel.name = "Spawned Barrel";
        }
}
```

This script will be attached to the same object as the BBTouchableButton script, so when that button receives a touch call, it will send the message "doButtonAction" to itself. This means that doButtonAction() will get called on this script.

The first thing you do is check to see if there are any spawned barrels already. You don't want to spawn barrels if there are still some out there that you already spawned.

The GameObject.Find() method returns the first object with the supplied name, if it does not find anything it returns null.

If there are no previously spawned barrels in the scene, then you spawn a couple. Your spawn method simply instantiates a prefab that you will hook up via the editor, and then names it "Spawned Barrel" so that you can easily find them later.

Take both the BBTouchableButton script and the BBSpawnBarrelsAction and attach them to your barrelButton. The only thing you need to do is hook up the barrel prefab to the BBSpawnBarrelsAction script. Find the barrel prefab and drag it onto the BBSpawnBarrelsAction script into the barrel prefab slot.

Now if you hit play and try it out, your button doesn't work!

What has happened is that your touch input controller is only looking at the main camera when it is raycasting. The main camera can't see your button. You need to add a second camera to your BBTouchInputController. Let's have a look at that script.

```
public class BBTouchInputController : MonoBehaviour {

        public Camera GUICamera;
        .
        .
        .

        public void handleTouchAtPointForAllCameras(Vector2 touchPoint) {
                if (this.cameraDidHandleTouch(GUICamera,touchPoint)) return;
                this.cameraDidHandleTouch(Camera.main,touchPoint);
        }

        public bool cameraDidHandleTouch(Camera cam, Vector2 touchPoint) {
                RaycastHit hit = new RaycastHit();
                if (Physics.Raycast(cam.ScreenPointToRay(touchPoint),out hit,↩
    Mathf.Infinity)) {
                        BBTouchable touchableObject =↩
    (BBTouchable)hit.transform.gameObject.GetComponent(typeof(BBTouchable));
                        if (touchableObject != null) {
                                touchableObject.handleTouch(hit.point);
                                return true;
                        }
                }
                return false;
        }
}
```

This looks like a bunch of changes but really it is very simple.

You added a public instance variable for the GUICamera so you can hook that up in the editor. You moved the raycasting code into its own method so that you can just send it any old camera, and if it successfully handles a touch, then it returns true, otherwise it returns false.

Then, in the handleTouchAtPointForAllCameras() method you first check to see if the GUICamera has any touches, and if not you check the main camera. You want to give the gui preference because it will be visually in front of the main camera scene.

Lastly, in the Update() method, just change the handleTouchAtPoint() method to the handleTouchAtPointForAllCameras() method.

Back in the editor, be sure to link the GUICamera object into the BBTouchInputController script. Once that is hooked up, you are ready to try it again. Now everything should work (see 7–32).

Figure 7–32. *Your very simple gui and your resultant spawned barrels*

Building for Your Device

So far you have spent the entire time inside the Unity editor. You have built your little game and tested it in the game preview window. At some point, you will want to test it on the device to make sure that it is behaving properly and performing well.

In Unity, this is really very easy. If you have already built things in Xcode for your device, (and you should have already done it at least once to get the Unity Remote working) then it will be very easy indeed. First, save your scene, then open the Build Settings found under the File menu. Drag your scene into the build settings window to add it to the scene list. Then press the build button. That is about it.

What Unity does is take all of your game data and build a big binary blob, it then wraps that in a tasty Cocoa/ObjC wrapper, and serves it up in an Xcode project. When the build is finished, you will have a new xCode project that is ready for you to add your certificates to and build for your device, just like any other iPhone project.

Unity projects cannot be used in the simulator, so don't bother trying that. Not that you need the simulator when Unity Remote is a far better simulation solution.

If you have been following along with the free desktop version of Unity, then you don't have the option to build for iPhone, but you can deploy to a slew of other platforms, like the web, which is a great way to get the word out about your game, build a web version and let people demo your game before buying it on the App Store.

Summary

This chapter has covered a huge amount of ground. You managed to build a working game-like application that had a fully animated character model, imported 3D assets, multi-camera rendering, and touch input handling.

All of this in less than a hundred lines of code.

This is the power of using Unity for your game development. All the hard stuff is already done for you, so all you need to do is build your game on top of it. I spent many years as a hobbyist, building little games here and there for the fun of it, but once the iPhone came along, I finally had a deployment platform for my games.

This is when I realized that mostly what I had been writing were game engines. I spent all of my time tweaking the material loading code so that it worked with PVRTC textures or adjusting the way my particle system handled its memory management, and I really spent very little time actually building my games. With Unity all that stuff becomes a very distant secondary consideration. Yes, you still need to worry about memory and texture compression, but Unity handles all the hard bits for you. Once I started using Unity, I stopped building game engines and started building games.

Hopefully, this shallow but broad introduction to Unity will pique your interest and show you how useful a tool like Unity can be.

If you are already hooked, and want to try more, here are some suggestions to help hone your Unity skills: In your game, change the touch input system so that it handles touch, down/touch, moved/and touch up. Use the character model (or make your own if you know how) and make an evil twin for the warrior to fight for domain over the land of the barrels. Add walls and rooms and expand the dungeon so you can go exploring. Add a health bar to your GUI. Or alternatively, scrap the whole thing and make your own game!

In closing, I want to offer my help: Feel free to email me at support@benbritten.com if you have any questions, or check out my game development blog: http://escfactory.com/blog. I often post tips and tricks there, and there are a few other people who post there as well, artists, writers, and sound people.

In addition, if you hang out on the Unity forums for even a few minutes (http://forum.unity3d.com) then you will notice that the Unity support team and the Unity community is incredibly helpful and generous with their time and expertise. The Unity forums were instrumental for me when I was picking up Unity for the first time, and I still constantly go there to find help when I get stuck.

Again, many thanks to Adam Taylor for the model/texture/animation work on the warrior model. You can check out some more of his work at his site: http://www.adamtaylorfolio.com.

Chuck Smith

Company: *Chuck Smith*
(www.chucksmith.de)

Location: *Berlin, Germany*

Former Life as a Developer: *I started my career developing a web front-end using Siebel and found that sitting behind a cubicle wasn't really for me. I then founded the Esperanto Wikipedia and took off to travel Europe for half a year to promote it and see more of the world. Since then, I've developed a complete e-commerce solution in PHP for a company in New York City and then moved to Heilbronn, Germany where I was a wiki researcher for two years mostly working in Java. After that, I lead the Ruby on Rails development team on a poker social networking site in Berlin. Finally, I became fascinated with the iPhone, jumped on board, and haven't looked back.*

Life as an iPhone Developer: *I am a freelance iPhone developer and developer of educational iPhone software such as Chess Player and German Course, as well as "game helpers" like Dominion Minion and Random Chess. I also do contract work writing iPhone credit-card applications. On the side, I coordinate an iPhone internationalization service (www.iphone-i18n.com) and am happy to report success: after iphone-i18n translated Harbor Master into German, it quickly rose to the Top 10 list in the German App Store!*

Apps on the App Store:

- *Games: Chess Player, Go Player, Dominion Minion, Random Chess*
- *Education: German Course and German Sex*

What's in This Chapter: *I will show you how to create a simple card game quickly and painlessly. You will create a menu to navigate to different scenes in the game. Then, you will see and appreciate how easy sprite manipulation can be using the Cocos2d library. Finally, you will add sound and learn how to port your app to Apple's ultimate gaming device, the iPad.*

Key Technologies:

- *Game Menu Creation*
- *Sprite Handling*
- *Sound Engine*

Chapter 8

Cocos2d for iPhone and iPad; It Is Easier than You Think

So, you've decided to write an iPhone game, but are scared off by the complexities of OpenGL ES? Quartz2D doesn't have enough power for you? The answer is cocos2d, which provides an abstraction layer, so you can easily use the power of OpenGL ES. This lets you focus on your game rather than the mathematics behind matrix transformations.

Origins of Cocos2d

Cocos2d originally began as an open source game library for Python. The iPhone port even uses the same API, but in Objective-C. It all started after many Argentine Python developers kept attending Pyweek every year and lamented the fact that every time they met, they had to recode everything from scratch, essentially "reinventing the wheel" each time: the menu, logic for manipulating scenes, sprites, animations, etc. In January 2008, fifty Python developers gathered in Los Cocos, a region in Argentina where six ambitious souls started writing an open source 2d game engine. It was then named cocos2d after its birthplace.

In March 2008, Apple released its SDK and they immediately started to port the code for the iPhone. They kept all the original principles of the Python version and made sure the project remained open source. In the early days, Apple's NDA was their biggest obstacle preventing them from sharing code with others and raising doubts about whether Apple would ever allow open source libraries on their platform. At this time, cocos2d development stayed underground until Apple gave the green light to share. Since Apple removed the restrictions, the community and codebase has steadily grown and now cocos2d v1.0 is planned to go live in May 2010.

NOTE: Some ambitious developers are hard at work on an Android version as well, but it is still in its very early stages at the time of this writing.

Why Use Cocos2d?

OpenGL ES is a very powerful low-level graphics engine which also has a very difficult learning curve. After an hour introductory lecture, I was even more confused by it than before. However, in just a few hours learning and using cocos2d, I already had playing cards spinning and moving around a screen. Sure, cocos2d won't give you the full power of OpenGL ES, but for more applications it will give you enough, and will greatly speed up your development time unless you already have a strong background in OpenGL. Benjamin Jackson summarized it best, "OpenGL is powerful, but hand-coding the same calls to its cryptic method names repeatedly will have any sane person leaving head-shaped holes in the wall before the first prototype is out the door[1]."

Another powerful feature of cocos2d is its inclusion of the popular physics libraries Chipmunk and Box2d. Many people choose Box2d because it was written in C++ instead of C. On the other hand, Chipmunk has been integrated into cocos2d longer, so there is more sample source code available which can make it faster to learn. That being said, the developer of Stick Wars recently migrated his app from Chipmunk to Box2d. Box2d is more powerful giving it a steeper learning curve, yet its documentation is more complete (http://www.cocos2d-iphone.org/forum/topic/762). From what I've seen, most developers prefer Box2d over Chipmunk, but a detailed discourse on this topic is beyond the scope of this chapter.

Getting Started with Cocos2d

Cocos2d development may use some concepts which may be unfamiliar to you if you have not done game development before. First of all, now in v0.99 of cocos2d, all cocos2d-specific objects start with CC. This will make it easier to see which parts of your code are dealing with the cocos2d API and which are native to the iPhone SDK.

At the highest level, you will work with CCDirector, CCScene, CCLayer, and CCSprite objects.

- The CCDirector looks over your entire program and controls the flow of scenes.

- A CCScene could be an intro page, menu, a level, a cutscene, or even a high scores page. They help you organize individual components of your game into logical units. See an example game flow in Figure 8–1. Each rectangle in that figure represents a different scene.

---

[1] Wolfgang Ante et al., *iPhone Cool Projects* (New York: Apress, 2009), p 109.

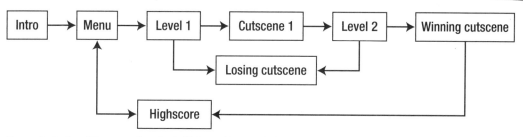

Figure 8–1. *Possible scene flowchart. (Taken with permission from rights owner:* `http://www.cocos2d-iphone.org/wiki/doku.php/prog_guide:basic_concepts.`*)*

- Within a scene, you can have multiple CCLayer objects. Each layer has the size of the entire screen area and can also include transparent or partially transparent sections which show the layer(s) behind it. You will define event handlers within layers, so this is where most of your programming will be done. A CCLayer can contain a CCLabel, CCSprite and even other CCLayer objects. A CCLabel is an object for displaying text. These can be used for displaying messages to the user or even just the score or other important details. Figure 8–2 shows how layers might look in an actual game.

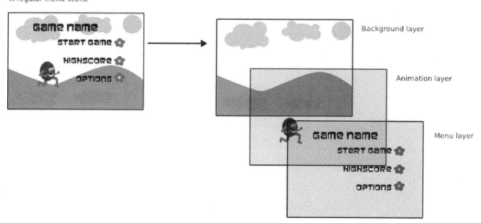

Figure 8–2. *Combining layers to make a scene. (Taken with permission from right owner:* `http://www.cocos2d-iphone.org/wiki/doku.php/prog_guide:basic_concepts.`*)*

- CCSprite objects are a way to store images in memory for easy manipulation. In this form, it is easy to move, rotate, scale, and animate them simply by calling simple methods. This is how a beginner game developer can make simple impressive animations without trekking to the local community college to enroll in a course of Linear Algebra.

Installing Cocos2d

Download the latest stable version of Cocos2d from http://www.cocos2d-
iphone.org/download. Unzip this and you're almost ready to go. Feel free to unzip this
file anywhere, because its location is not important.

Configuring Sample Code

Open the cocos2d-iphone.xcodeproj in XCode. cocos2d-iphone.xcodeproj is a sample
jungle gym where you can see examples of many different frameworks like in the virtual
Targets group in Figure 8–3. Since cocos2d is relatively new and documentation is
incomplete at the time of this writing, a critical tool to learning will be viewing sample
source code to learn what you need to continue your project. Unfortunately, this code
does not automatically work right out of the box, so you need to set it up. Fortunately, it's
quite simple: from the XCode menu, select **View ➤ Customize Toolbar**. Now drag the
Overview item to the far left place in the toolbar. This will help you to easily see which
targets you are building. When this is completed, your toolbar should look like Figure 8–4.

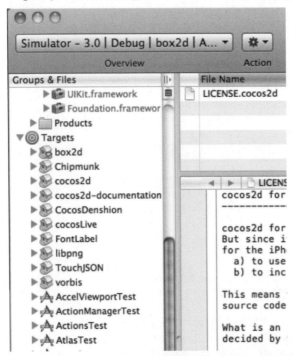

Figure 8–3. *Sample tests at your disposal in cocos2d-iphone.xcodeproj*

Figure 8–4. *Customized XCode toolbar to run cocos2d sample code*

Now that you have this set up, you will want to run the `HelloWorldSample`. From the Overview dropdown, choose `HelloWorldSample` for Active Target and then click this dropdown again and select HelloWorldSample for the Active Executable too. Now, click Build and Debug (or Build and Go depending on your version of XCode) and see the cocos2d splash screen followed by the words Hello World appear in your iPhone Simulator.

You will find the sample code for this app at `/tests/Samples/HelloWorld.m`.

This also means you can modify the sample code to play around with cocos2d. Find the following line of code and change "Hello World" to "Hello cocos2d" and then build this project again to see it in action.

```
CCLabel* label = [CCLabel labelWithString:@"Hello World" fontName:@"Marker Felt"
  fontSize:64];
```

Installing the XCode Project Templates

Let's install the cocos2d project templates into XCode to give you skeleton projects which you can use to jump start your new game idea. To do so, start Terminal, navigate to the folder with the unzipped files you downloaded, and enter the following command:

```
./install_template.sh
```

NOTE: If you want to uninstall these templates later, you can find them in the following folder on your hard drive:
`/Developer/Platforms/iPhoneOS.platform/Developer/Library/Xcode/Project Templates/Application`.

Starting a New Project

Here you will want to start a new project by clicking **File ➤ New Project**. After this, your window should look like Figure 8–5. If not, then you still need to install the XCode Project Templates as described in the previous section "Installing the XCode Project Templates."

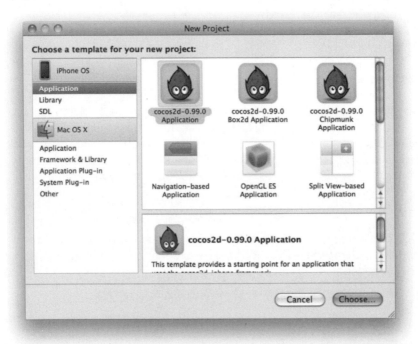

Figure 8–5. *Starting a new cocos2d project*

Here you will want to choose the cocos2d Application. You will only want the Box2d or Chipmunk application template if you are planning to have heavy physics elements in your game. At this point, a project skeleton will be created for you as in Figure 8–6. (See my comparison of Box2d and Chipmunk in the "Why use cocos2d?" section for more details about the other templates.) Under the `Classes` folder, you'll find `HelloWorldScene.m` and `.h` were auto-generated for you which you can now use to start building your game.

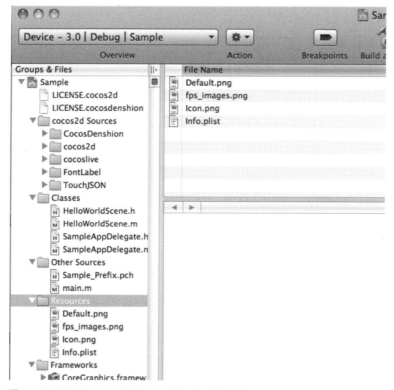

Figure 8–6. *Auto-generated cocos2d project skeleton*

Introduction to Video Poker

To demonstrate cocos2d, I will be using Video Poker as an example, since it is deep enough to be interesting, yet easy enough to explain cocos2d without too many distracting details. The player taps a Deal button which will then deal five cards. Then he may choose which cards to hold and tap the Deal button again. At this point, if the player has a hand which is a pair of jacks or better, then he will receive chips back according to Table 8–1.

Table 8–1. *Prize Table for Video Poker*

Hand	Prize
Royal flush	4000
Straight flush	250
Four of a kind	125
Full house	45
Flush	30
Straight	20
Three of a kind	15
Two pair	10
Jacks or better	5

The player will receive this many chips for the given hand.

Making a Scene

A scene is basically one screen of information. This could be a main menu, a level of a game, a game over screen, a high scores list, etc. Here you will start by making a main menu, so that the user can choose to either start a game or learn how to play or change options. This menu is an excellent opportunity to get your feet wet and learn how to switch between scenes.

To start, find the auto-generated HelloWorldScene.h and HelloWorldScene.m files in the Classes folder. Remove the lines in the init section and you can now use these files as a template for any scene you would like to create. Create empty files called HowToPlayScene.h and HowToPlayScene.m, copy the contents from HelloWorldScene.h and HelloWorldScene.m into them and set their object name to HowToPlay. Also, remember to import HowToPlayScene.h and change both occurrences of "HelloWorld" in the following line to HowToPlay as well.

```
HelloWorld *layer = [HelloWorld node];
```

Now you should have two files, which look like Listings 8–1 and 8–2. Also, notice the node method here. A CocosNode is basically the super-object of all cocos2d objects. Basically, if you want to draw it or it contains something, this will be a CocosNode. The node function is generally a factory method which returns a CocosNode. In the previous example, the HowToPlay layer will be initialized using the HowToPlay node.

Listing 8–1. *HowToPlayScene.h: Sample Scene Header File Template*

```
//  HowToPlayScene.h
//  Video Poker

#import "cocos2d.h"

@interface HowToPlay : CCLayer {
}

+(id) scene;

@end
```

Listing 8–2. *HowToPlayScene.m: Sample Scene Main File Template*

```
//  HowToPlayScene.m
//  Video Poker
#import "HowToPlayScene.h"

@implementation HowToPlay

+(id) scene
{
        // 'scene' is an autorelease object.
        CCScene *scene = [CCScene node];

        // 'layer' is an autorelease object.
        HowToPlay *layer = [HowToPlay node];

        // add layer as a child to scene
        [scene addChild: layer];


        // return the scene
        return scene;
}

-(id) init
{
        // always call "super" init
        // Apple recommends to re-assign "self" with the "super" return value
        if( (self=[super init] )) {
                // Put code to initialize cocos2d scene here
        }
        return self;
}

@end
```

In Listing 8–1, you first created a CCScene object and a CCLayer object to be placed within that scene. Then you added the CCLayer object as a child of the CCScene and finally returned the CCScene to the CCDirector. You will rarely deal with the CCDirector object directly, you'll only call it within a CCScene to replace it with another scene (more about this in the next section).

Creating a Game Menu

Python developers got tired of writing the same menu logic code every time they wrote a new game, so they made menu creation very quick and easy. Now let's create a menu item with the text "How to Play" which will call the function howToPlay. You just need the following line within a scene:

```
CCMenuItem *howToPlay = [CCMenuItemFont itemFromString:@"How to Play"
                                        target:self selector:@selector(howToPlay:)];
```

Now, let's add this to your project. Copy HelloWorldScene.m and .h again and call them MainMenuScene.m and .h. In this line, you're creating a CCMenuItem object. Don't forget to change the @interface and @implementation lines in MainMenuScene.m and .h respectively as follows:

```
@interface MainMenu : CCLayer

@implementation MainMenu
```

Now you want to add three menu items: Play Game, How to Play, and Options. So, you'll need to replace anything in your init function (MainMenuScene.m) and replace it with the code in Listing 8–3.

Listing 8–3. *Creating Your Game's Menu Items*

```
// New menu
CCMenuItem *playGame = [CCMenuItemFont itemFromString:@"Start Game"
                                        target:self
                                        selector:@selector(playGame:)];

CCMenuItem *howToPlay = [CCMenuItemFont itemFromString:@"How to Play"
                                        target:self
                                        selector:@selector(howToPlay:)];

CCMenuItem *options = [CCMenuItemFont itemFromString:@"Options"
                                        target:self
                                        selector:@selector(options:)];
```

Now that you have these menu items, you have to put them somewhere. Let's display them vertically down the center. First, you need to create a CCMenu object and initialize it with the menu items you already created. Next, the menu will need to align its items vertically. Finally, you need to add this menu as a child to the MainMenuScene, as you can see by Listing 8–4 and then you should run your app and see the result in Figure 8–7.

Listing 8–4. *Adding Menu items to a Menu and Adding it to the Scene*

```
CCMenu *menu = [CCMenu menuWithItems: playGame, howToPlay, options, nil];
[menu alignItemsVertically];
[self addChild:menu];
```

Now you need to create the functions that will be called when these buttons are pressed. To replace a single scene, you will have to run the following command:

```
[[CCDirector sharedDirector] replaceScene:[HowToPlay node]];
```

Now you see the first reference to the CCDirector. The CCDirector is used to keep track of the program's scenes internally. This function will change the current scene with a new scene you indicate. You'll finish the menu by creating a transition to the HowToPlay CCScene and then commenting out the transitions to the other CCScene objects that you want to add in the future, as demonstrated in Listing 8–5. This code should go under the init function of MainMenuScene.m.

Figure 8–7. *Main menu aligned vertically*

Listing 8–5. *Creating Functions for Menu Item Clicks*

```
-(void)playGame:(id)sender {
        // [[CCDirector sharedDirector] replaceScene:[PokerGame node]];
}

-(void)howToPlay:(id)sender {
        [[CCDirector sharedDirector] replaceScene:[HowToPlay node]];
}

-(void)options:(id)sender {
        // [[CCDirector sharedDirector] replaceScene:[Options node]];
}
```

Now you will just have to replace [HelloWorld scene] in Video_PokerAppDelegate.m with [MainMenu scene]. Next, add the Main Scene class to the App Delegate and you should be able to run the app and see the menu.

Since the code is in place, create PokerGameScene.h, PokerGameScene.m, OptionsScene.h, and OptionsScene.m in the same manner as you did in the "Making a Scene" section of this chapter. Finally, you can uncomment out the commented out lines in Listing 8–5.

Game Logic

Now that you have the basic navigation complete to get to the game, you can start working on the logic of the game itself. This will need to be done before you start playing with graphics. Since this chapter is about cocos2d, this will be a summary of how the game logic classes work. I would recommend copying the files Card.h, Card.m, Deck.h, Deck.m, SimpleHand.h, SimpleHand.m, and GlobalVariables.h from the sample source code into your project now. If you do not care about the game logic and just want to get back to the cocos2d API, you can skip ahead to the section "I Like The Sprites in You" later in this chapter.

Card

The smallest unit of data in this app is a card. This just contains the rank (like 2 or King) and suit (like heart or diamonds) of a card. You also need to add a simple boolean value to tell whether the card is locked into place before the second draw. So, you will create a Card class and add the following to the interface as seen in Listing 8–6.

Listing 8–6. *Creating Card object interface in Card.h*

```
@interface Card : NSObject
{
        NSUInteger rank;
        NSUInteger suit;
        BOOL locked;
}

@property BOOL locked;
```

Let's make a list of constants for card ranks and suits. While you're at it, you might as well add card hand values too. You'll make a file called GlobalVariables.h for this purpose in Listing 8–7.

Listing 8–7. *Constant for Global Variables in GlobalVariables.h*

```
#define JACK   11
#define QUEEN  12
#define KING   13
#define ACE    14

#define SPADES    1
#define HEARTS    2
#define CLUBS     3
#define DIAMONDS  4

#define HIGH_CARD          1
#define JACKS_OR_BETTER    2
#define TWO_PAIR           3
#define THREE_OF_A_KIND    4
#define STRAIGHT           5
#define FLUSH              6
#define FULL_HOUSE         7
#define FOUR_OF_A_KIND     8
#define STRAIGHT_FLUSH     9
#define ROYAL_FLUSH        10
```

Note that for the card ranks, you will be using the actual values for cards 2–10 and then Jack = 11, Queen = 12, King = 13, and Ace = 14. Most importantly, back in your Card.m file, you need a function to create a random card (see Listing 8–8).

Listing 8–8. *Functions in Card.M for Initializing Cards*

```
-(id) initWithRandomCard
{
        suit = arc4random() % 4 + 1;
        rank = arc4random() % 13 + 2; // Pick random card between 2 and ACE (14)
        return self;
}

-(id) initWithRank:(NSUInteger)cardRank andSuit:(NSUInteger)cardSuit
{
        rank = cardRank;
        suit = cardSuit;
        return self;
}

-(id)initWithCard:(Card *)myCard;
{
        rank = [myCard rank];
        suit = [myCard suit];
        return self;
}
```

Now you can set up a card, but you'll also need to access it. I have all my card images saved as two character filenames, so the Queen of Clubs is Qc.png, 2 of Spades is 2s.png and the Ten of Hearts is Th.png. First, let's make two classes to return the human-readable string representation for the rank and suit (see Listing 8–9).

Listing 8–9. *Making Human-Readable Description for Each Card in Card.M*

```
-(NSString *)humanRank
{
        switch (self.rank)
        {
                case 0:     return @"Error";
                case JACK:  return @"J";
                case QUEEN: return @"Q";
                case KING:  return @"K";
                case ACE:   return @"A";
                case 10:    return @"T";
                default:    return [NSString stringWithFormat:@"%d", rank];
        }
}

-(NSString *)humanSuit {
        switch (self.suit) {
                case 0:        return @"Error";
                case SPADES:   return @"s";
                case HEARTS:   return @"h";
                case CLUBS:    return @"c";
                case DIAMONDS: return @"d";
                default:       return @"Suit >4 Error";
        }
}

-(NSString *)description
{
        return [NSString stringWithFormat:@"%@%@",
```

```
            [self humanRank],
            [self humanSuit]];
}
```

Now you just need to add a few utility functions to Card.m for card locking, as shown in Listings 8–10 and 8–11.

Listing 8–10. *Making Human-Readable Description for Each Card in Card.M*

```
-(void)lock {
        locked = true;
}

-(void)unlock {
        locked = false;
}

-(void)toggleLock {
        locked = !locked;
}
Now we just need to declare what we have in Card.h.
```

Listing 8–11. *Declaring Variables and Prototyping Functions in Card.h*

```
#import <Foundation/Foundation.h>


@interface Card : NSObject <NSCopying>
{
        NSUInteger rank;
        NSUInteger suit;
        BOOL locked;
}

@property BOOL locked;

-(id)initWithRandomCard;

-(NSString *)humanSuit;
-(NSString *)humanRank;

@end
```

Deck

Now that you have cards, you need to put them in a deck. This will also simplify the logic of the rest of the app, because the deck can shuffle its own cards, etc. Let's create the header file. You just need a mutable array of cards and an indicator of the current card, as shown in Listing 8–12.

Listing 8–12. *Declaring Variables and Prototyping Functions in Deck.h*

```
#import <Foundation/Foundation.h>

@class Card;
```

```
@interface Deck : NSObject {
        NSMutableArray *cards;
        NSUInteger curCard;
}

@property (nonatomic, retain) NSMutableArray *cards;

-(void) shuffle;
-(Card *)nextCard;

@end
```

Let's set up an initial deck. You simply need to create all 52 cards, as shown in Listing 8–13.

Listing 8–13. *Initializing Cards in Deck.m*

```
-(id) init
{
        cards = [[NSMutableArray alloc] initWithCapacity:52];

        for ( int suit = 1; suit <= 4; suit++ )
        {
                for ( int cardRank = 2; cardRank <= 14; cardRank++ )
                {
                        Card *myCard = [[Card alloc] initWithRank:cardRank↩
  andSuit:suit];

                        [cards addObject:myCard];
                        [myCard release];
                }
        }

        [self shuffle];

        return self;
}
```

Now for the most important part: shuffling. Many programmers simply always go through each card and swap it with any other card. However, this will not get you a very random shuffle, because cards at the beginning have a bigger chance to be swapped than cards later in the deck. Instead, you need to shuffle in the following way, as shown in Listing 8–14.

Listing 8–14. *Shuffling Cards in Deck.m*

```
-(void) shuffle
{
        // Swap each card with a random card AFTER it to get an even random↩
  distribution.
        for ( int i = 0; i < 51; i++ )
        {
                [cards exchangeObjectAtIndex:i withObjectAtIndex:arc4random()↩
% (52 - i) + i];
        }

        curCard = 0;
}
```

Here you cycle through the cards, but you only swap it with a random card that comes *after* this card and then you keep swapping until the 51st card. You don't need to check the last card, because if you did, it would just swap with itself since there are no cards after it. Also, notice that I use arc4random() instead of rand() or random(). I do this for the following two reasons:

■ rand() must first be seeded by running arandom(time(NULL)); while arc4random() automatically seeds on its first run.

■ arc4random() has twice the precision of rand().

NOTE: For more details about shuffling algorithms and an amusing story about an online poker scam that profited from this mistake, see
http://www.cigital.com/papers/download/developer_gambling.php.

Now you just need a simple utility function to access the next card in the deck, as shown in Listing 8–15.

Listing 8–15. *Advance to Next Card in Deck.m*

```
-(Card *)nextCard
{
        return [cards objectAtIndex:curCard++];
}
```

SimpleHand

Now you need to calculate which hand the user has, so you'll know how much to reward depending on the hand. This is the heart of the game logic and can get somewhat complicated. First, you need to initialize with space for five cards, as shown in Listing 8–16.

Listing 8–16. *Initializing Hand in SimpleHand.m*

```
-(id) init
{
        cards = [[NSMutableArray alloc] initWithCapacity:5];
        [super init];
        return self;
}
```

Next, you want to create a function to add a card to this SimpleHand as can be seen in Listing 8–17.

Listing 8–17. *Add Another Card to Hand in SimpleHand.m*

```
-(void)addCard:(Card *)anotherCard
{
        [cards addObject:anotherCard];
}
```

After you have cards in your hand, you need to see if a player has Jacks or Better. You start by sorting the cards, so you can simplify your hand checking algorithms. Now you'll check to see if it is a Royal Flush, then a Straight Flush, Four of a Kind, etc. If it finds no hand value at all, then you can assume the hand was a pair of tens or worse (see Listing 8–18).

Listing 8–18. *Calculate Hand Rank in SimpleHand.m*

```
-(void)calculate
{
        SimpleHand *sortedHand = [[SimpleHand alloc] initWithHand:cards];

        // Sort cards to make hands easier to calculate
        [sortedHand sort];

        if ( [sortedHand isRoyalFlush] )     { handRank = ROYAL_FLUSH;      return; }
        if ( [sortedHand isStraightFlush] )  { handRank = STRAIGHT_FLUSH;   return; }
        if ( [sortedHand isFourOfAKind] )    { handRank = FOUR_OF_A_KIND;   return; }
        if ( [sortedHand isFullHouse] )      { handRank = FULL_HOUSE;       return; }
        if ( [sortedHand isFlush] )          { handRank = FLUSH;            return; }
        if ( [sortedHand isStraight] )       { handRank = STRAIGHT;         return; }
        if ( [sortedHand isThreeOfAKind] )   { handRank = THREE_OF_A_KIND;  return; }
        if ( [sortedHand isTwoPair] )        { handRank = TWO_PAIR;         return; }
        if ( [sortedHand isJacksOrBetter] )  { handRank = JACKS_OR_BETTER;  return; }

        [sortedHand release];

        // No hand found
        handRank = HIGH_CARD;
        return;
}
```

As shown in Listing 8–18, you first make another `SimpleHand` object called `sortedHand` which you then sort. Now you need an initWithHand method as seen in Listing 8–19.

Listing 8–19. *Initialize with Hand in SimpleHand.m*

```
-(id)initWithHand:(NSMutableArray *)myHand
{
        cards = [[NSMutableArray alloc] initWithArray:myHand];
        return self;
}
```

Next, you need a sorting function like in Listing 8–20.

Listing 8–20. *Simple Sort Function in SimpleHand.m*

```
-(void) sort
{
        [cards sortUsingSelector:@selector(compareDescendingTo:)];
}
```

You need a compare function in Card.h, since you have to sort at the Card level as in Listing 8–21.

Listing 8–21. *Simple Sort Function in Card.m*

```
-(NSComparisonResult) compareDescendingTo:(Card *)anotherCard
{
        if ( rank < [anotherCard rank] ) { return NSOrderedDescending; }
        if ( rank > [anotherCard rank] ) { return NSOrderedAscending; }
```

```
        // The value is the same
        return NSOrderedSame;
}
```

Here you only compare cards by their rank. In Poker, all cards of different suits are the same worth, so there is no need to sort by suit like you would in Bridge, for example. Now that your cards are sorted, you can determine the hand rank. The program starts by checking a royal flush as you can see from Listing 8–22.

Listing 8–22. *Check for Royal Flush in SimpleHand.m*

```
-(BOOL)isRoyalFlush
{
        return ( [[cards objectAtIndex:0] rank] == ACE &&↵
  [[cards objectAtIndex:1] rank] == KING
                        && [self isStraightFlush] );
}
```

Since the hand is sorted, you can check to see if the first card is an ace, the second card is a king, and the hand is also a straight flush; then it is a royal flush. How do you check for a straight flush? Have a look at Listing 8–23.

Listing 8–23. *Check for Straight Flush in SimpleHand.m*

```
-(BOOL)isStraightFlush
{
        return ( [self isFlush] && [self isStraight] );
}
```

Simple enough, check to see if the hand is a flush and a straight. How do you check for a flush? A flush is a hand where every card in your hand is the same suit, so if every card in your hand is a spade, then you have a flush. You check to see if the second, third, fourth, and fifth card are all the same as the first card. See Listing 8–24 to see how this was done.

Listing 8–24. *Check for Flush in SimpleHand.m*

```
-(BOOL)isFlush
{
        for ( int i = 1; i < 5; i++ )
        {
                if ( [[cards objectAtIndex:0] suit] != [[cards objectAtIndex:i] suit] )
                {
                        // If any suit doesn't match the 1st card, it's not a flush.
                        return false;
                }
        }

        // All suits match, this is a bona fide flush!
        return true;
}
```

A straight is a hand where each card forms a sequence like 9-8-7-6-5. Now it is incredibly useful that you sorted the cards! Therefore, you just have to check to see if each card is exactly one lower than the one before it. You also have to account for the rare possibility that a hand is 5-4-3-2-Ace. In this one rare case, it is useful for an ace to have a value of 1, so that the player can get credit for a straight. The problem is that

your sorting function already placed the Ace in the front like Ace-5-4-3-2, so you will
need a special test just for this condition. Also, note that straights that "wrap around"
like 3-2-A-K-Q are **not** valid in poker, so you do not need to check for this (see Listing
8–25).

Listing 8–25. *Check for Straight in SimpleHand.m*

```
-(BOOL)isStraight
{
        // Special boolean to check for A-5-4-3-2 straight -> 5-4-3-2-A
        BOOL aceAndFiveStart = false;

        if ( [[cards objectAtIndex:0] rank] == ACE && [[cards objectAtIndex:1] rank]↵
== 5 )
        {
                aceAndFiveStart = true;
        }

        // If 1st card is not exactly one less than current and the ace and five↵
don't start, not straight.
        if ( [[cards objectAtIndex:0] rank] != [[cards objectAtIndex:1] rank]↵
+ 1 && !aceAndFiveStart )
        {
                return false;
        }

        // See if 8-7-6-5-4
        for ( int i = 1; i < 4; i++ )
        {
                if ( [[cards objectAtIndex:i] rank] != [[cards objectAtIndex:i+1]↵
rank] + 1 )
                {
                        // The next card is not exactly one less than current one,↵
so not a straight.
                        return false;
                }
        }

        if ( aceAndFiveStart ) {
                // Save first card to put at the end.
                Card *aceCard = [[Card alloc] initWithCard:[cards objectAtIndex:0]];
                [cards removeObjectAtIndex:0];
                [cards addObject:aceCard];
                [aceCard release];
        }

        // All cards are in order, it's a straight!
        return true;
}
```

There are quite a lot of hand rank functions and I do not want to bog down the chapter
with them all, so I leave it as an exercise to the reader to go through all the methods in
SimpleHand.m to see how they work. I have made an effort to comment them well, so
they should be easy to figure out.

I Like the Sprites in You

Putting images into Sprite objects in Cocos2d is very powerful and one of the key building blocks of the architecture. This section will go through the process of loading, displaying, and manipulating sprites. This also includes how you can chain actions, either so that some actions immediately follow each other, or so that your sprite can walk and chew gum at the same time.

Load and Display a Sprite

You can load a sprite into memory with just one command:

```
CCSprite *mySprite = [CCSprite spriteWithFile:@"MySprite.png"];
```

Let's place the sprite in the center of the screen. First, you need to get the size of the screen. This can especially be important in differentiating an iPhone from an iPad. To do this, you get the winSize from the `CCDirector`. Then you set the position of the sprite to be half the width and height of the screen. By default, cocos2d will place the center of the sprite at the coordinates that you set for it, so keep this in mind when working with position. Also note that in Objective-C, you typically use CGPointMake() to create a CGPoint, but in cocos2d it is recommended to use ccp() to create a cocos2d point instead. After you have set the sprite's position, you can display it using the addChild function of the current CCScene, as shown in Listing 8–26.

Listing 8–26. *Display Sprite in the Center of Screen*

```
// ask director the window size
CGSize size = [[CCDirector sharedDirector] winSize];

// set position of image in center of screen
mySprite.position = ccp( size.width / 2, size.height / 2 );

// display image on screen in Z-Axis 0
[self addChild:newCardImage z:0];
```

> **NOTE:** ccp() is an abbreviation for a CoCos2d Point which is considered better style in Cocos2d programs instead of the standard Objective-C method CGPointMake(). If you are using Chipmunk, you will want to use cpv() instead for Chipmunk's cpVect.

Another nice feature of cocos2d is its automatic management of the Z-Axis. This basically means that the lower the number on the Z-Axis you place the image, the further back on the screen it appears. Thus, if you have a dog on Z-Axis 2, a tree on Axis 1, and the sky on Axis 0, the system will show the dog in front of the tree and the tree in front of the sky. This way you can have several nice flowing backgrounds to achieve a psuedo-3D effect in 2D games. Be aware though that the more Z-axes you use, the slower your game will perform. If you have an iPhone 3GS or later, you will want to test on the iPhone 3G and earlier to ensure that the game performs satisfactorily on older devices to reach the entire market and avoid bad reviews.

Manipulating Sprites

This is the real beauty of cocos2d. With very simple commands, you can perform many actions on your sprites with nice animations: rotate, move, scale, etc. So, let's say you have a CCSprite object called mySprite which you want to move to coordinates (25, 60), you can just use the following command:

```
[mySprite runAction:[MoveTo actionWithDuration:1.0 position:ccp(25, 60)]];
```

The runAction parameter tells the CCSprite to immediately run the following action. The actionWithDuration parameter tells the sprite how quickly it should move. In this case, it will take it one second to move to (25, 60).

Spawns

If you run multiple actions at the same time, then you can use a Spawn. Just add the actions you want in a Spawn object. These actions are like commands you give a sprite, so you can collect different commands into different variables and then combine them together into bigger commands. Let's say you want to show cards (of class CCSprite) spin while moving:

```
id deal = [MoveTo actionWithDuration:0.75 position:ccp(200, 100)];
id rotate = [RotateBy actionWithDuration:0.75 angle:360.0];
id spawn = [Spawn actions:deal, rotate, nil];
[card runAction:spawn];
```

This tells the card to move to coordinate (200, 100) and rotate itself a complete 360 degrees in 0.75 seconds. You can see multiple sprites in the middle of this action in Figure 8–8. You can add as many actions as you would like to be performed simultaneously to the Spawn. To let the system know that the action list is finished, you need to finish it with nil. Also note that if you set the actionWithDuration in one action to be different from another, then one action will continue while another has already stopped.

Figure 8–8. *Five sprites spinning and moving simultaneously*

Sequences

In the same way you can make actions happen simultaneously with a Spawn, you can make them happen one after another with a Sequence. Say you want to move a CCSprite called card in the form of a square, starting at the upper-left corner and then right, down, left, and back up:

```
card.position = ccp(100, 100);
id moveRight = [MoveTo actionWithDuration:0.5 position:ccp( 200, 100 )];
id moveDown = [MoveTo actionWithDuration:0.5 position:ccp( 200, 200 ) ];
id moveLeft = [MoveTo actionWithDuration:0.5 position:ccp ( 100, 200 )];
id moveUp = [MoveTo actionWithDuration:0.5 position:ccp( 100, 100 )];
id square = [Sequence actions:moveRight, moveDown, moveLeft, moveUp, nil];
[card runAction:square];
```

Now the card can move in a square around the screen in two seconds. If you want to call a method when you're done with a sequence, you have a problem, because you cannot just call an ordinary Objective-C function from a CCSprite. So, how can you do it? Well, you can use the CallFunc method like this which sends a selector to your sprite.

```
id sendAlert = [CallFunc actionWithTarget:self selector:@selector(sendAlert)];
```

Now that you have the action in sendAlert, you can sequence this with your preceding square action, so that the card will move in a square and then call the function sendAlert.

```
id squareAndAlert = [Sequence actions:square, sendAlert, nil];
[card runAction:squareAndAlert];

-(void) sendAlert {
        // Send alert here
}
```

You can also cause something to repeat a certain number of times or forever.

```
id rotate = [RotateBy actionWithDuration:1.0 angle:360.0];

// This will cause the card to rotate 5 times.
[card runAction:[Repeat actionWithAction:rotate times:5]];

// ...or you can choose to have this card rotate forever
[card runAction:[RepeatForever actionWithAction:rotate]];
```

Putting It All together

Now that you have the menu and the logic, let's create the heart of the game interface: PokerGameScene.h and .m which will inherit from CCLayer. You will need to allocate memory for the following:

- A deck (Deck)
- A simple hand (SimpleHand)
- Card images (NSMutableArray which will hold CCSprite objects)
- A deal button image (Sprite)

- A hand label (CCLabel) to show hand value

- First or second draw state (BOOL)

You will also need the following methods:

- for dealing a card and animating it onto the table

- toggling a card: lock or unlock it

- displaying the calculated value of a hand

You can find these object allocations and method prototypes of PokerGameScene.h in Listing 8–27

Listing 8–27. *Initialize Variables and Methods in PokerGameScene.h*

```
// When you import this file, you import all the cocos2d classes
#import "cocos2d.h"

@class Deck;
@class SimpleHand;

// PokerGame Layer
@interface PokerGame : CCLayer
{
        Deck *myDeck;
        SimpleHand *myHand;
        NSMutableArray *cardImages;
        CCSprite *dealButton;
        BOOL firstDraw;
        CCLabel *handLabel;
}

@property (nonatomic, retain) NSMutableArray *cardImages;
@property (nonatomic, retain) Deck *myDeck;
@property (nonatomic, retain) SimpleHand *myHand;
@property (nonatomic, retain) CCLabel *handLabel;

// returns a Scene that contains the HelloWorld as the only child
+(id) scene;

- (CGPoint)cardHomePoint:(NSUInteger)cardIndex locked:(BOOL)lockedVal;
- (void) dealCard:(NSUInteger)curCard;
- (void)animateCard:(NSUInteger)cardIndex;
- (void) toggleCard:(NSUInteger)cardIndex;
- (void) calculateHand;

@end
```

Now, for the moment you've been waiting for: PokerGameScene.m! You start by initializing the deck and simple hand in the init function (for more information about the Deck and SimpleHand classes, see the "Game Logic" section.). Just initializing the deck automatically shuffles it, so you can go ahead and take the first five cards and put it into your hand. Then you'll use your own calculate function to calculate the hand's rank (like is it two pair or a straight?). Listing 8–28 shows how this was done.

Listing 8–28. *Initialize Deck and Hand in PokerGameScene.m*

```
Deck *myDeck = [Deck new];
SimpleHand *myHand = [SimpleHand new];

for ( int a = 0; a < 5; a++ )
{
        [myHand addCard:[myDeck nextCard]];
}

[myHand calculate];
```

Now you'll calculate the home position of each card using a method called cardHomePoint. If the card is locked into place (so it won't get swapped out on the next deal), then this function will return a position somewhat lower than normal. Note that I will need to use the winSize function from the CCDirector to get the dimensions of the device as shown in Listing 8–29.

Listing 8–29. *Set Up Card Home Points*

```
// Calculate home point of card given its index
- (CGPoint)cardHomePoint:(NSUInteger)cardIndex locked:(BOOL)lockedVal {

        // ask director the window size
        CGSize size = [[CCDirector sharedDirector] winSize];

        NSUInteger multiplier = 1;

        // Move sprite lower for locked cards.
        if ( lockedVal ) { multiplier = 2; }

        // For each iPhone card, position it 80 pixels over
        CGPoint homePoint = ccp( (cardIndex + 1) * 80,↩
                                size.height / 2 - 50.0f * multiplier);

        return homePoint;

}
```

Before you add this next code, go ahead and copy the Images folder from my project into your project. Now load the card images that you need into memory as CCSprite objects and put them into the cardImages NSMutableArray. Next, place each card in the center of the screen, but 50 pixels off the top of the screen, so you can later spin them onto the screen to make it look like someone is dealing the cards. Then, put all the cards on Z-Axis 0, so they will appear under other sprites you put in later. Set these sprites' tags to 100-104 to make it easier to access them later if you want to change the cards on new draws. Finally, deal the cards onto the screen (see Listing 8–30).

Listing 8–30. *Load Card Sprites into Memory Using spriteWithFile and Deal Them Out*

```
cardImages = [NSMutableArray new];

for ( int a = 0; a < 5; a++ )
{
        CCSprite *newCardImage = [CCSprite new];

        // Load image of card
```

```
            newCardImage = [CCSprite spriteWithFile:[NSString stringWithFormat:@"%@.png",
                                            [myHand getCard:a]]];

            // Place card off screen centered on the top.
            newCardImage.position = ccp( size.width / 2, size.height + 50 );

            // Add card image to Z-Axis:0
            [self addChild:newCardImage z:0 tag:a+100];
            [cardImages addObject:newCardImage];
            [newCardImage release];

            // Animate card to screen
            [self dealCard:a];
            }
}
```

Here comes the fun part. The effect you want is for a card to move from offscreen to its home point in the middle, as seen back in Figure 8–8. You first set up a deal action to move the sprite from off screen to its card home point. Next, set up a rotate action to spin the card sprite 360 degrees. Note that you are setting both of these actions to happen in 0.75 seconds. Now you create a Spawn command to deal and rotate at the same time. Then, you choose the sprite you wish to deal (from the curCard parameter in the method), and run this spawn on it, as shown in Listing 8–31.

Listing 8–31. *Use Spawn to Deal a Card*

```
- (void) dealCard:(NSUInteger)curCard
{
        id deal = [CCMoveTo actionWithDuration:0.75
                                    position:[self cardHomePoint:curCard locked:NO]];

        float degrees = 360.0f;

        id rotate = [CCRotateBy actionWithDuration:0.75 angle:degrees];
        id spawn = [CCSpawn actions:deal, rotate, nil];

        [[cardImages objectAtIndex:curCard] runAction:spawn];
}
```

Events: Making It Interactive

This section describes how to detect mouse taps and drags as well as covering gotchas that are quite common among beginners on the platform. This will include how to drag a sprite under your finger and techniques for making this happen smoothly.

At this point, it may look nice to see the cards fly in on the screen, but you want to play, so you have to get ready for user interaction. A user can always do one of three things:

- Lock a card.
- Unlock a card.
- Deal new cards.

Remembering the rules, you will first get five cards, and then you can lock some into place and get new cards, similar to the way Yahtzee works. Of course, if someone locks a card, but changes his mind, he can unlock it. So, the user taps on a card to lock it. To accept taps, you first need to run the following line of code, preferably at the beginning of the init function:

```
self.isTouchEnabled = YES;
```

In the app, you don't need the accelerometer, but if you need it in your creation, use the following code:

```
self.isAccelerometerEnabled = YES;
```

Detecting Sprite Taps

You detect touches in the same way as ordinary iPhone development, through the ccTouchesBegan method. First you make sure it's a single tap, then get the coordinates of the touch and convert them to landscape mode. If the deal button was tapped, you will need to deal new cards. Otherwise, you check to see if any card was tapped (see the next section for details). If a card is tapped, and it can be locked (first draw), then the card moves down into the lock position or up if it is already locked, as can be seen in Figure 8–9 and Listing 8–32.

Figure 8–9. *Locking cards in preparation for second draw*

Listing 8–32. *Process Taps*

```
- (void)ccTouchesBegan:(NSSet *)touches withEvent:(UIEvent *)event
{
        // Get UITouch object
        UITouch *touch = [touches anyObject];
        NSUInteger numTaps = [[touches anyObject] tapCount];

        // Only process if single tap.
        if ( numTaps == 1 )
        {
                // Find point of touch
                CGPoint location = [touch locationInView: [touch view]];
                // Convert point to landscape mode
                CGPoint touchPoint = [[CCDirector sharedDirector] convertToGL:location];
```

```
        NSLog( @"You touched (%0.f, %0.f)", touchPoint.x, touchPoint.y );

        // See if deal button was tapped.
        if ( [self tappedSprite:dealButton withPoint:touchPoint] ) {
                [self dealCards];
        }

        // Check each card to see if it was tapped.
        for ( NSUInteger a = 0; a < 5; a++ ) {
            if ( [self tappedSprite:[cardImages objectAtIndex:a]
                          withPoint:touchPoint] ) {
                if ( firstDraw ) {
                        // Only lock and unlock cards
                        // if it's the first draw.
                        [self toggleCard:a];
                }
            }
        }
    }
}
```

In almost every game you will have to detect whether a sprite has been tapped or not. In the following tappedSprite function, you first get the size of the sprite with the contentSize method and its position with the position method. Then you create a rectangle object (CGRect) with the location data where the sprite is currently on screen. Once you have this information, the program then checks to see if the user has tapped somewhere between the upper-left and lower-right corner of this rectangle. See how you can do this in Listing 8–33.

Listing 8–33. *See if the Sprite Was Tapped*

```
- (BOOL)tappedSprite:(CCSprite *)curButton withPoint:(CGPoint)touchPoint
{
        CGSize sprSize = [curButton contentSize];
        CGPoint sprPos = [curButton position];

        // Make rectangle from size and position data.
        CGRect result = CGRectOffset(CGRectMake(0, 0,
                                sprSize.width,
                                sprSize.height),
                                sprPos.x-sprSize.width/2,
                                sprPos.y-sprSize.height/2);

        // See if touch is within rectangle.
        if ( touchPoint.x > result.origin.x &&
                touchPoint.y > result.origin.y &&
                touchPoint.x < result.origin.x + result.size.width &&
                touchPoint.y < result.origin.y + result.size.height )
        {
                NSLog( @"Tapped sprite" );
                return true;
        }
        else {
                NSLog( @"DID NOT tap sprite" );
                return false;
        }
}
```

Combining Many Actions Together

To deal out new cards, you first have to move all the unlocked cards (while rotating to get a better visual effect). Then, once the card is off screen, you have to change the card image to the newly dealt card and send it spinning back on screen. Once the cards come back, you need to call your function (calculate) to show the value of the hand (such as two pair or full house).

Listing 8–34. *Remove and Deal New Cards*

```
- (void) dealCards
{
        // If second draw, shuffle the deck to get ready for fresh cards.
        if ( !firstDraw ) {
                [myDeck shuffle];

                // Empty hand value display
                [handLabel setString:@""];
        }

        // Temporarily state that all cards are locked to check later if still true.
        BOOL allLocked = true;

        for ( NSUInteger a = 0; a < 5; a++ )
        {
                if ( [[myHand getCard:a] locked] )
                {
                        // Card is locked, unlock it for later.
                        [[myHand getCard:a] unlock];
                }
                else
                {
                        // Something is unlocked, so change all locked state to false.
                        allLocked = false;
                        [self animateCard:a];
                }
        }

        firstDraw = !firstDraw;

        // All cards are locked, so new cards will not need to be dealt.
        if ( allLocked ) {
                NSLog( @"ALL LOCKED" );
                [self calculateHand];
        } else {
                NSLog( @"NOT ALL LOCKED" );
        }
}
```

In Listing 8–34, you can see the line of code [self animateCard:a]; which calls the method in Listing 8–35. This method uses Spawn to send a card off screen, change the card, bring it back on screen and then display the value of the resulting hand. Using what you have just learned, you should be able to read the code in Listing 8–35 without any problems. Congratulations!

Listing 8–35. *Animate Card Off Screen and Then Back*

```
- (void)animateCard:(NSUInteger)cardIndex {
    // Card is not locked, swap it out.
    CGSize size = [[CCDirector sharedDirector] winSize];

    // Prepare CCMoveTo action to send card off screen
    id dealAway = [CCMoveTo actionWithDuration:0.75
                    position:ccp( size.width / 2, size.height - 25.0 )];

    id rotate = [CCRotateBy actionWithDuration:0.75 angle:360.0];

    id dealBack; // Initialize dealBack action

    // Prepare to move card back on screen in unlocked position.
    dealBack = [CCMoveTo actionWithDuration:0.75
                    position:[self cardHomePoint:cardIndex
                                       locked:firstDraw]];

    // Create spawns to send cards away and back on screen.
    id spawnAway = [CCSpawn actions:dealAway, rotate, nil];
    id spawnBack = [CCSpawn actions:dealBack, rotate, nil];

    // Switch sprite to new card from new deal
    id changeCard = [CCCallFuncN actionWithTarget:self
                                      selector:@selector(changeCard:)];

    // Display hand rank (like one pair or three of a kind)
    id showHandRank = [CCCallFunc actionWithTarget:self
                                      selector:@selector(calculateHand)];

    // Set up sequence to send cards away, change the card,
    // bring it back and show hand rank.
    id sequence = [CCSequence actions:spawnAway, changeCard,
                    spawnBack, showHandRank, nil];

    // Finally, run the above sequence for this card.
    [[cardImages objectAtIndex:cardIndex] runAction:sequence];
}
```

Switching a Sprite Image

Unfortunately, changing the image of a sprite is not as simple as one would hope. In this case, you also have to figure out which sprite is referenced by its node which is passed from the animateCard function. Since you set the tags of your card sprites to values of 100–104, you can subtract 100 from the tag to determine which card needs to be replaced. Then you replace the card in memory with the next card from the deck.

Finally, you have to change the actual image of the sprite. The image itself is stored in what is called the texture of the sprite. So, you need to use a new CCTextureCache object, add the new image to this, and then set that as the texture of your sprite as shown in Listing 8–36.

Listing 8–36. *Swap Card Image*

```
- (void) changeCard:(id)node {
```

```
    // Subtract 100, since we set card sprite tags to 100-104.
    int cardNum = [node tag] - 100;

    // Replace card at index with the next card in the deck.
    [myHand replaceCardIndex:cardNum withCard:[myDeck nextCard]];

    // Swap out images in the card sprite for the new card.
    [[cardImages objectAtIndex:cardNum]
      setTexture:[[CCTextureCache sharedTextureCache]
                                addImage:[NSString stringWithFormat:@"%@.png",
                                                [myHand getCard:cardNum]]]];
}
```

Adding Sound

To complete the gaming experience, you'll have to provide background music and sound in your game. Fortunately, once again cocos2d makes this extraordinarily easy. First, copy the contents of the Sound folder of the sample project into your project's Resources folder. Next, you need the following line of code to import the Cocos2d simple audio engine into PokerGameScene.m which is still called SimpleAudioEngine.h although Cocos2d classes generally start with CC:

```
#import "SimpleAudioEngine.h"
```

To play the card-slide.wav sound, you simply need the following line of code which you will put at the very beginning of the toggleCard function in PokerGameScene.m:

```
[[SimpleAudioEngine sharedEngine] playEffect:@"card-slide.wav"];
```

If you have headphones plugged in, you may see the following error:

```
AQMEIOBase::DoStartIO: timeout
2010-03-21 07:59:17.244 Video Poker[662:207] AQMEDevice::StartIO: error -66681
2010-03-21 07:59:17.245 Video Poker[662:207] AUIOClient_StartIO failed (-66681)
```

This error seems only to occur sometimes in the iPhone Simulator when headphones are plugged in. Some developers were able to get around this error by hacking with settings in the Audio MIDI Setup app, but I just tested without headphones or on the iPhone itself. This appears to be a bug in iPhone Simulator which will hopefully be fixed in a future release.

As for the game, I may be spoiled, but I've always liked game background music ever since Super Mario Bros. on the original Nintendo. Well, with just a couple short lines of code, your dreams can come true and you can have background music in your game too. Here you'll start playing an mp3 file which I called poker-music.mp3.

```
[[SimpleAudioEngine sharedEngine] playBackgroundMusic:@"poker-music.mp3"];
```

Now, I don't actually recommend stopping the background music while the game is in play unless you have a very good reason to do so, but I'll stop it in this app just to demonstrate how easy it is. Between hands while the hand rank is being displayed, I will stop the music and when the next hand is dealt, I want to continue it again. Therefore, change the lines in the if (!firstDraw) block of the dealCards function in PokerGameScene.m to the following code in Listing 8–37.

Listing 8–37. *Pausing and Resuming Background Music*

```
// If second draw, shuffle the deck to get ready for fresh cards.
if ( !firstDraw ) {
        [myDeck shuffle];

        // Empty hand value display
        [handLabel setString:@""];

        // Unpause background music
        [[SimpleAudioEngine sharedEngine] resumeBackgroundMusic];
} else {
        // Pause background music
        [[SimpleAudioEngine sharedEngine] pauseBackgroundMusic];
}
```

While I've only shown you the basics, the Cocos2d sound library can be very powerful including preloading music, adjusting music volume, looping music, and even muting all sounds. For more information, see the CocosDenshion Cookbook at http://www.cocos2d-iphone.org/wiki/doku.php/cocosdenshion:cookbook.

Supporting the iPad

Since Cocos2d v0.99rc was released on Feb 1, 2010, it has supported the iPad. In Apple's iPad Programming Guide, they show three ways to support the iPad from a current iPhone app.

- Create a Universal Application that works on both devices.

- Use a single project to build separately for each device.

- Use two projects and build separately for each device.

For the sake of simplicity and ease of use for the reader, I will create a Universal Application. Since many of you may be new to iPad development, I will also quickly explain how to port an iPhone app to the iPad. Note that this was written using the iPhone SDK 3.2 and details may have changed before this book's publication.

First, make sure that the Video Poker target is selected as the Active Target in the Overview, Now select the Video Poker Target and choose **Project ➤ Upgrade Current Project for iPad,** as shown in Figure 8–10.

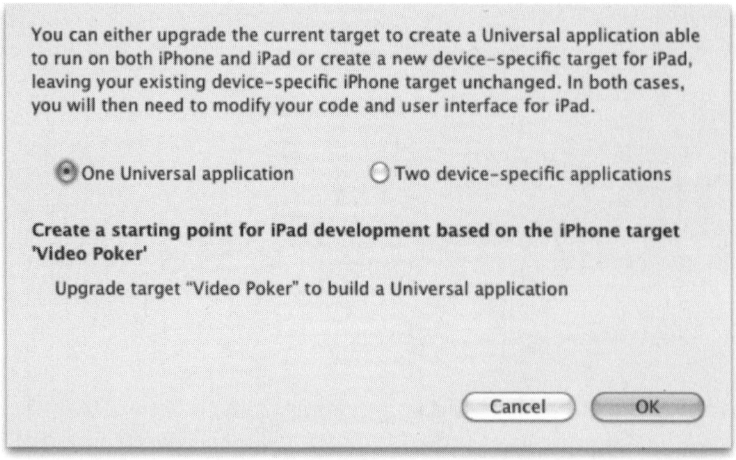

You can either upgrade the current target to create a Universal application able to run on both iPhone and iPad or create a new device-specific target for iPad, leaving your existing device-specific iPhone target unchanged. In both cases, you will then need to modify your code and user interface for iPad.

⊙ One Universal application   ○ Two device-specific applications

Create a starting point for iPad development based on the iPhone target 'Video Poker'

Upgrade target "Video Poker" to build a Universal application

(Cancel)   (OK)

Figure 8–10. *Dialog box to upgrade target for iPad*

Now let's run your new iPad app and see what you get in Figure 8–11.

Figure 8–11. *Rough menu after automated iPad upgrade*

It works, but looks a bit strange with the menu items so small. Let's increase the menu font. First, you need to determine if the app is being run on an iPad. Fortunately, Apple provides code which uses a new variable called UIUserInterfaceIdiomPad. Unfortunately though, since this is only available in the iPhone 3.2 or later, you will also have to run a preprocessor directive to check the IPHONE_OS_VERSION_MAX_ALLOWED value which must be greater than or equal to 30200, as shown in Listing 8–38. This directive tells the program to ignore this code if its iPhone OS is earlier than v3.2. Remember that the name of the OS is called iPhone OS, even if it is running on an iPod Touch or iPad (see Listing 8–38).

Listing 8–38. *Detecting if the User is on an iPad*

```
#if __IPHONE_OS_VERSION_MAX_ALLOWED >= 30200
if (UI_USER_INTERFACE_IDIOM() == UIUserInterfaceIdiomPad)
{
    // The device is an iPad running iPhone 3.2 or later.
}
else
{
    // The device is an iPhone or iPod touch.
}
#endif
```

Now you can add larger menu fonts in Listing 8–39 right before declaring all of your CCMenuItem objects in MainMenuScene.m which will result in a much better looking menu, as shown in Figure 8–12.

Listing 8–39. *Increase Font Only on the iPad*

```
#if __IPHONE_OS_VERSION_MAX_ALLOWED >= 30200
if (UI_USER_INTERFACE_IDIOM() == UIUserInterfaceIdiomPad)
{
        // The device is an iPad running iPhone 3.2 or later.
        [CCMenuItemFont setFontSize:64];
}
#endif
```

Figure 8–12. *A new, improved menu for the iPad*

Next, you need to look at what happened to your gameplay which you can see in Figure 8–13.

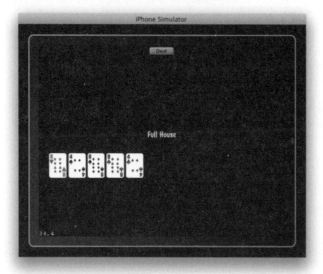

Figure 8–13. *Rough game after iPad project upgrade*

You need a larger Deal button, larger card rank text, and larger cards. First, start by increasing the size of the deal button. Normally you would use separate larger sprites, but to simplify things, just scale up the deal button to be a better fit for the iPad, as shown in Listing 8–40.

Listing 8–40. *Increase Size of Deal Button on the iPad*

```
#if __IPHONE_OS_VERSION_MAX_ALLOWED >= 30200
// Increase font size if user is on an iPad
if ( UI_USER_INTERFACE_IDIOM() == UIUserInterfaceIdiomPad )
{
    // The device is an iPad running iPhone 3.2 or later.
    [dealButton runAction:[CCScaleBy actionWithDuration:0.1f scale:2.0f]];
}
#endif
```

Next, you increase the font size for the card rank text. You need to substitute your current code in the init function of PokerGameScene.m to Listing 8–41.

Listing 8–41. *Increase Font size of handLabel on the iPad*

```
// create and initialize a Label
#if __IPHONE_OS_VERSION_MAX_ALLOWED >= 30200
    // Increase font size if user is on an iPad
    if ( UI_USER_INTERFACE_IDIOM() == UIUserInterfaceIdiomPad ){
        // The device is an iPad running iPhone 3.2 or later.
        handLabel = [CCLabel labelWithString:@"" fontName:@"Marker Felt"↵
fontSize:64];
    } else {
    // The device is an iPhone or iPod touch.
    handLabel = [CCLabel labelWithString:@""
                            fontName:@"Marker Felt"
                            fontSize:32];
```

```
        }
#else
        // The device is an iPhone or iPod touch earlier than v3.2
        handLabel = [CCLabel labelWithString:@"" fontName:@"Marker Felt" fontSize:32];
#endif
```

Now comes the hard part: the card images. I like the ratio of the card width to the iPhone's screen width, so the card images are 75×101 and the iPhone's screen is 320×480. The iPad's resolution is 1024×768. Fortunately, all you care about here are the widths, so you can put them into the simple equation in Figure 8–14.

$$\frac{75}{480} = \frac{x}{1024}$$

Figure 8–14. *Simple formula to calculate desired iPad image size*

Feeling lazy, I put this equation into Wolfram Alpha and it gave me the solution: x = 160. Luckily, my source images are much larger than that, so I shove them into the Mac app ResizeMe, which I bought to do mass resizing of photos and voilà, iPad-appropriate images. Now I rename all the images using Terminal.

```
for x in *.png; do mv $x Large-$x; done
```

Now, modify the cardHomePoint function in PokerGameScene.m to work for the iPad. Luckily, you only need to change the amount of pixels, so Listing 8–42 is the only code you have to add right before returning homePoint.

Listing 8–42. *Change Card Positions on the iPad*

```
#if __IPHONE_OS_VERSION_MAX_ALLOWED >= 30200
        // Increase font size if user is on an iPad
        if ( UI_USER_INTERFACE_IDIOM() == UIUserInterfaceIdiomPad ) {
                // The device is an iPad running iPhone 3.2 or later.
                homePoint = ccp( (cardIndex + 1) * 170.66667f,
                                 size.height / 2 - 100.f * multiplier );
        }
#endif
```

Finally, I need to modify the card file name in Card.m. Just add Listing 8–43 to the beginning of the description function, so it will return Large- at the beginning of the filename.

Listing 8–43. *Change Card Image Filename on the iPad*

```
#if __IPHONE_OS_VERSION_MAX_ALLOWED >= 30200
        // Increase font size if user is on an iPad
        if ( UI_USER_INTERFACE_IDIOM() == UIUserInterfaceIdiomPad )
        {
                // The device is an iPad running iPhone 3.2 or later.
                return [NSString stringWithFormat:@"Large-%@%@",
                        [self humanRank],
                        [self humanSuit]];
        }
#endif
```

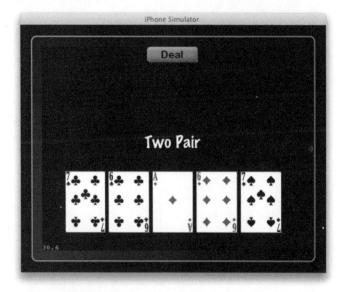

Figure 8–15. *Finished sample game for iPad*

Further Exploring cocos2d

Due to cocos2d's open vibrant community, there are many open source projects from which you can learn. If you are more interested in developing physics, Ray Wenderlich has a set of blog posts introducing the reader to cocos2d (http://www.raywenderlich.com/352/how-to-make-a-simple-iphone-game-with-cocos2d-tutorial) and then to Box2d (http://www.raywenderlich.com/457/intro-to-box2d-with-cocos2d-tutorial-bouncing-balls). Since 0.99 was just released at the time of this writing, there is not much current sample code online, but it should be easier to find by the time this book is in your hands.

I'd also highly recommend checking out the forum at http://www.cocos2d-iphone.org/forum/ if you have any further questions. The community is always very helpful and I look forward to seeing your next creation. In any case, you now have a good foundation to start a deeper exploration of the cocos2d framework. Remember, the most successful cocos2d app, StickWars (a castle defense game) stayed in the App Store's paid top ten list for three months. Hopefully your game will stay at least four months!

David Smith

Company: Traveling Classics

Location: Herndon, Virginia

Former Life as a Developer:

- *Ruby*
- *Java*
- *.NET*

Life as an iPhone Developer: I began iPhone development as a hobby in 2008 with an application I wrote while on a family vacation. Over the succeeding two years that hobby grew into a full-time profession, and I've now built a business large enough to support six employees. Our breakthrough moment was when our Audiobooks app was released and, in the absence of a marketing campaign, soared to become the number-one book app in the store. The App Store continues to be our focus, and while we dabble in some of the new awesome technologies that seem to be constantly appearing in the mobile space, Audiobooks is still our primary application.

Apps on the App Store:

- *Audiobooks (Books)*
- *AudioBookShelf (Books)*
- *Somewhere around 150 individual audiobook apps for specific titles (Books)*
- *PerDiem (Travel)*
- *PictureBooks (Education)*
- *ZenDraw (Entertainment)*
- *TweetThisSong (Entertainment)*

What's in This Chapter: A discussion of how to build an audio-focused application, including design considerations, a case study of our Audiobooks app, and a detailed guide on how to build your first audio player.

Key Technologies:

- *AVAudioPlayer*
- *UIKit*

Chapter 9

Creating an Audio-Centric App for the iPhone with AVAudioPlayer

I've loved audiobooks for years. When I used to commute hours into work, they kept me sane. Now that I make audiobooks apps, they keep me fed.

I remember how it felt when I first heard about the iPhone SDK. It was a combination of opportunity and intimidation. I think there was a collective appreciation that this was going to be huge, and that for probably the first time since the .COM bubble that individual developers could write some code and make their fortune. Well, that was the dream anyway.

To begin, I started creating what I think has become the "Hello World" of the iPhone, a Tip Calculator. This was never intended to see the light of day. Coming from a Java/Ruby background, just getting used to the conventions of Objective-C and its unique syntax took some time. That rite of passage behind me, I then started making my first app. It was a Per Diem calculator that allowed me to dive into things like database management and then tackling the App Store submission process. The best advice I was ever given in regard to doing first submission to the app store was to print out the directions, pick a quiet time in the day without distractions, and go through line by line, checking off each step as I read. The process is tricky to get right at first, but this method saved me from the headaches I hear lots of new developers have.

Audiobooks wasn't my first foray into iPhone development. However, it has certainly been my most successful. The idea for it came almost immediately when I first stumbled across the Librivox project. The Librivox project coordinates volunteers to narrate classic, public domain literary works, and then releases the recordings freely into the public domain. They have a catalog of over 3,000 works spanning most genres and topics. At once, I had the idea to write an app that would wrap this immense collection and make it accessible on the iPhone. The real wonder of the Librivox project is that it includes such a variety of works. There are famous novels, children's books, poetry, and non-fiction. This makes it an ideal venue to attract a diverse customer base. Plus, since it is all free content I could wrap it all in a free or $0.99 app.

At its core, Audiobooks is a simple application that lets the user browse/search through the Librivox collection. They can read book descriptions and choose what books they want to listen to. Then, the app downloads the book's mp3 contents and lets the user listen to the chosen classic.

This chapter will walk you through the design and development process of creating Audiobooks. I hope that at the end of it, you will have a good understanding of the challenges and opportunities in creating an audio-focused application. Specifically, this chapter will cover:

- UI Design for audio-centric apps

- Core APIs and frameworks needed

- Walk-through the development of a simple audio app

- Discuss the high-level aspects of the business of development

Design

At the core of building an application on any platform, but especially the iPhone, is the layout of the design and the user's interaction with it. It is essential to have a thoughtful examination of how the user will experience your applications content and be proactive about making that a positive experience.

Designing for Your Target User

The design of an audio focused application takes on a slightly different process than that of a more traditional, visually focused app. The UI of an audio focused application is more about getting the user set up to start listening. Once they begin listening, they typically turn off the display and stop interacting with the UI. This means that while most users' sessions are over 45 minutes, they will only see the UI for a few minutes.

The second major consideration in designing an application is to define the target audience. We were seeking to create an application with as broad an appeal as possible. That means that we can assume no prior experience or skills of our users. For us, that meant streamlining our application to be as simple as possible. The user is presented with a simple option to select how they want to browse for their titles. After a quick description to make sure they want it, then two to three seconds later they are listening.

Our Design Process

The iPhone's small screen means that each screen tends to have a highly focused purpose and use. When designing our applications we tend toward designing each screen's content individually. This helps us keep a focus on the goals that particular screen is trying to accomplish and ensure we don't include any extraneous content or functionality.

Home Screen

Most often, the first interaction the user has with the application and the screen is the Home Screen. Because it is the first place the user lands when launching the app, it needs to load quickly and provide simple navigation to the other parts of the app. Our initial attempts at this page rendered it too simple. We just included the Titles, Authors, and Most Popular links plus a link to the Library. It quickly became clear that this would be insufficient. Our initial user feedback was that they wanted as many different ways to navigate through our 3,000 books as possible. So we added the Languages, Narrators, Genres, and Surprise Me features (see Figure 9–1).

Figure 9–1. *Home screen*

Surprise Me is a feature that bears some further discussion. This is a simple link that randomly selects a book for the user to try. It is a simple idea that took only a few minutes to implement. However, it has routinely been referenced as one of the "most fun" parts of Audiobooks. It takes the task of browsing and makes it feel like a game. It almost feels like a slot machine, because you can keep hitting it again and again until you find a book you like. Generally, whenever you can find a way to make a mundane part of your app (in this case, browsing through thousands of books) into something that is more interactive I find users really enjoy it.

Book Selection Screens

The actual browser screens in Audiobooks follow a very simple UI. They each include a Search bar at the top to allow the user to quickly filter down lists of potentially thousands of books. Secondly, a section navigator on the right side is included that lets the user quickly scan through the contents, organized by name (see Figure 9–2).

Figure 9–2. *Book Selection screens*

Getting this window to display with acceptable performance was made possible by the introduction of Core Data in the 3.0 release of the SDK, specifically by using a NSFetchedResultsController. This class provides a wrapper for accessing your core data store that performs smart caching and paging of the rows in your database. Using this, the phones can display a 3,000 row table view and scroll through it without delay.

Book Information Screen

Once the user has selected a book, a screen sharing the details of the book is provided. This is one of the few places where we decided to embellish the look of the UI. Generally, our UI is simple and straightforward, focused on getting the user to their audio. Also, because the user won't be spending much time looking at it, a more utilitarian UI makes sense. For this screen, however, the user is actually reading through a reasonably long bit of text and making a decision about whether to download this book or not. Therefore, we decided to keep with the generally bluish tones of the standard iPhone tab bar, but texturize and embellish the background and buttons. Our goal for this is similar to the goals of a book's cover. We want the user to be attracted to the aesthetics of the imagery so that they are more inclined toward listening to our books (see Figure 9–3).

Figure 9–3. *Book Information screen*

Player Screen

The player screen is the most streamlined of the screens. The goal here is to provide the typical playback controls (play, pause, skip, and rewind) and the core-related functionality. We experimented here with a variety of designs, ranging from the very intricate to the downright plain looking. In the end, we settled on a very simple black background with gray/white buttons. We felt this spartan approach was reminiscent of the iPod app and would hopefully make it very clear about how to use this screen. We also didn't want to have too much going on with this screen since the users were most often going to immediately lock the device screen once they start listening (see Figure 9–4).

Figure 9–4. *Player screen*

Another aspect of this screen that took a lot of discipline to achieve was cutting back on the number of added embellishments. It can be tempting to go crazy in Photoshop, adding more and more detail to a screen until it becomes gaudy.

Implementation

The iPhone SDK provides a variety of ways to play audio. These are all essentially differing levels of abstraction on top of the Core Audio framework (see Figure 9–5).

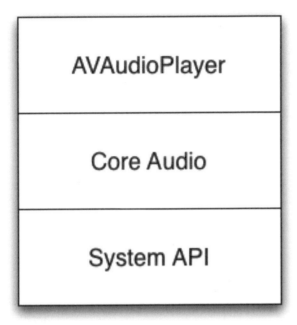

Figure 9–5. *iPhone OS Audio stack*

The Core Audio framework provides total control over audio playback, but does it at the price of complexity. This framework requires the direct management of the audio data and playback. The use of Core Audio usually only makes sense if you need that level of control on the audio session. Generally, I find that using the AVFoundation classes is much more productive. My initial experiments with using Core Audio directly lead to a lot of headaches and complications. If simple playback and control is all that is required, AVFoundation is the way to go.

AVFoundation is a collection of utility classes that hide the details of Core Audio away from the developer and let them get on with development. For playback, the primary class to look at is AVAudioPlayer. This provides a clean and straightforward interface for playing back a variety of formats of sound. The supported file formats (as of SDK version 3.0) are shown in Table 9–1.

Table 9–1. *Supported Audio Formats in SDK Version 3.0*

Format	Usual Extensions
MPEG-1, Layer 3	.mp3
MPEG-2 or MPEG-4 ADTS	.aac
AIFF	.aif,.aiff
CAF	.caf
WAV	.wav
MPEG-4	.m4a, mp4

Example Project

The creation of our Audiobooks application involves a lot of file management and interactions with web services to allow the user to navigate through the thousands of audiobooks in our collection. However, the core capability of our application is that it can play and manage a user's place in MP3 files. I will now walk through the creation of a simple application that does just that. It will provide basic playback controls for play, pause, skip forward, and back. Plus, it will include basic bookmarking to keep the user's place and resume where they left off.

Getting Started

To demonstrate how to use AVAudioPlayer in a simple application I will now discuss the creation of an application that provides for playback of an MP3 file. This will include the following:

- Player initialization and setup
- Playback controls (Play, Pause, Skip Forward, and Skip Back)
- On screen display of time elapsed and remaining
- Setting up the correct audio session

This tutorial assumes that you have Xcode and iPhone SDK 3.0 or greater installed on your development machine.

To get things started, let's launch Xcode and create a new project (File ➤ New Project), select a "View-based Application," and then name it AudioExample, as shown in Figure 9–6.

Figure 9–6. *Create a new view-based application*

This will have give you a basic template from which to set up your project. Run your application now (Build ➤ Build and Run) and you will see a basic flashlight app with a plain gray background (see Figure 9–7).

Figure 9–7. *Starting point*

Setting Up the UI

The UI will have the following controls:

- Three UIButtons
    - Play & Pause
    - Skip Forward
    - Skip Backward
- Two UILabels
    - A time elapsed label
    - A time remaining label

First, you will set up the outlets for the UI controls. Open the file AudioExampleViewController.h found in the Classes group, as shown in Figure 9–8.

Figure 9–8. *Basic application classes*

Add to this file the IBOutlet declarations for the UI elements. You don't need outlets to the back and forward buttons since they are not changed during execution.

These declarations will look like the following code:

```
IBOutlet UIButton* playPauseButton;
IBOutlet UILabel* timeRemaining;
IBOutlet UILabel* timeElapsed;
```

and should be added inside of the @interface block.

Next, add the IBAction methods for the buttons to call when clicked. You need one of these for each of the buttons.

```
-(IBAction)playPauseButtonClicked;
-(IBAction)forwardButtonClicked;
-(IBAction)backButtonClicked;
```

Now let's add some UI elements to control and display the playback of our file. Locate and open the AudioExampleViewController.xib file in the Resources group (see Figure 9–9).

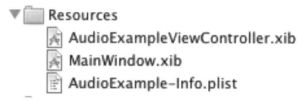

Figure 9–9. *UI resource classes*

This will bring up the Interface Builder, where you can connect the outlets to actual UI controls. Drag from the Library panel the three Round Rect Buttons and give them titles corresponding to the three functions the app has (see Figure 9–10).

Figure 9–10. *Playback controls*

Next, add two UILabels to display time elapsed and remaining. This should result in a UI that looks like Figure 9–11.

Figure 9–11. *Full UI*

Now connect these controls to their corresponding outlets in the view controller. This is done by control-clicking on the File's Owner element in the main Interface Builder window and then dragging from the corresponding outlet to the desired control. This process is repeated until all of the controls in the view controller have been matched up with their physical control (see Figure 9–12).

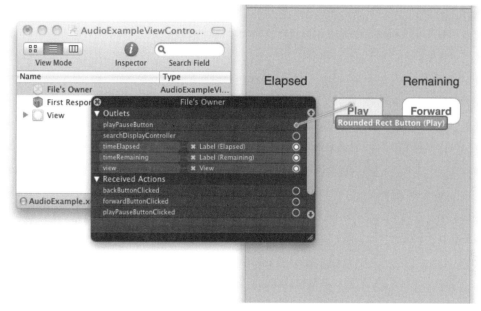

Figure 9–12. *Connection IBOutlets*

Next, connect the IBActions to their controls, Touch Up Inside method, as shown in Figures 9–13 and 9–14.

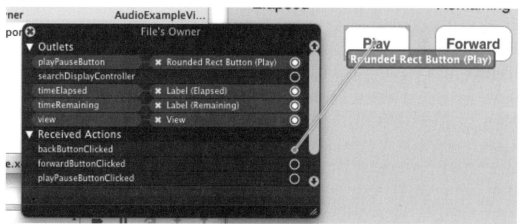

Figure 9–13. *Connecting IBActions (Step 1)*

Figure 9–14. *Connecting IBActions (Step 2)*

Coding the Audio Player

You can now begin to implement the various methods needed to set up playback. First, you need to quickly add an example mp3 file to use during playback. This can be any supported file you need. For this example, I have a file named example.mp3 that will be added to the project. To add a file to the project control-click on the Resources group and select Add ➤ Existing Files… then browse to your file and select it.

Next, you need to add the AVFoundation framework to your project. This is done by control-clicking the current target and then selecting Get Info (see Figure 9–15).

Figure 9–15. *Setting the options for the target*

Then, add the AVFoundation Framework in the Linked Libraries area (see Figure 9–16).

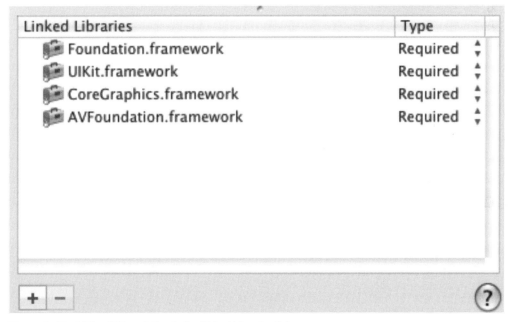

Figure 9–16. *Adding AVFoundation to the Linked Libraries list*

The AVFoundation classes provide wrapper classes for simple audio playback and recording. The main class you will be concerned with is AVAudioPlayer. This provides a mechanism to playback any supported media file and then control and monitor its state.

You then import the AVFoundation classes in AudioExampleViewController.h.

```
#import <AVFoundation/AVFoundation.h>
```

In order to control the playback, once you have begun playing you will need to retain a reference to the player. Add an AVAudioPlayer variable to the view controller for this purpose.

```
AVAudioPlayer* player;
```

Connecting the Play/Pause Button

First, let's fill in the body of the playPauseButtonClicked method. This method will be called whenever the play/pause button is pressed. To start this, set up an AVAudioPlayer and begin it playing. The body of this method will look like the following code:

```
-(IBAction)playPauseButtonClicked {
        NSBundle* bundle =[NSBundle mainBundle];
        NSString* path = [bundle pathForResource:@"example" ofType:@"mp3"];
        NSURL *url = [NSURL fileURLWithPath:path];

        player = [[AVAudioPlayer alloc] initWithContentsOfURL:url error:nil];
        [player play];
}
```

> **NOTE:** Replace the string @"example" and @"mp3" with the filename and extension of the media you are going to play.

If you run the app now and hit the play button, your sound file should begin playing. You may have noticed, however, that your playPauseButton still says "Play". To fix this, you need to update the label of the button based on the player state. Add this to the end of the playPauseButtonClicked method.

```
if([player isPlaying]) {
        [playPauseButton setTitle:@"Pause" forState:UIControlStateNormal];
} else {
        [playPauseButton setTitle:@"Play" forState:UIControlStateNormal];
}
```

Now the label updates correctly, but when you click the pause button it just keeps playing. To pause playback, you need to check to see if the player has been initialized and if it has then to select pause. Otherwise, select initialize and play. Replace the original initialization with this one.

```
-(IBAction)playPauseButtonClicked {
  if(player == nil) {
    NSBundle* bundle =[NSBundle mainBundle];
    NSString* path = [bundle pathForResource:@"example" ofType:@"mp3"];
    NSURL *url = [NSURL fileURLWithPath:path];
    player = [[AVAudioPlayer alloc] initWithContentsOfURL:url error:nil];
  }
  if([player isPlaying]) {
    [playPauseButton setTitle:@"Play" forState:UIControlStateNormal];
    [player pause];
  } else {
    [playPauseButton setTitle:@"Pause" forState:UIControlStateNormal];
```

```
        [player play];
    }
}
```

Run the application now to see that it is functioning correctly. You can start and stop playback as you like by clicking the playPauseButton.

Connecting the Skip Controls

Next, let's set up the skip forward and backwards methods. This is done by filling out the backButtonclicked and forwardButtonClicked methods.

```
-(IBAction)forwardButtonClicked {
        if(player != nil && [player isPlaying]) {
                player.currentTime += 30;
        }
}
-(IBAction)backButtonClicked {
        if(player != nil && [player isPlaying]) {
                        player.currentTime -= 30;
        }
}
```

These check to see if the player is set up and playing before adjusting the currentTime attribute. This is measured in seconds.

Providing Player State in the UI

Now it's time to make those time elapsed remaining labels update as the file is played. The AVAudioPlayer provides no mechanism for getting updates on playback position so instead you set up a timer to update the display once per second. Add this call to the initialization section of your playPauseClicked method directly after the initialization of the player.

```
[NSTimer scheduledTimerWithTimeInterval:1.0 target:self selector:@selector(onTimer)
    userInfo:nil repeats:YES];
```

Then, add the onTimer method to actually update your display.

```
-(void)onTimer {

  if(player != nil && [player isPlaying]) {

    float remainingTime = player.duration - player.currentTime;
    timeElapsed.text = [NSString stringWithFormat:@"%0.1f",player.currentTime];
    timeRemaining.text = [NSString stringWithFormat:@"-%0.1f",remainingTime];

  } else {
    timeElapsed.text = @"";
    timeRemaining.text = @"";
  }

}
```

Understanding Audio Sessions

The iPhone SDK uses audio sessions to determine how the device should be respond to various audio impacting events. These are described in Table 9–2.

Table 9–2. *AudioSession Types*

Session Type	Allow Other Audio	Input/Output	Respect Sile Switch
kAudioSessionCategory_AmbientSound	Yes	Output only	Yes
kAudioSessionCategory_SoloAmbientSound	No	Output only	Yes
kAudioSessionCategory_MediaPlayback	No	Output Only	No
kAudioSessionCategory_RecordAudio	No	Input Only	No
kAudioSessionCategory_PlayAndRecord	No	Input and Output	No

For the purposes of this example application, you would choose the kAudioSessionCategory_MediaPlayback category, because you want playback to not mix with the iPod application and for playback to continue whether or not the silent switch is set.

Add the Audio Toolbox framework to your current target then add the following after your player initialization code in playPauseButtonClicked. The first step creates a variable with the correct session value. Then you initialize an AudioSession with all default settings. Next, you set the session to your desired mode. Finally, you activate the session.

```
UInt32 category = kAudioSessionCategory_MediaPlayback;
AudioSessionInitialize(NULL,NULL,NULL,NULL);
AudioSessionSetProperty (kAudioSessionProperty_AudioCategory, sizeof (category),
    &category);
AudioSessionSetActive (true);
```

Now, you have a fully working audio application. The finished result should look like Figure 9–17.

Figure 9–17. *Final App*

Summary

Our Audiobooks application has been a massive success. It has stood as the number one Book app and has hundreds of thousands of downloads. It was initially created in around five days of full-time effort and has now become successful to such a degree that it supports a small company of three. This is truly a remarkable aspect in the App Store. There is a lot of talk about how iPhone apps are a gold rush, so there is a lot of exuberance. While this is no doubt correct, there are a lot of very disappointed developers out there, many of who came to the platform expecting quick riches and automatic success.

For me, the App Store has shown that when individual developers can be made accessible to customers, customers get exactly what they want. I think the real uniqueness of the App Store is that it has created the first software ecosystem where customers feel comfortable working with small indie developers (because they have Apple acting as curator), and so the brilliant ideas of developers can be immediately tried. Coming into that kind of market requires that developers be creative (it is hard to succeed if you are just copying other successes). For developers to be agile, you have to be first to market and then iterate to stay ahead. Finally, be realistic and don't put all your eggs in one basket. Audiobooks was my eighth app. Keep trying! Eventually if you have the right skills and good ideas, the marketplace will reward you.

Joost van de Wijgerd and Arne de Vries

Company: *eBuddy*

Location: *Amsterdam, the Netherlands*

Former Life as a Developer: Joost has been designing and developing Java applications since 1996. His areas of expertise are server side development, high performance java, and scalable architectures. Joost is an Open Source advocate and has been active in and working with Open Source Java projects since 2000. Most notably, is his work on the Spring Framework of which he was one of the early adopters as well as one of the founders of SpringSource, the commercial company built around the product. At eBuddy, Joost is responsible for the overall architecture of the eBuddy server platform.

Arne finished his Master's degree on Telematics at Twente University in Enschede, the Netherlands in 2008. He started with iPhone development in 2007 as part of his Master's thesis project, and at the same time worked as lead iPhone developer at Mobilaria, Enschede, creating the basis for their streaming radio applications that are now available in the AppStore. Arne has been working at eBuddy since 2009 as lead iPhone developer, taking over the development of the eBuddy iPhone applications.

Life as an iPhone Developer: Arne created the basis for multiple streaming-radio iPhone applications, using an adaptive bit-rate switching technique developed during his Master's-thesis project.

Apps on the App Store:

- *eBuddy Messenger (Social Networks)*

- *eBuddy Pro Messenger (Social Networks)*

What's in This Chapter: This chapter describes the implementation of Push Notifications in the eBuddy iPhone application. It discusses both server side and client side aspects of the Apple Push Notifications framework.

Key Technologies:

- *Apple Push Notifications*

- *Java 6*

- *Apache Mina*

Chapter 10

Implementing Push Notifications at eBuddy

In this chapter we would like to share our experiences with implementing push notification for the eBuddy iPhone application. While being relatively late to market with our iPhone application, we were the first free Instant Messaging application to have push notifications. To get there, we had to overcome a number of hurdles yet we have learned a lot in the process. Since supporting push notification requires an application to have a server side component, we would like to tell our story from the client development and server development perspectives. We were both part of the core development team that created the eBuddy iPhone application and we also currently continue to work on extending and improving its functionality.

Introduction to eBuddy

eBuddy was founded in 2003 as e-Messenger and created the world's first, independent, web browser-based Instant Messaging service for MSN. The company was rebranded in 2006 from e-Messenger to eBuddy and now enables millions of users worldwide to chat free of charge in one aggregated interface on multiple networks besides MSN, such as AIM, Google Talk, Yahoo!, Facebook, MySpace, Hyves and ICQ, without having to download or install any application on their computer. The eBuddy web application is mostly used in public places where users are not allowed to install applications, or where firewalls block connections to popular chat networks, like companies and schools.

eBuddy also offers a web application optimized for mobile phones (eBuddy Lite), and chat clients for mobile phones supporting mobile Java (J2ME), Android phones, and the iPhone. We have been the most downloaded Java application on getjar.com since January 2008, and send more than ten billion chat messages all over the world each month. Our free iPhone application has been downloaded more than three million times and our paid iPhone application with special features like push notification for a longer time is seeing good uptake.

The company eBuddy is located in the heart of Amsterdam, and at the time of writing employs over 60 people from which around 20 people are full-time developers.

The eBuddy Messenger

The eBuddy Messenger is a Multi Network Instant Messaging Client meaning you can add multiple accounts to your eBuddy ID account. The account details are remembered, so the next time you log in to eBuddy you will be automatically logged in to your IM Network accounts. The different applications will show you an aggregated list of all your buddies and their status (online, away, offline, etc). The server part of the eBuddy service is written in Java. When you log in to one of our clients, the client connects to one of these servers and the server then creates the actual connections with the IM networks. Most of our clients offer, besides chatting of course, managing your buddies (adding, blocking, and deleting them), starting group chats, managing your different IM accounts, and setting your displayname, personal message, and status. Some of the clients also support setting your display pictures, sending pictures, and video chatting.

The eBuddy iPhone Application

There are two eBuddy iPhone applications: the free version called eBuddy Messenger and a paid version called eBuddy Pro Messenger. eBuddy Messenger has all of the basic chat features: sending messages, smileys, and buzzers; managing buddies and IM accounts; setting your personal information like displayname, personal message, and status; starting and chatting in group chats; viewing pictures and web sites inside the application, etc. The eBuddy Pro Messenger can also send pictures to your buddies, set your display picture, and offers a longer Push timeout than the free version.

Due to the nature of the iPhone environment, the application on the device will shutdown and be removed from memory when the user goes to the Springboard or when there is a period of inactivity; no applications other than Apple's own applications can exist in the background. At these moments, the application will lose the connection with our server. In order to solve this lack of applications running in the background, Apple chose to offer the Push Notification Service, so users can still receive messages for applications that are not running. When a disconnect from a client application is detected, all incoming messages and some events (such as network disconnects) are sent to the iPhone using these push messages.

We created a specialized server component called the Push Server to support the Push functionality for the iPhone. The iPhone application connects to the Push Server directly, and the Push Server connects to one of the normal servers. After it is detected that the iPhone application was shut down or got disconnected in some other way, the session on the Push Server stays alive for a specific amount of time that can be set by the user from within the application. We keep the state of the session in memory because of performance reasons, but it would also be possible to keep the state in a database. Figure 10–1 shows how this works.

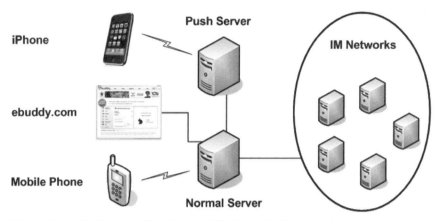

Figure 10–1. *eBuddy connection diagram while the application is running*

Figure 10–2 shows how the messages arrive on the iPhone as Push Notifications when the eBuddy application is not running and there is no connection between the iPhone and the eBuddy Push Server available.

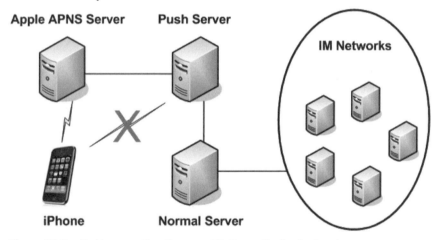

Figure 10–2. *eBuddy connection diagram while the application is closed*

Apple Push Notification Service

Through Push Notifications Apple provides application developers with a tool to communicate with their users even when the application is not active on the device. This is a very powerful feature since it enables long-running sessions while saving battery life. An obvious drawback for application developers is that you need a server-side component to facilitate the communication between your application and the iPhone. Apple acts as a middleman to deliver messages to the device.

The Communication Flow

The iPhone Dev Center web site gives an excellent explanation[1] about the Apple Push Notification Service (APNS) which we will quickly reiterate here.

1. First, the application must register itself with APNS.

2. APNS will return a token that can be used to send notifications to the device.

3. The application must communicate this token to the server side component.

4. The server side component must create a TLS (secure) connection to APNS using the Provider certificate.

5. During the lifetime of the session, the server side component must send messages to APNS in a binary format.

6. The user will be presented with a Push Notification on the iPhone and gets the opportunity to start the application; if the application is running a callback method will be called.

Another important aspect to consider is feedback. Since the server keeps a client session online while the application on the iPhone is off, it could happen that a user either disables push, or deinstalls the application altogether. Apple uses the feedback service to provide the application with feedback on messages that couldn't be delivered to the device for one of the reasons previously stated. The server will then terminate the session.

The Client Implementation

To register for push notifications, the application has to start by requesting a device token from the device, which you can do by calling a method on the UIApplication. This is best done when the application is starting up in the applicationDidFinshLaunching method of your UIApplicationDelegate. In this method, you can specify for which types of notifications you want to register.

■ *Alert*: The user gets a pop-up when the notification is received, with either one or two buttons. When one button is shown, clicking it will dismiss the alert. When two buttons are shown, the first dismisses the alert while the second button opens the application.

■ *Badge*: The push notifications change the badge number on the applications icon on the Springboard.

---

[1] Apple Push Notification Service Programming Guide

- *Sound*: A sound is played and/or the phone vibrates when the push notification is received.

To register for all three types, format your call like this:

```
- (void)applicationDidFinishLaunching:(UIApplication *)application {
        [[UIApplication sharedApplication]
        registerForRemoteNotificationTypes:UIRemoteNotificationTypeAlert|
        UIRemoteNotificationTypeBadge|UIRemoteNotificationTypeSound];

        // other initialization code…
}
```

BACKWARDS COMPATIBILITY

Use the following line of code to check whether the operating system supports push notifications:

```
[[UIApplication sharedApplication] respondsToSelector:
@selector(registerForRemoteNotificationTypes:)]
```

This way it is possible to register for push notifications on operating systems that contain this functionality, and still support older operating systems (OS 2.x) that don't support push notifications.

You have to call this method on the UIApplication every time the application starts; calling this method when running the application for the first time will pop-up an alert to the user giving a choice whether to allow or deny push notifications to be sent. If the user gives the green light for push notifications, the phone will call a callback function that has to be implemented by your UIApplicationDelegate:

```
- (void)application:(UIApplication *)application
didRegisterForRemoteNotificationsWithDeviceToken:(NSData *)deviceToken;
```

In this callback, the deviceToken variable is passed, which contains the token that the server has to include when sending push notifications to that specific phone. Inside the body of this method, you may want to include your logic for communicating the device token to the server. This can be done however you prefer; you probably already have a client-server communication protocol in place. To convert the deviceToken object to a string you can simply use [deviceToken description]. If something went wrong registering for remote notifications, the phone will call the following method on your UIApplicationDelegate:

```
- (void)application:(UIApplication *)application
didFailToRegisterForRemoteNotificationsWithError:(NSError *)error;
```

The error variable contains the reason why the phone couldn't register for remote notifications. In the body of this method, you may want to notify the user that something went wrong, for instance by showing an alert.

Although we try to prevent it, it can be possible that the phone receives a push notification for the application, while the application is running. This can happen, for example, when the connection with the server is lost and the server thinks that the application is closed, or when a push message sent when the application was actually closed got delayed somewhere on its way from the eBuddy servers, via the Apple Push Notification servers, to the phone. To prevent this notification from being shown to the user (which could be confusing for the user when the application is already running), you can implement the following method in your UIApplicationDelegate:

```
- (void)application:(UIApplication *)application
didReceiveRemoteNotification:(NSDictionary *)userInfo;
```

The userInfo variable contains the information in the push notification (alert text, sound, badge number, etc). Based on what you put in your push notifications server side, you can put some logic inside the body of this method if you want. If you do not implement this method, the phone will not show the push notification to the user.

It is also possible to launch the application directly from a push notification by touching the View button. In this case, the method that's called in your UIApplication delegate is not the normal - (void)applicationDidFinishLaunching:(UIApplication *)application, but a different method is called that also provides the information in the push notification:

```
- (BOOL)application:(UIApplication *)application
didFinishLaunchingWithOptions:(NSDictionary *)launchOptions {
        NSDictionary *remoteNotificationDictionary = [launchOptions
        objectForKey:@"UIApplicationLaunchOptionsRemoteNotificationKey"];
        NSArray *infoArray = [remoteNotificationDictionary objectForKey:@"info"];

        // code to handle the push message information

        return TRUE;
}
```

You can get the dictionary containing the push message information by getting the object for the UIApplicationLaunchOptionsRemoteNotificationKey key from the passed dictionary. This dictionary is exactly the same as the JSON dictionary you created server side and sent to Apple. You use the info field to pass in a custom array that contains information about what to do with this message; for example, immediately open the chat with the buddy that sent the message, and show a chat bubble with a spinner in it to indicate that new messages for this buddy are being retrieved (see Figure 10–3). Note that this method is the same as the method to support custom URL schemes (for example ebuddy://), so if you implemented support for that you will have to make a distinction somewhere in this method.

Figure 10–3. *Opening the chat from a push message showing a spinner*

The eBuddy Push Implementation

When we decided to implement the iPhone application, we already had a number of other clients, on web as well as mobile, and a stable server environment. Most of the functionality was already thought out and developed for the other applications so it would just be a matter of copying and building them into the iPhone app.

The iPhone deployment environment has however some unique properties that we needed to address. Since only one application can be active at one time we suddenly had to deal with a lot of disconnected clients. It used to be an exceptional case when a client suddenly disconnected during a session but now with the iPhone it would become a rule rather than an exception.

Another feature of the iPhone was the Push functionality. In order to support this, we needed to support a new type of endpoint to relay our messages. Suddenly it also became important to actually know if a client was online or not. Another side effect of Push and the ability for a client application to be offline would be that the session duration was expected to grow exponentially, 24 hours online would become the norm.

These requirements made us decide to define a new component in the backend architecture: the Push Server. The Push Server will extend the normal protocol with Push related functionality. This component would also be responsible to implement the contract between the iPhone and the backend. The contract consists of two integration points:

- Definition of the protocol between iPhone and server.

- Definition of the payload to be send to APNS.

Client / Server Protocol

The iPhone communicates to the eBuddy Backend via a JSON API. We have extended the API to add the push settings. The API message structure is defined as follows:

```
{
        "action" : "push_settings",
        "seq" : 12,
        "parameters" : {
                "push_destination" : "<DEVICE_TOKEN_HEX>",
                "push_type" : "iphone",
                "push_timeout" : "60"
        }
}
```

The action and seq dictionary entries are part of the eBuddy protocol, but the parameters dictionary is push-specific.

- push_destination: This parameter contains the device token as a hexadecimal string (64 characters long). This device token was obtained from APNS via the SDK method described earlier.

- push_type: Since you need support for multiple applications (for instance eBuddy Pro Messenger is a separate application in the app store) the client needs to tell the server which application channel it needs to use to send Push Notifications.

- push_timeout: The application gives users the opportunity to select how long they want to receive push notifications after they were last seen online, as shown in Figure 10–4.

Figure 10–4. *Setting the push timeout in the free eBuddy application*

Server to APNS

Our server code is all developed in Java. We use the excellent Apache MINA framework as a basis for all our networking code. Within the MINA framework, we created the following classes (see Figure 10–5).

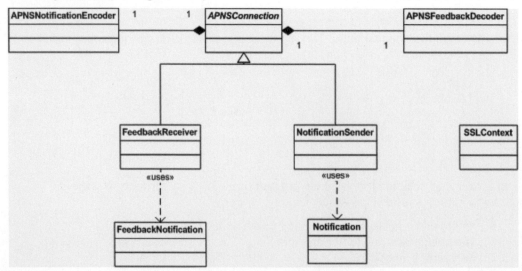

Figure 10–5. *Server class structure*

- APNSConnection
- APNSNotificationEncoder
- APNSFeedbackDecoder
- SSLContext
- FeedbackReceiver
- NotificationSender
- FeedbackNotification
- Notification

The server component communicates with the APNS via a binary protocol. This protocol consists of a header containing the device token and a payload of 256 bytes at maximum. The payload is a JSON dictionary object that contains a mandatory dictionary named aps. We set the following values for the keys, as shown in Table 10–1.

Table 10–1. *Values for the Standard aps Dictionary*

Key	Value type	Comment
alert	String or dictionary	Uses the alert key as a dictionary where we provide the body field as follows: ${from} + ": " + ${msg}.
badge	number	Provides the number of waiting messages.
sound	String	Always sends "message.aif" or buzz.aif.

For the sound, you can specify a sound file inside your application bundle, or specify "default" to play the default iPhone alert sound. Besides the aps dictionary, it is possible to pass some custom data, as shown in Table 10–2.

Table 10–2. *Values for the Custom Dictionary*

Key	Value type	Comment
Info	String, array or dictionary	We provide an array with the necessary information to open the correct chat directly when the application is started from the push notification.

When the phone is in sleep, it will display the push message in the unlock screen, making the slider the action button to open the application and view the message, as shown in Figure 10–6. To not open the application, simply lock the phone again; the next time you unlock it, the slider will function as unlock again.

Figure 10–6. *Push message in sleep mode*

When the user has the Springboard or another application open, the push message is shown over it and requiring the users action immediately. When the user touches the View button, the application for which the push message was received is opened. On the springboard, the badge icon is immediately updated on the application's icon, as shown in Figure 10–7.

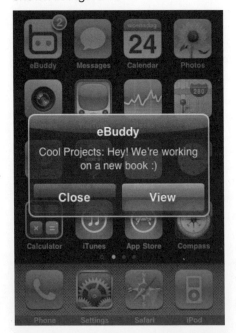

Figure 10–7. *Push message on the springboard*

It is also possible to localize the push messages you send to the users. This can be done in two ways: either by passing the phones localization setting to the server, or by sending a language string which is specified in the `Localizable.strings` files in the applications bundle. To let the server know what the current locale is, you would have to pass the value obtained from `[[NSLocale preferredLanguages] objectAtIndex:0]` in a message from the client to the server. Using this value, the server can send a localized version of the message in the push notification. You can let your application listen to the notification named `NSCurrentLocaleDidChangeNotification` to detect the user changing the current locale, after which you can send the new setting to the server again. If the server doesn't have a translation for the current language, it should send the message in one of the mainstream languages like English or Spanish.

The other way to support localization is by using a language key in the `Localizable.strings` files in your applications bundle. This way you can localize both the alert message and provide a customized, localized value for the action button, which is the button that will open your app when the user taps it. You will have to pass a dictionary as the value for the alert field in your aps dictionary, configured as shown in Table 10–3.

Table 10–3. *Values for the Custom Dictionary*

Key	Value type	Comment
body	string	The text of your alert message, or not present when using `loc-key`.
action-loc-key	string or null	The (localized) value for the action button. If null, then only one button is displayed saying "Dismiss".
loc-key	string	Key to a localized string in `Localizable.strings` in the application bundle. Use %@ or %n$@ for passing arguments.
loc-args	array of strings	An array of the arguments to use in the localized string specified in `loc-key`.

To give you an example, we send a message saying `"Your %@ account %@ got disconnected from eBuddy"` when one of your accounts gets disconnected while you are in push mode. The first argument is the network (e.g., Facebook or MSN), the second argument shows the username used for that specific account. Configure the aps dictionary as follows to send this message:

```
{
        "aps" : {
                "alert" : {
                        "action-loc-key" : "",
                        "loc-key" : "AccountDisconnectedKey",
                        "loc-args" : [ "MSN", user@example.org ]
                },
                "sound" : "default"
        }
}
```

This push message will show the user the message "Your MSN account user@example.org got disconnected from eBuddy" and play the default alert sound. It will show only one button displaying a localized version of "Dismiss" that dismisses the alert, because we specified an empty string for the action-loc-key in the dictionary.

Next, we send a somewhat similar push message when we completely log the user out of eBuddy (see Figure 10–8). For example, the following displays: "You were automatically logged out of eBuddy", along with a Dismiss button. The aps dictionary is configured as follows:

```
{
        "aps" : {
                "alert" : {
                        "action-loc-key" : "",
                        "loc-key" : "AllAccountsDisconnectedKey",
                },
                "sound" : "default"
        }
}
```

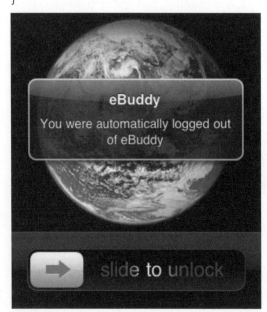

Figure 10–8. *Localized push message in sleep*

Because there is no action key provided in the dictionary, this push message will not display the "slide to view" slide, but sliding it will just unlock the phone.

Fitting the Parts Together

Because the push server and the iPhone application were developed at the same time, the iPhone application had to communicate with the normal backend servers at first, and at a certain moment in time be switched to the push server. Since the push server was a completely newly developed server system, this of course caused some issues when the switch was made.

One of the most important problems we needed to solve was to detect whether the iPhone is connected or not. This may sound simple but mobile phones have notoriously bad network connections and it is not always easy to determine whether the user has closed the app or is simply walking through a tunnel. In the end, we opted for a model where the client regularly pings or polls the server to let it know that it is still there. If no ping or poll occurs for a period of say 20 seconds, we consider the session offline and it will start to send push notifications.

Changes along the Way

Of course, when you have an application in the App Store, as a developer you constantly want to update, improve, and extend functionality of this application. At eBuddy, we have a team of developers working on improving the client constantly, and this process also sometimes influences the working of the push notifications. In the following, you find some examples of what we encountered when developing new stuff for the eBuddy iPhone application.

Introducing eBuddy Pro

In the beginning, we only had the free eBuddy Messenger application to worry about. This meant one configuration on our servers that kept one connection to the Apple Push Notification servers over which all the push messages were sent. Then our product managers thought it was a good idea to start making some money on this application, and introduced another application called eBuddy Pro Messenger. eBuddy Pro Messenger would contain more fancy features like sending pictures, setting your display picture, and all sorts of other customization. Besides these fancy features, one of the most requested features was, as our users called it: longer push. At that moment, we offered a period of one hour for the users of our free application that they would stay online after closing the application. Keeping a user online after it closes the application increases the load on our servers, because they still had to keep the connections to the IM networks open. For eBuddy Pro Messenger the so called push timeout would be raised to three days. This basically meant that if a user logs in once every 72 hours, eBuddy Messenger will keep its session on the IM networks online forever!

Next to that, with introducing more applications we had to overcome another hurdle as well. When there was only one application, we would only have certificates for one application for the connection with the Apple servers as well. But with more than one application, the application needed to identify itself whether it was eBuddy Messenger or eBuddy Pro Messenger: the server needs to use the certificates created for this specific application.

Each application needs to make its own secure connection to the Apple servers. You can create more than one connection to the APNS but it's a best practice to create one connection per server and push your notifications over that connection. Each application has one certificate for the development environment and one for the production environment. We used the application ID in the `Info.plist` file to identify the developer account: `[[NSBundle mainBundle] objectForInfoDictionaryKey:@"CFBundleIdentifier"]`. Each application has its own application ID, usually formatted as `com.yourcompany.uniquename`. You set this up in the iPhone Developer Program Portal. The server then has to send the push messages for this client session via the proper connection to the Apple servers to make them arrive at the device.

MULTIPLE APPLICATIONS

When designing your server components for Push Notifications, keep in mind that you might be adding other applications in the future, and that you need to maintain multiple connections to Apple's servers. Changing this afterwards is a lot more work than implementing it right from the start!

Extending the Beta Program

As most developers know, Apple has a restriction of one hundred devices you can use for development and beta testing. The reasoning behind this is that you cannot add unlimited devices to your beta program and in that way start distributing your application through other ways as the Apple App Store. In order to prevent developers to simply add a device, create a build for it and then delete the device from the list again, they let each device you add count for a complete year, regardless of whether you delete it or not.

DELETING DEVICES

As a developer, you get a chance to delete devices from the list once a year. When this time has come (you get a notice in your iPhone Developer Program Portal; see Figure 10–9), be sure not to add any devices before you cleaned up the list; it will take away your possibility to remove any devices from the list.

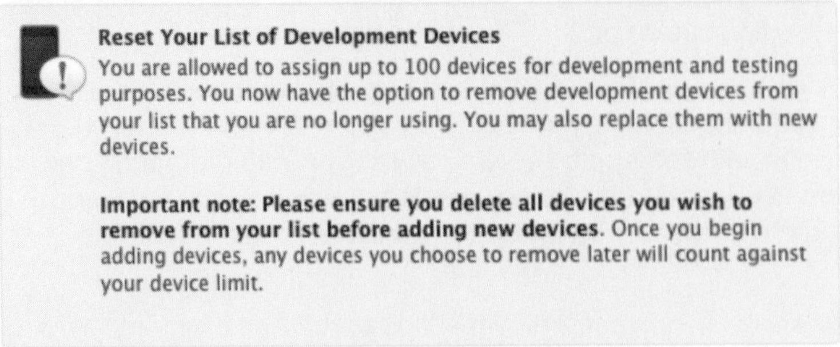

 Reset Your List of Development Devices
You are allowed to assign up to 100 devices for development and testing purposes. You now have the option to remove development devices from your list that you are no longer using. You may also replace them with new devices.

Important note: Please ensure you delete all devices you wish to remove from your list before adding new devices. Once you begin adding devices, any devices you choose to remove later will count against your device limit.

Figure 10–9. *Apple Development Devices Announcement*

At eBuddy, we have a pretty big user base and want to be able to thoroughly test our applications before we release it. For this, we started a beta program which of course contains all the company employees that own an iPhone or iPod Touch, and besides that a number of selected users that were willing to test the new releases of the eBuddy iPhone application before we would submit it to the AppStore. Unfortunately, some of the users that we selected lost interest in testing our beta applications shortly after they were added to the beta program, or only signed up to take a sneak peek at our new features and left it at that. Meanwhile, they were still taking up a slot of our valuable one hundred devices.

To workaround this limitation, we simply paid the $99 fee and created another developer account. Of course, this solution didn't come without problems: different developer accounts mean different certificates, provisioning profiles and private keys, as well as two different groups of beta testers that need different builds to install. We use automated build scripts that monitor our revision control system, and automatically create builds for code we submit. Both developer accounts are registered to eBuddy, and Apple automatically names your distribution certificate after your company. XCode will not build your project in Distribution mode if there are two distribution certificates in the keychain with the same name. This meant creating different keychains that only contain the private keys and certificates for the appropriate developer account, and importing them into the keychain before building and then deleting them after building.

Another problem was that by introducing a new developer account, we also got extra certificates to let our servers connect to the Apple Push Notification servers, like we had with introducing the eBuddy Pro application. More configurations had to be introduced server side, and the client had to be able to identify to which account it belongs and communicate this to the server.

On the server side, this meant adding another set of APNS endpoints, but after we changed our architecture once to accommodate the eBuddy Pro Messenger version it was just a matter of configuring two more endpoints.

Summary

In this chapter, we showed you how to start implementing support for Push Notifications in your iPhone application, how to set up your server side component, and how to configure the messages you want to send to the iPhone. We hope we helped you on your way in creating a Push Notification service for your own application. To conclude, we would like to give you some nice numbers: in total, we process around 13 billion messages a month through eBuddy, of which around one eighth are sent or received

Index

■ B

H

 I

N

∎P

V

W

You Need the Companion eBook

Your purchase of this book entitles you to buy the companion PDF-version eBook for only $10. Take the weightless companion with you anywhere.

We believe this Apress title will prove so indispensable that you'll want to carry it with you everywhere, which is why we are offering the companion eBook (in PDF format) for $10 to customers who purchase this book now. Convenient and fully searchable, the PDF version of any content-rich, page-heavy Apress book makes a valuable addition to your programming library. You can easily find and copy code—or perform examples by quickly toggling between instructions and the application. Even simultaneously tackling a donut, diet soda, and complex code becomes simplified with hands-free eBooks!

Once you purchase your book, getting the $10 companion eBook is simple:

❶ Visit **www.apress.com/promo/tendollars/**.

❷ Complete a basic registration form to receive a randomly generated question about this title.

❸ Answer the question correctly in 60 seconds, and you will receive a promotional code to redeem for the $10.00 eBook.

THE EXPERT'S VOICE™

233 Spring Street, New York, NY 10013

Offer valid through 11/10.